The Global Financial Crisis

What Have We Learnt?

Edited by

Steven Kates

School of Economics, Finance and Marketing, RMIT University, Melbourne, Australia

Edward Elgar

Cheltenham, UK • Northampton, MA, USA

Published by
Edward Elgar Publishing Limited
The Lypiatts
15 Lansdown Road
Cheltenham
Glos GL50 2JA
UK

Edward Elgar Publishing, Inc.
William Pratt House
9 Dewey Court
Northampton
Massachusetts 01060
USA

A catalogue record for this book
is available from the British Library

Library of Congress Control Number: 2011925798

ISBN 978 0 85793 422 2 (cased)

Typeset by Servis Filmsetting Ltd, Stockport, Cheshire
Printed and bound by MPG Books Group, UK

Contents

Figures and tables

FIGURES

TABLES

Contributors

Peter J. Boettke is BB&T Professor for the Study of Capitalism at the Mercatus Center at George Mason University and University Professor of Economics at George Mason University.

Tim Congdon is an economist and businessman, who has for over thirty years been a strong advocate of sound money and free markets in the UK's public policy debates. He was a member of the Treasury Panel of Independent Forecasters (the so-called 'wise men') between 1992 and 1997. Often regarded as the original 'Thatcherite monetarist', he founded the economic research consultancy Lombard Street Research in 1989. A collection of his papers, with the title *Keynes, the Keynesians and Monetarism*, was published in September 2007. His latest work, on *Central Banking in a Free Society*, was published by the Institute of Economic Affairs in March 2009. He writes columns on economics for *Standpoint* and the IEA's journal, *Economic Affairs*. He was awarded the CBE for services to economic debate in 1997.

Horst Hanusch was born in 1942 and submitted his dissertation in 1971 (Dr. rer. pol.). From 1974 to 2010 he was Full Professor of Economics at the University of Augsburg. He is Secretary General of the International J.A. Schumpeter Society, of which he was co-founder in 1986. He is co-editor of the *Journal of Evolutionary Economics*, which he founded in 1991. His fields of research include: innovations and technical progress in neo-Schumpeterian economies; efficiency in the public sector; tax policies and structural change. His publications include: *The Legacy of Joseph A. Schumpeter* (ed.) (1999); *Economic Evolution, Learning, and Complexity* (ed.) (2000); *Applied Evolutionary Economics and the Knowledge-based Economy* (ed.) (2006) and *The Elgar Companion to Neo-Schumpeterian Economics* (ed.) (2007).

Steven G. Horwitz is Charles A. Dana Professor of Economics at St Lawrence University in Canton, NY and an Affiliated Senior Scholar at the Mercatus Center in Arlington, VA. He is the author of two books, *Microfoundations and Macroeconomics: An Austrian Perspective* (2000) and *Monetary Evolution, Free Banking, and Economic Order* (1992), and he has written extensively on Austrian economics, Hayekian political economy, monetary theory and history, and the economics and social theory of gender and the family. He has a PhD in Economics from George Mason University and an AB in Economics and Philosophy from The University of Michigan. He is currently working on a book on classical liberalism and the family.

Steven Kates is Senior Lecturer in Economics at the School of Economics, Finance and Marketing at RMIT University in Melbourne. For most of his career he worked for the private sector, having been for a quarter of a century the Chief Economist for the Australian Chamber of Commerce and Industry. His professional interests have therefore been closely related to the formation of economic theory in line with the needs of policy. His *Say's Law and the Keynesian Revolution* discussed the loss to economic theory of the disappearance of the classical theory of the cycle. As well as editing this collection, his *Free Market Economics: An Introduction for the General Reader* was also published in 2011. He describes himself as a classical economist.

Steve Keen is Associate Professor of Economics and Finance at the University of Western Sydney, and author of *Debunking Economics*. He has over forty academic publications on topics as diverse as financial instability, the money creation process, mathematical flaws in the conventional model of supply and demand, flaws in Marxian economics, the application of physics to economics, Islamic finance, and the role of chaos and complexity theory in economics. Since 2006 he has been publishing a monthly report explaining the economic dangers of excessive private debt. He is a specialist in Minsky's Financial Instability Hypothesis, and produced the first mathematical model of a debt-induced economic crisis in 1995.

J.E. King teaches economics at La Trobe University in Melbourne. A strong believer in pluralism in the teaching of economics, he has sympathies with several heterodox approaches, including institutional and ecological economics. His principal attachments, however, are with post-Keynesian and Marxian political economy, with Michał Kalecki serving as a bridge between them.

Mervyn K. Lewis is Professor of Banking and Finance in the School of Commerce at the University of South Australia. Previously he was Midland Bank Professor of Money and Banking at the University of Nottingham and Course Director of the MBA in Financial Studies. He was also a Consultant to the Australian Financial System Inquiry, Visiting Scholar at the Bank of England and inaugural Securities Commission–University of Malaya Visiting Scholar. In 1986 he was elected a Fellow of the Academy of the Social Sciences in Australia. Professor Lewis has authored or co-authored 21 books, 63 articles and 74 chapters. Recent volumes are *Handbook of Islamic Banking* (2007), *Islamic Finance* (2007) and *Untangling the US Deficit: Evaluating Causes, Cures and Global Imbalances* (2007). His latest volume is *An Islamic Perspective on Governance* (2009).

William J. Luther is a Mercatus PhD Fellow at George Mason University He has been a Fellow with the American Institute for Economic Research. He conducts research in monetary theory and history, political economy and Austrian economics.

Robert E. Prasch is Professor of Economics at Middlebury College where he teaches monetary theory and policy, macroeconomics, American economic history, and the history of economic thought. He is the author of over ninety academic articles, book chapters and book reviews, in addition to multiple editorials and interviews in newspapers, radio, and online media including *The Huffington Post* and *Common Dreams*. The most recent of his three authored or co-edited books is *How Markets Work: Supply, Demand and the 'Real World'* (2008). He has also served on the editorial boards of the *Review of Political Economy* and the *Journal of Economic Issues*, and as president of the Association for Evolutionary Economics (AFEE). Previous to Middlebury College, he taught at Vassar College, the University of Maine, and San Francisco State University. His PhD in economics is from the University of California, Berkeley.

Martin Ricketts is Professor of Economic Organisation and Dean of the School of Humanities at the University of Buckingham. He is a graduate of the Universities of Newcastle and York. He has published papers in public finance, public choice, the new institutional economics and Austrian economics. He is a Trustee and Chairman of the Academic Advisory Council of the Institute of Economic Affairs. His publications include *The Economics of Energy* (with Mike Webb) (1980); *Neoclassical Microeconomics* (ed.) (1988); *The Many Ways of Governance: Perspectives on the Control of the Firm* (1999) and *The Economics of Business Enterprise* (3rd edn 2003).

Rodolfo Signorino is Associate Professor of Economics at the Law Faculty of the University of Palermo, Italy. He has published in the areas of Classical and Sraffian economics and the methodology of economics. He is also author of a two-volume intermediate textbook, *Istituzioni di Economia Politica.*

Daniel J. Smith is the Oloffson Weaver Fellow of Political Economy and PhD Candidate in Economics at George Mason University. He is conducting research in the fields of political economy, and law and economics.

Nicholas A. Snow is a Mercatus Center PhD Fellow at George Mason University. He is conducting research in the fields of political economy and Austrian economics.

Florian Wackermann holds a Diploma in Economics from the University of Augsburg in Germany and a Master in Business Administration from the University of Rennes in France, which he accomplished as part of a joint programme of 'French–German management'. He has also received a Master's degree in Economics from Wayne State University in Detroit, USA. Dr Wackermann accomplished his PhD in Economics in 2010 under the supervision of Professor Horst Hanusch on the question of whether governments can foster innovation by securing existential risks of individuals. He has worked intensively in the fields of the economics of innovation and public sector management with a focus on agent-based modelling and the economic approaches to policy questions.

Charles J. Whalen is an economist residing in upstate New York. When his chapter was written, he was Executive Director and Professor of Business and Economics at Utica College. He worked previously at the Institute for Industry Studies at Cornell University, the Levy Economics Institute of Bard College, and at *BusinessWeek*, where he served as associate economics editor. He has written extensively on institutional economics. He describes himself as a post-Keynesian institutionalist, influenced by institutional labour economists in the tradition of John R. Commons and by post-Keynesian macroeconomists such as Hyman P. Minsky.

L. Randall Wray is Professor of Economics at the University of Missouri–Kansas City, Research Director of the Center for Full Employment and Price Stability, and Senior Scholar at the Levy Economics Institute of Bard College. A student of Hyman Minsky, Jan Kregel and Marc Tool, Wray works within the post-Keynesian and institutionalist traditions.

Acknowledgements

Books, especially collections of articles, do not happen by themselves, but require the willing assistance of quite a few others along the way. There are therefore a number of others to whom I wish to express my gratitude for their assistance in getting this completed and within the tight time frames that were set.

I am, of course, indebted to the authors whose papers are found in this volume. Not only have they provided me with their articles on time and within the deadlines set, but each has written a chapter that has looked at the Global Financial Crisis in ways that are well outside the mainstream but from within distinct and recognized divisions of economic theory as it now is. These were truly the alternative perspectives that were sought, and each of these chapters has provided a different and deeply insightful discussion of the economic circumstances we have had to deal with over the period since the GFC began.

I am also especially grateful once again to Edward Elgar for his personal support for this project. I am also grateful for the highly professional group at Edward Elgar Publishing for their assistance in seeing this through to its final completion.

But it is to my family that I owe a special measure of gratitude and in this I include my now adult children Benjamin and Joshua. The book is, however, dedicated to my wife, Zuzanna, whose contribution has been her warm encouragement in allowing me the time to see this through to the end. My debts to her, as I have said before, extend far beyond her help in seeing this book finally into print.

Introduction

Steven Kates

> Oh happy people of the future, who have not known these miseries and perchance will class our testimony with the fables.
>
> Petrarch on the Great Plague

The Global Financial Crisis (GFC) has come and gone, leaving behind a trail of damage and destruction that will take many years to repair. From the latter half of 2008 through until the first few months of 2009, the world's economy experienced an almost total breakdown of its financial and credit creation system. This was the GFC itself. But even when the financial crisis had departed and receded into history, the resulting recession has left every economy significantly worse off than it had been before. Unemployment is higher, growth is less robust, public debt has increased and the future seems less secure.

The basics of what went wrong to set the GFC in motion are now generally accepted. It was the combination of sub-prime mortgages in the United States, the securitization of such mortgage debt, followed by the worldwide sale of such assets which formed a large component of the balance sheets of financial institutions, large and small. When housing prices in the US collapsed, it left many of these assets nearly valueless, some actually valueless. The subsequent seizing up of the global financial system caused trust in even what were formerly the most rock solid financial institutions to disappear. Since no one knew who was solvent and who was not, credit creation across the world ground almost to a halt.

With the collapse of credit, productive activity, investment and employment all fell. While there were variations in the size and extent of the downturn, no part of the global economy was spared, with one forecast following another predicting a cataclysm to rival the Great Depression or possibly even worse. Already, only two years later, it is hard to conjure the panic that was almost universally experienced in the face of such uncharted waters, especially amongst those responsible for the formation of our economic policies. No one was sure where the world's economy was heading and no one knew with certainty what to do. The policies based on standard economic theory have seemed inadequate to the task in dealing with the problems that arose and which we now have. For those contributing to this volume, the fault lies in economic theory itself.

THE FOUR POLICY PHASES OF THE GFC AND SUBSEQUENT RECESSION

Four distinct phases surrounding the GFC and the subsequent policy response have contributed to and further amplified this mistrust of standard economic theory. There is, first, a strong belief amongst many of these authors that the economic theory that guided policies during the period leading up to the GFC were profoundly wrong. These authors argue that the management of our economies had in itself contributed to the financial meltdown which occurred and indeed made it inevitable.

Then, secondly, there are those who believe that once the financial meltdown commenced, the policies adopted during the GFC to restore calm were badly designed and poorly constructed. They believe that the theoretical considerations that went into these policies were misconceived. Rather than helping to solve such problems for the long term, the actions taken during the height of the crisis to bring the GFC to an end have themselves created conditions that will see similar problems repeated sooner rather than later.

Thirdly, there are those who believe that the policy actions taken since the end of the GFC to restore the needed integrity to financial markets have been misguided and inadequate. It is argued that there were lessons we ought to have learnt and used to frame new regulatory policies that have been ignored. Instead, the policy post-mortems and the regulatory response have done little that will make any significant difference to the future and have made another downturn along similar lines not only inevitable but likely to be sooner rather than at some stage long into the future.

Then finally, there are critics of the policies that were adopted once recessionary conditions had set in, to place our economies on a stronger platform for growth and to return unemployment to the lower rates that had prevailed in the period leading up to the GFC. These were the stimulus packages that were adopted almost universally as an integral part of the programme of recovery. It is argued that these policies have been an unmitigated failure which should lead to a search for a more secure theoretical foundation on which future policies ought to be based.

This book, like its predecessor, is about the adequacy of economic theory.[1] It is about the usefulness or otherwise of existing textbook economics to make sense of and then provide guidance to those who must decide on what actions need to be taken. But while every author in this volume disagrees with the standard mainstream model, it should also be understood that the different authors in this collection do not necessarily agree with each other. There is, in fact, a very wide disparity of views amongst contributors. The perspectives provided in these chapters range across the entire breadth of economic theory from free market to highly interventionist. The intention in putting this collection together has been to provide a single platform for the different sets of views that are often drowned out by the standard bearers of the mainstream.

Moreover, even before our present problems commenced, all of the economists whose chapters are found in this volume have had longstanding beliefs that today's standard economic models are inadequate, if not actually wrong. It is the ideas and theories of these economists, all of whom are serious scholars, which are being employed to provide alternative explanations of the economic events of the past two years and to discuss what we have learnt during this time.

THE STANDARD MODEL

But to understand the nature of this criticism, it is first necessary to understand the structure of mainstream economic theory. The focus here is placed on the introductory macroeconomic model taught to first year economists. This model, although refined with additional features and nuance in later years of study, nevertheless provides the core conceptual reasoning that underpins the shared framework of both academic economists and the makers of economic policy. It is what every economist learns and is the basis for the macroeconomics of virtually every student who has taken only a single course in economics.

The relevant theory is often called Keynesian, after the English economist John Maynard Keynes. It was his *General Theory of Employment, Interest and Money*, published in 1936, that became the point of origin for the standard macroeconomic model now in general use. Although there are fundamental disagreements amongst economists over the message that Keynes was trying to impart, there is no disagreement that it is from Keynes's scholarly work that modern macroeconomic theory began its voyage.

Yet in saying this, it should be emphasized that a significant proportion of those who describe themselves as followers of Keynes would not accept many, and possibly most elements of the standard macroeconomic model as their own.

The model that has descended to the modern textbook level is generally referred to as the neo-classical synthesis, the melding of Keynesian ideas with the ideas of Keynes's predecessors. As taught today, within this neo-classical model, the single most important factor in understanding fluctuations in the level of output is fluctuations in the level of aggregate demand, the demand for everything produced.

Moreover, the underlying assumption in such models is that in an economy in recession, if it were left to itself, the level of aggregate demand would not recover, or if it did, the recovery process would take far too long. Active government involvement to restore economic growth is seen as essential and overwhelmingly beneficial.

Even where supply-side factors may in the first instance have caused the economy to slow and unemployment to rise, for example through the higher cost of oil, it is nevertheless from a stimulus to aggregate demand that the solution is to be found. The basic framework for discussing macroeconomic theory and policy today is generally through a model based on aggregate supply and aggregate demand (AS–AD). To raise output and push employment higher requires an increase in either aggregate demand or aggregate supply, that is, either through an increase in total spending or an increase in the underlying productivity of the economy.

Positive changes in aggregate supply are, however, either relatively long-term in nature – such as requiring an increase in physical capital, improvements in technology or increased workplace skills and abilities – or are related to factors largely beyond the reach of a national economy, such as a general fall in the price of oil. Indeed, improvements in workplace productivity can even lead to a fall in the demand for labour.

It is for this reason that policies based on AS–AD are generally related to aggregate demand. These are seen to be more immediate and available for adjustment by those who manage the domestic economy. They are also seen as being more able to provide a direct stimulus to the level of economic activity since a response from business as an intermediary is not required but can be applied directly by the government on its own using its vast powers to spend.

Aggregate demand is related to expenditure. Increasing the level of spending is seen as the key to increasing the level of economic activity. Going back to its origins in the early Keynesian models, the components of aggregate demand are identified as consumption, investment, government spending and net exports (exports minus imports). The standard formulation as an equation, with national output designated by the letter Y, is this:

$$Y = C + I + G + (X - M)$$

It is entirely arguable that this is not an equation at all but an identity. The level of GDP is *defined* by the sum of consumption, investment, government spending and net exports but is not directly governed by them, which is why the same expression used in the national accounts is presented as an accounting identity:

$$Y \equiv C + I + G + (X - M)$$

But in treating this expression as an equation, economic policy has been designed to raise the level of production on the left-hand side by increasing the elements that appear on the right-hand side. Therefore, to raise the level of national output, policy has been centred around raising expenditures by consumers, investors, governments and international buyers of domestically produced goods and services. The more that is spent, the faster the economy would be expected to grow, with the faster growth rates leading to a rise in the number of persons employed.

TEXTBOOK EXAMPLES

Some examples from modern texts by leading authors provide an indication of the instruction given to economics students. The first is from the fourth edition of Gregory Mankiw's *Principles of Economics* (Mankiw, 2007: 772):

> Any event or policy that raises consumption, investment, government purchases, or net exports at a given price level increases aggregate demand.

Similarly, in the text co-authored by Ben Bernanke, the Chairman of the Federal Reserve in the United States, we find the same sentiment (Frank and Bernanke, 2007: 826):

> For any given value of inflation, an exogenous increase in spending (that is, an increase in spending at given levels of output and the real interest rate) raises short-run equilibrium output, shifting the aggregate demand (AD) curve to the right.

In a text co-authored by John Taylor, who had devised the Taylor Rule used in interest rate determination around the world, we find this (Taylor and Moosa, 2002: 310):

> Imagine that government expenditure rises. We know from our analysis of spending balance in the previous chapter that an increase in government expenditure leads to an increase in real GDP in the short run.

Then in the eighteenth edition of Samuelson (first published in 1948 and now Samuelson and Nordhaus, 2005: 489) is found:

> Only with the development of modern macroeconomic theory has a further surprising fact been uncovered: Government fiscal powers also have a major *macroeconomic* impact upon the short-run movements of output, employment, and prices. The knowledge that fiscal policy has powerful effects upon economic activity led to the *Keynesian approach to macroeconomic policy*, which is the active use of government action to moderate business cycles.

There are no end of caveats to these bare statements found in each of these texts as well as in the many others that tell the same story. And it is even more so the case that the further one studies economics, the more qualifications to these basic statements there are. But in the end there is no practical point to discussing aggregate demand and public expenditure unless the conclusion being reached is that in recession one of the actions that governments can take is to raise the level of its own demand. Standard macroeconomic theory is unambiguously clear: higher public spending during recession is one of the actions governments should consider when unemployment rises and the level of economic activity falls.

The fact that governments around the world have done exactly this is directly related to the economic theory that economists are almost universally taught. Governments have not taken this course on their own initiative. In increasing the level of public spending, they have taken the advice of their professionally trained economic advisors. If these policies are seen to have failed, there will be a major case to answer that it was the economic theories encouraging these actions that will have themselves been shown to have failed.

REGULATION

Just as important as the issue of the fiscal stimulus has been, so too has been the role of regulation of markets, and in particular financial markets. Although there have already been various actions taken to deal with perceived vulnerabilities, over the longer term there are certain to be ongoing debates on what governments can and should do to minimize economic instability while still maintaining healthy rates of growth.

Within economic theory there is a strong predisposition towards a generally hands-off approach to economic management. For most economic activities, the economist's response is to assume that intrusive regulation of markets is unnecessary and, whatever might be the perceived benefits, will tend to do more harm than good.

For all markets, it is assumed that the participants know more than any outsider could possibly know. Moreover, about the unknowable future, the assumption is that since no one can know what is going to happen next, and all actions based on the future must of their nature be a form of guesswork, markets are able to adjust to circumstances more smoothly, with more accuracy and with more assurance than any group of government officials could ever hope to do. If such judgements are left to people with their own money on the line, the incentive to get things right will lead to the optimal outcome, although surprises will frequently upset many an applecart along the way.

Regulators are too distant and lack the requisite knowledge to make appropriate real-time decisions. Regulation therefore inhibits markets and leads to a sub-optimal outcome. The economy is worse for there being too many regulations, and regulations of the wrong kind.

There is also the role of self-interest to be considered. Within economics, it is generally assumed individuals acting on their own behalf and risking their own money will be prudent in the risks they take. Government intervention by a nine-to-five bureaucracy will in most instances create more harm than good. Indeed, not only would such attempts at detailed regulation of markets cause them to perform poorly, they are unnecessary because the market itself is its own discipline.

It is now a central question whether the current crisis in the United States began because of the actions of market participants in the finance industry and the housing market, or whether it was due to specific decisions by governments that allowed, if not actually caused, forces to be unleashed that would otherwise have been contained. Many policy questions will ride on the answer to just this question alone.

Even recognizing the harm that has been done by the global downturn, the question still remains whether the business cycle is the price that must be paid for the benefits that accrue when markets are allowed to find their own level. Cyclical activity may be impossible to avoid. If there is little that can be done to prevent periodic downturns, or to dampen their amplitude, then intrusive regulation will only limit growth in real incomes but do nothing to prevent the instability and personal insecurities that are embedded in the nature of things.

There is therefore the predisposition within the economics mainstream towards the self-regulation of markets where a culling process of the unprofitable and less competent is expected to ensure that those who should not be in business are removed and the capital they have been employing set free for other businesses to use in their stead. That is part of what the recessionary phase of the cycle is intended to achieve.

The basic framework of a free enterprise economy is tied to the ancient notion of the 'invisible hand'. Adam Smith's most famous passage even today remains an important part of an economist's understanding of the operation of markets:

> [A merchant] generally, indeed, neither intends to promote the public interest, nor knows how much he is promoting it. . . . He intends only his own security; and by directing that industry in such a manner as its produce may be of the greatest value, he intends only his own gain, and he is in this, as in many other cases, led by an invisible hand to promote an end which was no part of his intention. Nor is it always the worse for the society that it was not part of it. By pursuing his own interest he frequently promotes that of the society more effectually than when he really intends to promote it. (Smith, 1976 [1776]: Book IV, Chapter II)

An important modern manifestation of this principle is referred to as the 'efficient market hypothesis'. Financial markets are so well constructed, it is argued, that all of the relevant information available is already part of the price of any financial product. No one can enter the market with more knowledge; increased regulation can only make markets less efficient since those who do the regulating will never know as much as those who are already engaged in the market and have their own money at stake.

It is this conclusion which is embedded within standard neo-classical theory that the global financial crisis has put on notice. Are there regulations that can be introduced that will make economies perform better, make them less susceptible to downturns, and which will make whatever downturn that does occur shallower and shorter?

Or is the attempt to add new regulations of financial markets to those which already exist futile? Would such regulations only cause net harm by reducing the ability of markets to respond to changed circumstances and limit financial market innovation? Would such regulation in fact diminish economic stability and make jobs less secure?

These are questions of the greatest significance which will be discussed for years on end just as similar questions were discussed following the Great Depression. These are the kinds of questions that are a perennial part of the discourse amongst economists.

THE INVITATIONS TO PARTICIPATE

All of the chapters in the present volume were specially written for this collection. Each of those who have contributed to this volume received some variant of the following letter which was emailed to a number of economists identifiable from their previous writings for their rejection of the standard neo-classical model. The message line read: 'Seeking your contribution to an Elgar publication on the World Financial Crisis'. The following represents the relevant part of the letters that were sent, with the example being the letter written to those who had contributed to the previous volume:

> It is now more than a year ago that I wrote to ask if you would be able to participate in a collection of articles I was then putting together on the Global Financial Crisis. It has now been published as *Macroeconomic Theory and its Failings: Alternative Perspectives on the Global Financial Crisis* (Edward Elgar 2010). What I believe made this collection unique is that it examined from a non-mainstream perspective the economic theories and public policies used to deal with the GFC.
>
> Following the successful publication of this first collection, Edward Elgar has agreed to publish a follow up collection that continues to examine from a non-mainstream perspective the economic theories and public policies used to deal with the GFC but with the added perspective that the last eighteen months have given us. I am therefore hopeful that you will again be able to participate in this collection.
>
> The core aims of this second volume will be, firstly, to examine the causes of the downturn now that we have had a longer perspective on events, and then, secondly and more importantly, to provide a critical examination of the approaches taken by governments to reverse the economic downturn that reached its lowest point at the beginning of 2009.
>
> The specific questions to be addressed in each article could include a discussion of, but would not necessarily be limited to the following which I believe are the central issues at the present:
>
> - given the perspective of hindsight, how would you now explain the origins of the Global Financial Crisis?
> - what, in your view, caused the world's economies to stabilise?
> - which policy measures taken by governments have provided the greatest contribution to stabilisation and in what way have they contributed?
> - in contrast, have any of the measures taken by governments added to the economic problems that must now be dealt with and, if so, which policies were these and what have been their harmful effects?
> - what lessons have we learned about economic management and stabilisation policies during the GFC?
> - given your own theoretical perspective, what should policy-makers now do to assist in the recovery process?
> - do you believe regulatory changes are needed and, if so, what kind of regulatory changes should be introduced?
>
> The article is not intended to require much if anything in the way of research. It seeks a brief summary of the framework you bring to economic issues and the application of this framework to the questions that have been outlined above.
>
> The article should also not include statistics or mathematical analysis. The intention is to make each as accessible as possible to the widest range of readers, many of whom will not be economists but all of whom will be deeply interested

> in understanding the different perspectives on our current economic and financial circumstances.
>
> This book is also intended to be of enduring interest long beyond the present when economic growth, prosperity and a feeling of general optimism have returned. It is intended to be a reflection of how contemporary issues were viewed from different economic traditions during the early months of 2011.
>
> Let me just add that this collection is intended to include only those who have an economic perspective that would not be described as part of the mainstream neo-classical tradition. No one, for example, contributing to this volume would normally employ a standard textbook neo-classical model in trying to explain economic events or to formulate economic policy.

The enduring interest in a volume such as this is in having a series of essays contemporary with the events of the Global Financial Crisis. A major part of its value is to provide conceptual guidance to those who are making policy decisions to bring this recession to an end and then to ensure that mistakes that were made are not repeated.

LONGER-TERM PERSPECTIVE

But there is a longer-term perspective that is also an important part of the direct intent of putting these contributions together which is almost entirely unrelated to policy. The aim is to provide economists, historians and others in the future with a date-stamped on-the-ground perspective of these events as they were experienced by members of the economics community at the time.

None of us contributing to this volume know what will happen in the years to come. If we think in terms of the timeline of the Great Depression, the chapters have been written during the middle of 1931 while the world's economies were worsening but had not touched bottom. How comparable this is to that earlier timeline we cannot as yet know.

Even the name we use to describe our current situation has changed. The original period of economic upheaval has taken as its name, the Global Financial Crisis. But while this term is still used, the phrase now used more often is The Great Recession, in recognition that the depth and severity of the Great Depression are very unlikely to be repeated, but that this has been a very sustained period of economic disturbance far worse than any other since the 1930s. But we who have written our articles at the start of 2011 are in the dark about what will come next.

It is for those who live in times to come that this book is to an important extent intended. A major part of the reason that this collection has been brought together is to assist those who are interested in looking back at us from some vantage point in the future to do so. These are date-stamped articles that reflect the beliefs and attitudes of those who are living through these times. That is part of the value that these articles provide.

PERSPECTIVES ON THE CURRENT CRISIS

In spite of its reputation for disagreement, economics is no more fractious than any other science but with this one difference. It is within the public arena and amongst non-economists that a significant part of our economic debates take place. Moreover, the answers that economists provide have a major impact on the lives of millions. The conclusions reached by economists matter.

There is a mainstream. There are textbook theories and practices that are learned and understood by all economists. But whatever is the mainstream at any moment in time, some economists reach the conclusion that the mainstream – the core beliefs of the profession – is, in some important ways, wrong. This has always been the case. It is how economic theory develops. Some members of the profession disagree with the mainstream position, and over time their points of view becomes the mainstream in its place.

It is the macroeconomic side of these economic theories that is now under the microscope in this volume by economists who take sharply different points of view from the majority of the profession. But the different perspectives provided in this volume are not from a single direction but are from across the entire range of positions found in different economic traditions. The different traditions from which the chapters in this volume have been written are listed below in alphabetical order:

- Austrian
- Classical
- Environmental
- Institutionalist
- Marxist
- Minskyite
- Monetarist
- Post-Keynesian
- Schumpeterian.

No attempt is made to define any of these in this introductory chapter. That is for each author to take up on his own. The list of contributors provides a brief statement of the intellectual allegiances of each of the authors. Readers with a greater knowledge of economic theory and its sub-divisions will have no difficulty in recognizing the different points of view.

And although one might describe some of the members of this list as 'schools' of economic thought, it would be too confining in most cases to be constrained in that way. As the chapters make clear, there are overlapping points of view and a number of key concepts that are shared across a number of the perspectives presented. Each of the authors has been allowed to describe their own approach to economics in their own way. The chapters have been put in alphabetical order according to the author's name. No precedence has been given to any point of view.

But what is important is that each of the authors as a representative of one of these perspectives has something of value to contribute to this debate. For each of these, there is a historical tradition that goes back in time to the earlier years of the study of economics. Each of the economists is the present incarnation of a perspective on economic issues that has been pursued by a succession of economists who have learned their economics within those traditions. None of these perspectives was the invention of the economist who has written the chapter for this publication. Each is a descendant from a longer, older, deeper tradition.

Even so, amongst economists there is a common language. We can speak with each other because, by being economically trained, there is a framework within which discourse can take place. But when all is said and done, within each tradition there is a separate means of understanding the various dynamic operations of an economy. There are important differences on what matters and how it matters. There are differences over what governments can successfully do and what they cannot. There are differences over the consequences of different policies and there are differences over how policies will matter in the short run in comparison with the long run. There are differences in the categories in which to classify and aggregate. There are, in fact, differences over whether discussing economic issues in terms of aggregates is even coherent.

Yet so far as this collection is concerned, it has been designed to be read widely by those with no economic training whatsoever. The purpose has been to make these chapters accessible so that the different points of view can be understood by the interested non-economist. There would, in fact, be no point in having put this volume together if its only audience were other economists. The aim is to reach beyond the confines of the economics discipline to the wider community to present the diversity of views amongst economists on these major questions.

There is, it should be understood, not just one single school of economic thought. There isn't a single answer given by economists to the complex and perplexing issues that surround us. There is a wide variety of possible policy responses that ought to be examined and considered.

Those who make policy decisions usually do not have prior training in economics. They should therefore be aware of these other perspectives which are too often obscured by the mainstream. The narrowness of policy debates has often led to the adoption of a course of action that may have long-term consequences and potentially cause major damage to our productive potential because other options were not considered.

The aim of this book is to bring into focus views of other traditions within economics that those who must make policy in the midst of the rush of events would seldom consider in the normal course of events. But given the complexity of the task before us, and the distinct possibility that the policies which have so far been adopted will fail to bring about the desired result, this collection of articles has been brought together to ensure that we have comprehensively examined the effects of the policies that have already been put into practice and that alternative perspectives are examined as future decisions are made.

NOTE

1. Although this volume is linked thematically and by the overlap of many of the contributors with the volume published at the start of 2010, *Macroeconomic Theory and its Failings: Alternative Perspectives on the Global Financial Crisis*, this should not be seen as the second in a series. The chapters in the previous volume represented an immediate response to the GFC that was then at its peak of intensity. This volume contains a more reflective view of what took place and offers a more considered response to the events of the past two years. This introduction, however, follows the outline of that earlier volume.

REFERENCES

Frank, Robert H. and Ben S. Bernanke (2007), *Principles of Economics*, 3rd edn, New York: McGraw-Hill.

Kates, Steven (ed.) (2010), *Macroeconomic Theory and its Failings: Alternative Perspectives on the Global Financial Crisis*, Cheltenham, UK and Northampton, MA, USA: Edward Elgar Publishing.

Mankiw, N. Gregory (2007), *Principles of Economics*, 4th edn, Mason, OH: Thomson South-Western.

Samuelson, Paul A. and William D. Nordhaus (2005), *Economics*, 18th edn, Boston, MA: McGraw-Hill Irwin.

Smith, Adam (1976 [1776]), *An Inquiry into the Nature and Causes of the Wealth of Nations*, edited by Edwin Cannan, Chicago, IL: University of Chicago Press.

Taylor, John B. and Imad Moosa (2002), *Macroeconomics*, 2nd edn, Milton, Qld: John Wiley and Sons.

1. Been there done that: the political economy of déjà vu

Peter J. Boettke, Daniel J. Smith and Nicholas A. Snow

> In spite of the incredible reputation of the General Theory, I could not find in it a single important doctrine that was both true and original. What is original in the book is not true, and what is true is not original. In fact, even most of the major errors in the book are not original, but can be found in a score of previous writers.
>
> Henry Hazlitt (1995 [1960]: 3)

> We have been going back and forth for a century. I want to steer markets (Keynes). I want them set free (Hayek).
>
> John Papola and Russell Roberts (2010)

1 INTRODUCTION

In the midst of the current financial crisis the economics profession has seen a monumental resurrection of Keynesian ideas. The debate, which Keynes started back in the 1930s, is being picked up again, not where it left off, but in exactly the same place it started. While Keynesian theories were carefully critiqued by new classical economists and in the most part discarded by the profession, Keynesian models and prescriptions became a staple of politics and macroeconomic textbooks. Obviously, neither side of the debate articulated their views adequately and on the same terms. If the economics profession is going to escape this perpetual déjà vu of cycling through the same debate every time an economic crisis emerges, the profession must discard entrenched ideologies and turn back to the sound but creative application of basic economics.

On 17 October 1932, D.H. MacGregor, A.C. Pigou, J.M. Keynes, Walter Layton, Arthur Salter and J.C. Stamp (MacGregor et al., 1932) posted a letter in *The Times* articulating what they believed was one of the primary causes for the continuation and severity of the Great Depression: private spending. They were deeply concerned by the fall in consumption at that time, and believed government action was necessary to counteract this fall in aggregate demand, '[t]he public interest in present conditions does not point towards private economy; to spend less money than we should like to do is not patriotic' (MacGregor et al., 1932: 13). They continued further:

> Moreover, what is true of individuals acting singly is equally true of groups of individuals acting through local authorities. If the citizens of a town wish to build a swimming-bath, or a library, or a museum, they will not, by refraining from doing this, promote a wider national interest. They will be 'martyrs by mistake' and, in their martyrdom, will be injuring others as well as themselves. Through their misdirected good will the mounting wave of unemployment will be lifted still higher.

While they thought most of their fellow economists would agree with them, they did anticipate some dissent. T.E. Gregory, F.A. von Hayek, Arnold Plant and Lionel Robbins (Gregory et al., 1932) responded in *The Times* on 19 October 1932. Gregory et al. took issue with MacGregor et al.'s lack of understanding of the difference between consumption and real investment. Instead, they argued that investment was crucial to lengthening the process of production. While increased consumption would fuel immediate consumption industries, it would not provide the incentive for productive long-term investments. Gregory et al. disagreed with MacGregor et al.'s insistence that government had both the capacity and the incentive to use deficit spending to increase aggregate demand. Gregory et al. (1932: 10) believed that '[i]f the Government wish to help revival, the right way for them to proceed is, not expenditure, but to abolish those restrictions on trade and the free movement of capital (including restrictions on new issues) which are at present impeding even the beginning of recovery.'

The exchange on the pages of *The Times* between Keynes (MacGregor et al., 1932) and Hayek (Gregory et al., 1932) was just the start of what was to become one of the most important public policy debates of the century, one that would continue until even the present day.[1] While Keynes's ideas had a deep influence on the economics profession, it arguably had an even bigger impact on public policy, where, once adopted, it never waned despite scholarly rejection. Keynes's deficit spending prescriptions effectively eliminated the budget constraint of public officials, engendering a dramatic jump in the growth of government deficit spending and the size of government in general (Buchanan and Wagner, 2000 [1977]; Buchanan et al., 1978; Hayek, 1976: 90). As Cochrane (2009) explains,

> [f]iscal stimulus can be great politics, at least in the short run. The beneficiaries of government largesse know who wrote them a check. The businesses and consumers who end up getting less credit, and the businesses that can't sell them products, can only blame 'the crisis', and call up their congressmen to get their own stimulus.

It is important to note, as Skidelsky (2009: 103) points out, that many of Keynes's followers bastardized his theory in order to justify policies that even Keynes did not approve of (also see Leeson, 1997; 1999). Towards the end of his life, even Keynes questioned the desirability of having government take more than 25 per cent of national income (Skidelsky, 2009: xvi). Skidelsky (2009: 103) does admit, though, that Keynes was partially at fault for this because Keynes, in his hurry to get policies enacted, did not insist on close adherence to his theories (also see Leijonhufvud, 1968).

A few economists saw through the alluring Keynesian promises of growth-inducing profligacy and levied a decisive critique of Keynesian economics and its followers, which became known as the 'New Economics'. Henry Hazlitt was one of the most thorough critics of Keynes, publishing both an almost line-by-line refutation of Keynes's *General Theory* (1959) and an edited volume of the critics of Keynesianism (1995 [1960]). Despite the severe shortcomings found in the Keynesian model by its critics, revealing the fallacy of the Keynesian system, Keynesian ideas have witnessed a surge in popularity in the wake of the current financial crisis, especially in the political arena. Looking over the debates that occurred in the past and comparing them to those occurring today, one cannot help but get a feeling of déjà vu that we are, once again, embarking on the economically dangerous road of deficits, debt and debasement (see Smith, 1776; Beaulier and Boettke, 2009).

Nearly eight decades after the onset of these Keynesian ideas, the debate over the efficacy of public spending during economic downturns is once again in full swing. In the *Sunday Times* a debate broke out between economists led by Tim Besley and Lord Robert Skidelsky respectively. Besley et al.'s letter on 14 February 2010 warns the UK against the problems that plague governmental fiscal policies. Along with 19 other co-signers, he states '[i]n order to restore trust in the fiscal framework, the government should also introduce more independence into the generation of fiscal forecasts and the scrutiny of the government's performance against its stated fiscal goals.' Robert Skidelsky, along with 56 co-signers (among them Brad DeLong and Nobel Laureate Joseph Stiglitz), fired back on 18 February 2010:

> They seek to frighten us with the present level of the deficit but mention neither the automatic reduction that will be achieved as and when growth is resumed nor the effects of growth on investor confidence. How do the letter's signatories

> imagine foreign creditors will react if implementing fierce spending cuts tips the economy back into recession? To ask – as they do – for independent appraisal of fiscal policy forecasts is sensible. But for the good of the British people – and for fiscal sustainability – the first priority must be to restore robust economic growth. The wealth of the nation lies in what its citizens can produce.

Another example of the return of this debate came when, in a recent issue of *The Economist*, economists Brad De Long and Luigi Zingales (Lane et al., 2009) debated the desirability of Keynesianism. De Long asserts that the issue comes down to Say's Law, about which he claims, '[a]nyone who uses his or her eyes can determine that Say's law is in general false.' Much of the Keynesian refutation of Say's law is suspect, as Hazlitt (1995 [1960]: 6) pointed out, 'Keynes "refuted" Say's Law only in a sense in which no serious economist ever maintained it.' In reality, the Keynesians, even today, are adhering to the same distorted interpretation of Say's Law (see Horwitz, 1997; Kates, 1998).

Zingales was more on the mark. He claims the only way 'we are all Keynesians now' is in the sense that politicians and the general public are drawn into the Keynesian mentality. As he said (Lane et al., 2009),

> Keynesianism has conquered the hearts and minds of politicians and ordinary people alike because it provides a theoretical justification for irresponsible behaviour. Medical science has established that one or two glasses of wine per day are good for your long-term health, but no doctor would recommend a recovering alcoholic to follow this prescription. Unfortunately, Keynesian economists do exactly this. They tell politicians, who are addicted to spending our money, that government expenditures are good. And they tell consumers, who are affected by severe spending problems, that consuming is good, while saving is bad. In medicine, such behaviour would get you expelled from the medical profession; in economics, it gives you a job in Washington.

Despite the fact that these Keynesian ideas have once again gained prominence among even some notable economists, we would be reckless to discard the lessons from the past and re-embrace these ideas. Arguments made and the lessons learned have not been retained, and once again we are heading down the path of fiscal profligacy, and capricious government intervention. These misguided policy recommendations, which are all too quickly embraced by politicians eager to curry favor with special interest groups, come at precisely the time when basic economics shows the need for fiscal austerity and political stability.

The remainder of this chapter will explain the evolution of the Keynesian ideas and show that some modern economists re-adopted the Keynesian tenets, almost wholesale, when the current financial crisis hit. We will examine the modern arguments advanced by Keynesians such as Paul

Krugman and Brad DeLong, and demonstrate that they are essentially making the same arguments that were advanced in the past. We show that the critiques levied by Keynesian critics back in the 1950s are just as relevant and devastating to Keynesian propositions today as they were in the past but need to be more creatively presented in order to catch hold.

2 KEYNESIAN HISTORY

John Maynard Keynes published his *General Theory* after the worst period of the Great Depression had ended and recovery had commenced. In the *General Theory*, Keynes holds that the economy is primarily in a state of unemployment equilibrium, rejecting the classical model of full equilibrium. Many of these ideas directly called into question the common beliefs in economics, not just at the time, but even today. As Frank Knight (1937) noted, '. . . Mr Keynes's own doctrines are, as he would proudly admit, among the notorious fallacies to combat which has been considered a main function of the teaching of economics.'

The economy is mired in a chronic state of recession because of excess savings and thus a lack of consumption and investment. According to Keynes, investment falls short of savings because of the decreasing Marginal Efficiency of Capital as more investment is made in the same homogeneous capital, as well as the capriciousness of the determinates of the interest rates (Shackle, 1973; Skidelsky et al., 2010: 92). The lack of consumption and investment in turn leads to unemployment and a slowdown in production, decreasing income and consumption even further. The only way out of this 'paradox of thrift' is for government to run budget deficits during times of economic recession to increase consumption and investment. Even if the public money is not channeled into productive investments it would still do its job in jump-starting consumption and production by creating jobs. Keynes argued that budget deficits could be afforded because they would later be made up by budget surpluses in better economic times.

In the wake of the *General Theory* came many attempts at interpreting Keynes's ideas, engendering an extensive body of newly inspired macroeconomic work. As Paul Samuelson (1988) observed, '[t]he Keynesian revolution was the most significant event in 20th-century economic science'. In the first few decades after the *General Theory* was published, the followers of Keynes sought not only to clarify what Keynes had said but also to understand and account for the counter-arguments being made at that time.

Essentially the early Keynesians believed the economy was inherently unstable and subject to shocks due to their belief that investment was erratically influenced by 'animal spirits', and thus subject to huge swings based upon artificial considerations. Once out of equilibrium, they believed, the economy would take a long time to recover on its own, if at all, as Keynes held that there was no inherent tendency back to full employment equilibrium in the free market. Thus they argued that government intervention was required to restore effective aggregate demand in order to bring the economy back to full employment, and they believed that this was best achieved through fiscal, rather than monetary policy. As Keynes (1932: 60) wrote, '. . . there will be no means of escape from prolonged and perhaps interminable depression except by state intervention to promote and subsidise new investment'.

By the 1950s many believed that Keynes and his followers had won the day. Samuelson (1955) showed that 90 per cent of American economists accepted the 'neo-classical synthesis', meaning they generally accepted the classical model for microeconomic issues and the Keynesian model for macroeconomic issues. In the neo-classical synthesis, macroeconomics takes precedence over microeconomics, especially during economic downturns, because unless the economy is in macroeconomic balance, microeconomic market forces won't operate. While this last point is similar to the new classical perspective, it is important to note a point that Boettke (2009b) makes that distinguishes the two approaches:

> while there may be macroeconomic problems, there are only microeconomic explanations and solutions. Aggregate variables do not interact with one another independent of the choices of individuals. And those choices are guided by the incentives actors face, and the informational signals they receive. In short, economics is about exchange and the institutions within which exchanges take place. It is all about property rights, relative prices, the lure of profit and the penalty of loss.

In the long run the classical model was correct but economists seemed to believe the Keynesian model was necessary for short-run aggregate phenomena. In other words, though it was generally held that fiscal austerity and balanced budgets were economically desirable, these fundamentals should be abandoned in times of economic hardship. As Hayek (1995 [1966]: 241) wrote, the *General Theory*, '. . . more than any other single work', furthered the '. . . ascendancy of macroeconomics and the temporary decline of microeconomic theory'.

Despite this dominance in macroeconomics from the 1950s to the 1970s, there were a few lone voices making important criticisms of the Keynesian theory. On 31 December 1965, *Time* magazine quoted Milton Friedman as declaring '[w]e are all Keynesians now', but Friedman corrected the quote by providing the context in a letter to the editor on 4 February 1966, writing,

> You quote me [Dec. 31] as saying: 'We are all Keynesians now'. The quotation is correct, but taken out of context. As best I can recall it, the context was: 'In one sense, we are all Keynesians now; in another, nobody is any longer a Keynesian.' The second half is at least as important as the first.

Friedman was referring to the fact that even though Keynesian ideas were on the way out in the profession because they could not be grounded in microeconomic foundations, in times of economic turmoil economists and politicians would still turn in desperation back to the empty, but alluring, Keynesian promises. By the 1970s Keynesian ideas were thought to have been relegated to the history of economics within the profession, though they were never eradicated from politics or textbooks. Friedman's monetarist counter-revolution helped illustrate many of the flaws with the Keynesian models and helped pave the way for a revival of the classical approach which became known as the 'New Classical' school, led by Robert Lucas. Lucas and Sargent (1978) rejected the Keynesian model as well as attempts to modify it:

> existing Keynesian macroeconomic models cannot provide reliable guidance in the formulation of monetary, fiscal, or other types of policy. This conclusion is based in part on the spectacular recent failures of these models and in part on their lack of a sound theoretical or econometric basis. Second, on the latter ground, there is no hope that minor or even major modification of these models will lead to significant improvement in their reliability.

The massive inflation, and even stagflation, of the 1970s, coupled with the theoretical contributions of the Monetarists and New Classical Economics, led to a shift in macroeconomic thinking (Buchanan, 2001 [1986]: 324). A renaissance of the market economy shifted the macroeconomic view of the role of government. They held that government intervention inhibited the self-correcting tendencies of the market. What was needed, especially in times of economic recession, was not more government intervention, but less government intervention. Keynesian theorists were forced back to their drawing boards because they had no way to incorporate these microeconomic foundations into their aggregated macroeconomic models while retaining the traditional Keynesian governmental panaceas they favored.

The New Keynesian theorists ended up adopting some key features of the New Classical School. Namely, they attempted to titivate the Keynesian models by incorporating microeconomic foundations. The New Keynesian literature has attempted to 'search for rigorous and convincing models of wage and/or price stickiness based on maximizing behaviour and rational expectations' (Gordon, 1990). So while Keynes described the economy as inherently out of equilibrium, with no tendency towards it, New Keynesians view the market as always tending towards equilibrium, just that certain rigidities prevent the market from equilibrating automatically, leaving some room for government intervention, but, as Cochrane (2009) explains, 'not to rescuing the ancient view that fiscal stimulus is important'.

3 THE CURRENT CRISIS AND THE RETURN OF BASIC KEYNESIAN IDEAS

There are still modern adherents of Keynesianism who attempt to defend the traditional Keynesian prescriptions despite the many theoretical shortcomings of the outmoded model. Additional layers of sophistication and technicality have been added, but they are still built upon the same debunked Keynesian foundations. As John Cochrane (2009) points out about the theories used to debunk Keynesiansim, '[t]his is not fancy economics. Most of my arguments come from simply asking where the money is going to come from, simple arithmetic.' To their credit, some modern adherents of Keynesianism such as the above-mentioned New Keynesians, have outright rejected Keynesian tenets and prescriptions that have failed to find support in basic microeconomic theory.

Modern Keynesians have also attempted to justify stimulus policies based upon modern government capabilities. Just as Mises (1952: 69) said of Keynes and his *General Theory*, '[w]hat he really did was to write an apology for the prevailing policies of governments', so too are ideas of modern Keynesians. These theories hold that with advances in oversight and accountability practices, political pitfalls that have plagued past stimulus attempts, such as stimulus funds being directed to politically motivated projects rather than towards productive investments, can be avoided. The Internet, better accountability standards and refined management techniques, they argue, can ensure that stimulus funds are funneled only to those projects that are ensured to meet a minimum requirement of productivity (Summers, 2008). While certainly appealing, the blunders and earmarks that characterized the recent stimulus packages suggest that even the Internet and advanced management techniques cannot ensure against political shenanigans and defalcations (de Rugy, 2010; Newton-Small and Scherer, 2009). Furthermore, even if modern proponents of Keynesianism solve the public choice critiques, they still have failed to address the even more devastating critiques. Horwitz (2010a) stresses the importance of the epistemic problem faced by stimulus programs, 'the important question is not "how many jobs?" *but "which jobs?"* Jobs are easy to create; the right jobs are not and require the distributed intelligence of the marketplace.'

Despite some of the valiant attempts to address and account for past critiques of Keynesian ideas, when a crisis hits, any progress is thrown out the window in favor of the politically popular Keynesian solutions. Despite the long history of unanswered critiques, and failed attempts that forced even the old proponents of Keynesianism to reject old Keynesian tenets, the promise of economic recovery through fiscal profligacy proves too enticing to resist. Modern Keynesians, when it comes to economically trying times, are making the very same mistakes as their predecessors. In response to the current crisis they have offered up essentially the same Keynesian nostrums. Just like the Keynesians of yesterday they seek the miracle of turning stone into bread (Mises, 1948), but have failed to explain how this miracle is to happen. As many of the old critics of the Keynesian system have pointed out, they keep trying in vain. In this section we will demonstrate that the Keynesian framework failed to stand up to basic economic critiques in the past, and that modern manifestations of Keynesianism still fail this test, and thus are inappropriate and even pernicious, especially in a downturned economy.

3.1 The Framework

Little has been added to the traditional Keynesian framework since the 1950s. Despite its lackluster performance, and the inability of proponents to provide a microeconomic justification for it, stimulus is still the proffered solution for an economic downturn. Larry Summers (2010) directly makes the case for Keynesian remedies:

> It is important to recognize that the ultimate consequences of stimulus for indebtedness depend critically on the macroeconomic conditions. When the economy is demand constrained, the impact of a dollar of tax cuts or expansionary investment will be at its highest and the impact on deficits at its lowest.

As Keynes et al. (MacGregor et al., 1932) argue, the solution for economic woes cannot be found in the private economy, and government must step in to boost consumption in order to put the economy on the path to recovery. This same argument is once again being used to argue for Keynesian-inspired stimulus. Paul Krugman (2010a) argues, 'Penny-pinching at a time like this isn't just cruel; it endangers the nation's future. And it doesn't even do much to reduce our future debt burden, because stinting on spending now threatens the economic recovery, and with it the hope for rising revenues.'

Krugman's quote bears a close resemblance to Keynes (1932: 61): 'The voices which – in such a conjecture – tell us that the path of escape is to be found in strict economy and in refraining, wherever possible, from utilizing the world's potential production, are the voices of fools and madmen.'

Larry Summers (2010) echoes this same sentiment, arguing that there is a strong case for temporary stimulus if there are rigid interest rates and excess capacity, because the short-run multiplier is likely to be higher than average. Christina Romer (2009a) stresses the inability of the private sector to recover from the current economic crisis without the assistance of government-directed stimulus:

> With the dramatic fall in household wealth and the rapid spread of the downturn to our key trading partners, there was no realistic prospect that the private sector would generate a turnaround in demand any time soon. Thus, although stabilizing the financial system and helping distressed homeowners was essential, it would not be enough. We needed to bring in the other main tool that a government has to counteract a cataclysmic decline in aggregate demand: fiscal stimulus.

Robert Frank (2009) chimes in as well, defending the case for stimulus:

> The only remaining major component of aggregate demand is government spending. Stimulus proponents, following John Maynard Keynes, believe that increased government spending – financed by borrowed funds or printing new money – is the only way to bolster aggregate demand and end the downturn quickly. Recent results suggest that this strategy is working.

Despite all these prominent economists defending stimulus today, the Keynesian case for stimulus has been carefully refuted, both in the past and in modern times. John Cochrane (2009) lays out three of the most poignant arguments against Keynesian stimulus:

> First, if money is not going to be printed, it has to come from somewhere. If the government borrows a dollar from you, that is a dollar that you do not spend, or that you do not lend to a company to spend on new investment. Every dollar of increased government spending must correspond to one less dollar of private spending. Jobs created by stimulus spending are offset by jobs lost from the decline in private spending.
>
> Second, investment is 'spending' every bit as much as is consumption. Keynesian fiscal stimulus advocates want money spent on consumption, not saved. They evaluate past stimulus programs by whether people who got stimulus money spent it on consumption goods rather than save it. But the economy overall does not care if you buy a car, or if you lend money to a company that buys a forklift.

> Third, people must ignore the fact that the government will raise future taxes to pay back the debt. If you know your taxes will go up in the future, the right thing to do with a stimulus check is to buy government bonds so you can pay those higher taxes. Now the net effect of fiscal stimulus is exactly zero, except to raise future tax distortions. The classic arguments for fiscal stimulus presume that the government can systematically fool people.

So, Keynesian proponents must assume that government has better incentives and a better capacity than the private sector to direct resources to their most productive use. Eugene Fama (2009) echoes this point,

> Even when there are lots of idle workers, government bailouts and stimulus plans are not likely to add to employment. The reason is that bailouts and stimulus plans must be financed. The additional government debt means that existing current resources just move from one use to another, from private investment to government investment or from investment to consumption, with no effect on total current resources in the system or on total employment.

Then Keynesians must assume that savings is an actual leakage from the economy, but that hardly is the case. Tyler Cowen (2010) argues, '[c]orporations with cash surpluses are not destroying real resources, nor are they stuffing cash in their mattresses. They are investing in financial assets.' Rizzo (2010a) adds to this explanation:

> unemployment of resources, including labor, is not always pure idleness. We are living in conditions of real uncertainty. A bubble has burst, the domestic auto industry faces uncertain prospects, tax rates are on the way up – how far and in what respects is anyone's guess – we have just faced a possible healthcare transformation with its unique costs and taxes, European debt problems are becoming manifest, and more.

Finally, Keynesian proponents must also assume that people do not take into consideration that the stimulus must be paid back eventually in the form of higher taxes. In attempting to measure the multiplier effect of stimulus dollars during peacetime, Robert Barro (2009) got a number that was insignificantly different from zero, due to the fact that people foresee the growth in taxes to pay for the stimulus.

Mario Rizzo (2010b) questions the Keynesian tendency to disband economic theory during downturns, asking '[w]hen does the Keynesian moment end – and the ordinary laws of economics retake the stage?' Rizzo (2010c) also questions the ability of government to actually cut government spending during good economic times to make up for financial profligacy during economic downturns due to entrenched special interest groups. If there are any reductions, they 'will be half-measures taken half-heartedly. *So over the long run the size and scope of government will expand permanently*' (Rizzo, 2010d, emphasis in the original). Freedman et al. (2010) find that without a political regime that ensures that deficits do not continue to grow once the economy improves, the long-run costs of deficit spending during a recession can exceed the short-run benefits.

The Keynesian model, at its best, is still an over-simplified and overly aggregated schematic that is built upon highly idealized assumptions of benevolence and omniscience. This was a severe problem for Keynes, whose main criticism of the classical school, according to his biographer Robert Skidelsky (2009: 82), was that it 'used models which assumed certain things which did not occur in the real world'. As Hayek (1995 [1966]: 242) noted on the aggregation of Keynes's model:

> His final conceptions rest entirely on the belief that there exist relatively simple and constant functional relationships between such 'measurable' aggregates as total demand, investment, or output, and that empirically established values of these presumed 'constants' would enable us to make valid predictions. There seems to me, however, not only to exist no reason whatever to assume that these 'functions' will remain constant, but I believe that microtheory had demonstrated long before Keynes that they cannot be constant but will change over time not only in quantity but even in direction.

Keynes, while criticizing classical economists for assuming full employment, embraced an equally unrealistic assumption of full unemployment of all resources. As Hayek (1995 [1966]: 243) argues, this assumption,

> is not only at least as unlikely to be true in fact as the former; it is much more misleading. An analysis on the assumption of full employment, even if the assumption is only partially valid, at least helps us to understand the functioning of the price mechanism, the significance of the relations between different prices and of the factors which lead to a change in these relations. But the assumption that all goods and factors are available in excess makes the whole price system redundant, undetermined and unintelligible. Indeed, some of the most orthodox disciples of Keynes appear consistently to have thrown overboard all the traditional theory of price determination and of distribution, all that used to be the backbone of economic theory, and in consequence, in my opinion, to have ceased to understand any economics.

Keynes also did not foresee the public choice issues that emerge in contemporary democratic settings in which public policy is actually formed and implemented, instead assuming that policy was crafted by a small group of relatively wise and enlightened people (Buchanan et al., 1978: 16). The case for Keynesianism was also grounded in a closed economy model, and as Niall Ferguson (2009) points out, we are in 'a globalized world, where uncoordinated profligacy by national governments is more likely to generate bond-market and currency-market volatility than a return to growth.'

The Keynesian model also fails to account for how government intervention in the economy distorts the incentives to invest. Not only did Keynesian-inspired stimulus during the Great Depression fail to help the economy improve (Romer, 2009b), Keynesian policies adversely affected investment because businessmen were scared to undertake long-term projects with the uncertainty created by the constant political manipulation of the economy (Higgs, 1997). People make decisions based upon relative prices, and when government intervenes in the economy, distorting relative prices, it incentivizes people to behave in unpredictable ways, leading to what economists refer to as the problem of 'unintended consequences'. Keynesian models avoid taking into account these relatives price effects and the toll they take on the economy. As Lee Ohanian (2009) argues,

> the old Keynesian model does not come anywhere close to meeting today's standards for economic analysis. Economics is about incentives: the incentives for households to work, consume and save, and the incentives for business to hire workers and invest in plants and equipment. These incentives are remarkably absent from the macroeconomics of yesteryear. And modern economic analysis shows that the impact of government spending on the economy depends on what it is being spent on and how it ultimately is paid for.

3.2 The Causes of the Crisis

There is a wide range of explanations offered for the current financial crisis. Some of the competing narratives advanced are new, relying on modern conditions or innovations for their explanation, while others echo explanations that have been advanced to explain past economic downturns. The traditional Keynesian explanation for the severity of the Great Depression, as outlined in Keynes et al.'s letter in *The Times* blaming private sector spending, is once again being advanced, as Martin Wolf (2010) argues: '[w]hat we are seeing, in short, is an epidemic of private sector frugality'.

Some of the most widely cited explanations include blaming complex and poorly understood financial instruments (Foster, 2009) and private sector greed (Kotlikoff, 2010: 31). While arguments for greed and stupidity are tempting, they fail to explain why these components of human nature, which are omnipresent, all of a sudden lead to a financial meltdown, and thus fail to adequately explain the root causes, leading to misguided policy recommendations. Similarly, some explanations focus on the deregulation of the financial sector, which in turn let loose private sector greed

(Skidelsky, 2009: 44). In an op-ed in the *New York Times*, Krugman (2009) blames the deregulation of the financial system for partially being at fault for the onset of the financial crisis:

> America emerged from the Great Depression with a tightly regulated banking system. The regulations worked: the nation was spared major financial crises for almost four decades after World War II. But as the memory of the Depression faded, bankers began to chafe at the restrictions they faced. And politicians, increasingly under the influence of free-market ideology, showed a growing willingness to give bankers what they wanted . . . And the bankers – liberated both by legislation that removed traditional restrictions and by the hands-off attitude of regulators who didn't believe in regulation – responded by dramatically loosening lending standards. The result was a credit boom and a monstrous real estate bubble, followed by the worst economic slump since the Great Depression.

Similarly, the lack, or insufficiency, of regulation is often advanced as an alternative, or contributing factor to the financial crisis as well (Bernanke, 2010). Contrary to this claim, many economists have actually found that contradictory, complex, and constantly changing regulation led to the financial industry troubles. Klein (2010) challenges this explanation by looking at some basic measures of the magnitude of financial regulation, such as the number of federal registry pages, the amount of federal spending on finance and banking regulation, as well as other metrics for the growth of government. Klein finds no trend to indicate that there actually was a period of decline, or even lack of growth, in government programs or financial regulation. The deregulation and free market sentiments were stronger in rhetoric than in actual practice.

Levine (2010a) stresses that innovation is a constant in all industries, and that yes, it does have risks and sometimes leads to product misuse, but that claiming financial innovation inhibits economic growth is like claiming that medical research does not advance human health because sometimes drugs are abused. Financial innovation, just like innovation in any other sector, is a necessary component of economic growth.

Another explanation offered for the current crisis is that large capital inflows from foreign nations, due to a global savings glut, lowered interest rates and led to a rise in mortgages and a decline in lending standards (Greenspan, 2010). Taylor (2009) finds that there is no empirical evidence to support this argument, and that the evidence actually points to a saving shortage. The 'savings glut', even if it were conceivable in a world of scarcity, to the extent it exists outside the United States was offset by the saving shortage in the United States.

A more comprehensive understanding of the financial crisis requires taking a broader perspective of the political economy of the events preceding the crisis. Only with this perspective can the role that government, and in particular Keynesian-inspired policies, played in creating the regulatory and institutional conditions that set the stage for the real estate bubble and its subsequent collapse be seen. In this section we discuss what we hold to be the primary causes of the start and continuation of the financial crisis; namely inflationary policies, policies that led to the housing bubble, and the regulatory regime.

3.2.1 Inflationary policies

In response to the recession of 2001, the Federal Reserve pushed down the federal funds rate, the primary target rate of the Federal Reserve, from 6 per cent in January 2001, where it had hovered in between 4.5 and 6.5 per cent since the end of 1994, to hover around 1 per cent by around July 2003, its lowest rate in 40 years (Roberts, 2010). It even reached negative rates when adjusted for inflation (FRED, 2010). The artificially low interest rates and inflation spurred investments for which the economy did not have real resources to complete. In other words, the cheap availability of loans encouraged entrepreneurs to collectively make investments that exceeded the resources of the economy, and the productive and technological capacities of the economy. While an un-manipulated interest rate would have risen, operating as a brake on the economy to curtail malinvestment and overinvestment, and would have allocated loanable funds to only their most valuable projects (Hayek, 1975 [1933]: 94), the artificially low interest rates prevented this rationing device from operating to choke off superfluous investment.

Taylor (2009) finds that the excess monetary expansion was the main cause of the boom and the subsequent bust. Using the Taylor rule, a monetary policy rule that accounts for inflation and the interest rate, a rule that the Federal Reserve has followed for roughly the last 20 years, Taylor compares the actual federal funds rate with the federal funds rate that should have been targeted according to the rule. Taylor finds that there was a significant deviation from the prescriptions of the Taylor rule, indicating that monetary policy was too easy according to what historical experience dictates it should be. Using a model, Taylor then estimates what housing starts would have been had the Taylor rule been followed, and then charts them against the actual housing starts, showing that the low interest rates were indeed a key factor in the housing bubble.

Europe offers further empirical evidence to indict inflationary policies in the financial crisis. Rajan (2010) argues, '[c]ountries that had strongly negative real policy rates – Ireland and Spain are primary exhibits – had a housing boom and bust, while countries like Germany with low inflation, and therefore higher real policy rates, did not'. A working paper by two authors at the European Central Bank (Maddaloni and Peydro, 2010) establishes a causal connection between the inflationary policies of the ECB and the FED and the subsequent decline in commercial, mortgage and retail lending standards.

This was also recognized by Mises (1948) when he said, 'John Maynard Keynes, late economic adviser to the British Government, is the new prophet of inflationism.' The arguments by modern Keynesians are similar to the original arguments Keynes himself made. As Mises (1949: 787–93) also wrote, 'Keynes did not add any new idea to the body of inflationist fallacies, a thousand times refuted by economists . . . He merely knew how to cloak the plea for inflation and credit expansion in the sophisticated terminology of mathematical economics.' Economists like Mises knew the true effects of inflation.

Inflation, as Hayek argued, is a lot more destructive than just a rise in the general price level. Inflation necessarily creates changes in relative prices, causing people to adjust their behavior, which in turn creates even more distortions that ripple through the economy, pushing the economy to a position that is inconsistent with the underlying preferences and technology. Much of the concerns of Keynesians, such as unemployment, are often caused by this inflationary distortion of relative prices. As Hayek (1974) noted in his Nobel lecture,

> We have indeed good reason to believe that unemployment indicates that the structure of relative prices and wages has been distorted (usually by monopolistic or governmental price fixing), and that to restore equality between the demand and the supply of labour in all sectors changes of relative prices and some transfers of labour will be necessary.

The problem with inflation, and why it adversely affects relative prices, is that it ripples through the economy, distorting the information signals which prices represent. Hayek (1945) carefully detailed the important role that prices play in the economy by transmitting dispersed knowledge of time and place to the relevant economic actors. As Hayek (1941: 64) notes:

> But general price changes are no essential feature of a monetary theory of the trade cycle; they are not only unessential, but they would be completely irrelevant if only they were completely 'general' – that is, if they affected all prices at the same time and in the same proportion. The point of the real interest to trade cycle theory is the existence of certain deviations in individual price relations occurring because changes in the volume of money appear at certain individual points; deviations, that is, away from the position that is necessary to maintain the whole system in equilibrium.

Easy money policies fuel speculation and investments that fall beyond what would be encouraged by un-manipulated market prices. Savings represents the amount of future goods that consumers desire, and the interest rate adjusts to allocate the available savings among the competing investment projects. Excessive investment in a stable monetary regime, as mentioned above, would be discouraged by rising interest rates. In an inflationary environment this check on investment never operates, and thus, more investment projects are undertaken then dictated by consumers' desires for future goods. This leads to an eventual economic bust as investors realize that they undertook investments for which consumers were not actually leaving unconsumed (i.e. saving) enough real resources for all of them to be carried out. A policy of accelerating inflation may delay this bust, but the heavy economic and thus political costs of increasing inflation will eventually force a shift in policy that will unmask the investment errors. During the bust, resources will be channeled back into the projects that are in alignment with customer preferences and savings, absent further distortionary monetary or fiscal policy (see Garrison, 2001).

Inflation also bears additional costs, besides the relative price manipulations that undermine the epistemic function of prices. There are costs of avoiding inflation, which involve both the cost of tax lawyers and accounts, as well as the economic cost of investors refraining from particular investments, or altering their investment and consumption plans in order to obtain favorable tax treatment. There is the search for otherwise unproductive assets whose use lies solely in their ability to hold value during inflationary times. There are 'shoe leather costs', which are the costs associated with people having to run to the bank more frequently during inflationary times. In addition, there are also 'menu costs', which comprise the costs associated with price changes necessitated by inflation, such as having to reprint menus in order to reflect higher prices. Accountancy costs emerge because the relative price distortions don't equally affect all goods at the same time, so it undermines the accuracy of the information conveyed by financial statements. Accountancy costs are exacerbated by the fact that these distorted financial statements are then used to make future plans, meaning that inflationary distortions are carried forward. Finally, bouts of inflation also undermine the reliability of contracts, making private actors more wary of engaging in long-term contracts, as well as raising the costs of contract negotiation and enforcement.

3.2.2 Housing bubble

The easy money and artificially low interest rates spurred a bubble in the housing sector, where the ten-city composite index realized an average annualized rate of return of 13 per cent from June 2001 to June

2006 (Murphy, 2008). There were several factors that concentrated the excess currency, or overinvestment, into the housing sector. First was Fannie Mae and Freddie Mac, both government-sponsored enterprises that were chartered by Congress with the intent of providing liquidity, stability and affordability to the mortgage market in order to promote access to mortgage credit (Fannie Mae, 1954; Federal Home Loan Mortgage Corporation, 1970). In other words, the political purpose of these government-sponsored enterprises was putting mortgages into the hands of people who would otherwise have been denied a mortgage in the free market due to insufficient income, an unstable job, or lack of assets (cf. Block et al., 2008). In fact, these agencies were given a target requirement for the number of loans they made to borrowers with below median income for the area, which rose to 55 per cent in 2007 (HUD, 2008). They accomplished this by participating in the secondary market for mortgages or by buying up bundled mortgages from banks, either through outright purchase or by swapping them for a mortgage-backed security that promises the originators a guaranteed rate of return. Both of these courses of action shelter the originating bank from the risks of its mortgages as the risk is transferred to Fannie and Freddie.

Fannie and Freddie were equipped with several privileges unavailable to market institutions in order to carry out this goal. One of the most favorable privileges was that Fannie and Freddie were implicitly backed by the US taxpayers, meaning that while the stockholders maintained any gains, there was an implicit federal guarantee for any losses that resulted from the mortgages. Privatizing gains and socializing losses obviously in and of itself sets up the perverse incentives for excessive risk-taking. Fannie and Freddie were also able to borrow funds at a rate that was only slightly above the federal funds rate, a rate that was significantly lower than the rate available to market institutions (Bernanke, 2007). With these special provisions, Fannie and Freddie were in control of a combined $1.8 trillion in assets by 2003 (Frame and White, 2005). To put that in perspective, based purely upon assets, they were respectively the second and third largest companies in the US at that time. Between 1998 and 2003, when the housing market began to soar, they were the most frequent buyers of loans (Roberts, 2010). In return for these privileges, the government ensured that they would have the ability to influence the policies of Fannie and Freddie through the presidential appointment of five members of both Fannie's and Freddie's board of directors and through the Department of Housing and Urban Development.

Another factor that channeled overinvestment into the housing industry was tax code manipulation. To encourage house ownership, the US government has kept an extremely popular deduction for mortgages, while renting has not received similar treatment (Norberg, 2009). In 1997, home ownership was again encouraged through the tax code through the abolition of the capital gains tax on real estate investments, while it was maintained for other types of investments (Roberts, 2010). Just this change in 1997 is estimated to have increased the number of homes sold by 17 per cent (Bajaj and Leonhardt, 2008). Nobel Laureate Vernon Smith (2007) wrote that the 1997 tax break was the cause that fueled the 'mother of all housing bubbles'.

Of course, the view that government programs that distorted relative prices in order to influence private actors' decisions is not new; in fact, Henry Hazlitt, in his famous *Economics in One Lesson* (1979 [1946]: 47), warned that:

> Government-guaranteed home mortgages, especially when a negligible down payment or no down payment whatever is required, inevitably mean more bad loans than otherwise. They force the general taxpayer to subsidize the bad risks and to defray the losses. They encourage people to 'buy' houses that they cannot really afford. They tend eventually to bring about an oversupply of houses as compared with other things. They temporarily overstimulate building, raise the cost of building for everybody (including the buyers of the homes with the guaranteed mortgages), and may mislead the building industry into an eventually costly overexpansion. In brief in the long run they do not increase overall national production but encourage malinvestment.

This goes beyond just the housing bubble. Any artificial changes to the rate of interest will have a similar, and often devastating, effect. Hazlitt (1959: 385), in his almost point-by-point refutation of Keynesian fallacies in *The Failure of the 'New Economics'*, notes:

> It is hard to believe that Keynes is as naive as he pretends, and that he is not laughing up his sleeve. The rate of interest – the valuation of time and all investments – is to be taken out of the market and put completely in the hands of the state. But Keynes ignores the complete interconnectedness of all prices. This especially includes the price of capital loans, any State tinkering with which must necessarily affect and distort all prices and price relationships throughout the economy.

It is important to remember that the downturn is the recovery; the boom is where the problems emerge. The recession that results in the popping of the bubble is the market correcting itself. Thus as Rothbard (1962: 860) notes:

> It should be clear that any governmental interference with the depression process can only prolong it, thus making things worse from almost everyone's point of view. Since the depression process is the recovery process, any halting

> or slowing down of the process impedes the advent of recovery. The depression readjustments must work themselves out before recovery can be complete. The more these adjustments are delayed, the longer the depression will have to last, and the longer the recovery is postponed. For example, if the government keeps wages rates up, it brings about permanent unemployment. If it keeps prices up, it brings about unsold surplus. And if it spurs credit expansion again, then new malinvestment and later depressions are spawned.

Thus, any attempts to use government to interfere with the market adjustments will make things worse. These are exactly the policies that the Keynesians prescribe to, and to which we now turn.

3.2.3 Regulatory regime

During a recession, whenever laws and regulations become highly sensitive to political manipulation or popular opinion, oftentimes the first people blamed as the culprits are businessmen and women. When popular sentiments such as this are combined with a political administration that demonstrates a willingness to intervene in the economy in order to appease these sentiments, it creates a highly unpredictable business atmosphere. So precisely when political officials should be setting an environment in which entrepreneurs feel safe to undertake investments, they often create an atmosphere that discourages investment. Robert Higgs (1997) finds that this phenomenon, known as 'regime uncertainty,' helps explain the magnitude and length of the Great Depression because of the constantly changing regulatory and legal framework in response to the recession. Policies that have been pursued before and during the current financial crisis have led to greater uncertainty for investors as well.

Ross Levine (2010b) finds that policymakers and regulators had a hand in creating conditions that led to the financial crisis by maintaining policies that encouraged destabilizing policies. Capital requirement regulations required investors to use the Securities and Exchange Commission (SEC)-created National Recognized Statistical Rating Organizations (NRSRO) for security ratings. The NRSRO has limited competition in the credit rating industry to just a few key players. In 2000 there were only three recognized agencies and no justification or list of criteria for becoming recognized (White, 2009). By sheltering the credit ratings from competition, entry and innovation, these regulations reduced the reputational incentives of the protected rating agencies to accurately rate securities. Other policies such as the Recourse Act, which revised the Basel regulations, gave banks the incentive to hold mortgage-backed securities over individual mortgages and commercial loans by changing their relative capital reserve requirements (Friedman, 2009; Roberts, 2010). As Friedman (2009) stresses, regulation homogenizes, mandating what regulators believe to be prudent banking practices on the entire system. If the regulators are wrong, the whole system is at risk. One of those misguided policies that encouraged systematic risk was the de facto policy of the federal government to bail out large or politically connected firms over the past three decades (Roberts, 2010). Following an implicit policy to bail out firms if they suffer extreme losses, but allowing them to enjoy all upside profits, mollifies the prudence inspired by the profit and loss system, encouraging more risky behavior.

In addition to regulations that played a role in leading to the financial crisis, there has been a flux of new regulations after the initial onset of the financial crisis that have created uncertainty for investors. The Obama administration's continuing lambasting of profit-seeking businessmen and women has in particular created an atmosphere of uncertainty. Alan Meltzer (2010) points to several factors that increased economic uncertainty in the wake of the start of the financial crisis. The passage of the healthcare bill produced uncertainty for employers, especially those considering hiring new employees, as there was significant doubt about the Congressional Budget Office (CBO)'s estimates of the total cost that would be borne by employers. In addition, the estimates for the healthcare bill also depended upon cutting spending in politically popular areas in the future and other generous assumptions, creating uncertainty about future tax hikes or inflation in order to fund it, along with rising uncertainty about future Social Security and Medicare obligations (Holtz-Eakin, 2010). The auto bailouts, which transgressed the rule of law in order to hand out political favors to politically powerful unions over bondholders, put further doubts into the minds of investors (King Jr, 2009). Amity Shlaes (2010) compares the adverse effects of government-induced uncertainty in the Great Depression as well as following the onset of the financial crisis, concluding that:

> Mr Geithner is gradually discovering that to recover, the market needs a specific kind of confidence. It is not something Washington can hand down. It is not even demand confidence – the confidence of the consumer who wants to shop. The confidence relevant to recovery is the confidence of the investor and the saver. It comes only when an administration in Washington demonstrates reliability and restraint.

These insights that government intervention in the economy can inhibit investors from investing and preventing recovery were stressed by past critics of Keynesianism. These flaws in the policy prescriptions stemming from the Keynesian ideas have long been refuted. Economists have seen through the inconsistencies since Keynes's *General Theory* itself. As economist David McCord Wright (1958) noted,

> If consistency is the bane of little minds, Lord Keynes had certainly a great one. No one who studies the work of John Maynard Keynes can fail to be impressed by the frequent brilliance of his insights and the usefulness of many of his tools of analysis. But he lacked that sober quality which causes a man to sit down and carefully consider the consistency of his various successive theories and pronouncements.

Chicago economist Frank Knight (1937), in his review of the *General Theory*, had little respect for Keynesian policy prescriptions from the view of economics when he said, 'I can only comment that phrases like socialization of investment, with no indication of what procedure is in mind, sound (to me) more like the language of the soap-box reformer than that of an economist writing a theoretical tome for economists.' This seems relevant to today, with many of the modern proposals from modern Keynesians.

Economists F.A. Hayek and William Hutt had legitimate fears about the outcomes of government intervention inherent in the Keynesian policies. Hayek (1941) noted, '[a]re we not even told that, "since in the long run we are all dead", policy should be guided entirely by short-run considerations? I fear that these believers in the principle of *après nous le deluge* may get what they have bargained for sooner than they wish.' And Hutt (1995 [1954]) worried,

> Actual policies have, for decades, been based precisely upon the politically attractive rule, justified by Keynesian teaching, that disharmony in the wage-rate structure must not be tackled but offset; whilst the current tendency is to assume dogmatically with no examination of the institutional and sociological factors involved, that to advocate wage and price adjustments is to recommend the conquest of the moon.

These fears have often manifested themselves in reality when Keynesian policies were implemented. Henry Morgenthau, the treasury secretary under Franklin D. Roosevelt, said in 1939, '[w]e are spending more money than we have ever spent before, and it does not work . . . We have never made good on our promises . . . after eight years of this administration we have just as much unemployment as when we started . . . and an enormous debt, to boot' (Schram, 2009). This led Hazlitt (1995 [1960]: 10) to wonder, '[b]ut whatever the full explanation of the Keynesian cult, its existence is one of the greatest intellectual scandals of our age'.

4 CONCLUSION: LACK OF CREATIVITY

In the progression of economic ideas, some ideas are discarded as theoretically unsound and empirically invalid. Keynesianism is one of those ideas that was found lacking and was therefore appropriately discarded. Yet, it has shown a bewildering tendency to re-emerge during times of economic hardship, precisely when a return to basic economics is needed most. Its promises to turn stone into bread are too enticing to refrain from entertaining. As Peter Boettke (2010) stresses,

> what we need in extraordinary times is simple economics; as simple economics is far from simple minded. In times of crisis it is too often assumed we need extraordinary and complex theories but what we really need is cool-headed and basic economic principles. As economists we tell our students in principles courses that incentives matter and we should know this is true even in times of crisis. When we forget and discard the basic principles of economics we make the very crisis we wish to solve worse.

Throughout history, fiscal profligacy and government interventionism have caused the decline and the downfall of many societies. While the theories that promise abundance out of scarcity are intoxicating, they are based upon false premises, which violate the fundamental lessons of basic economics. Heedless attempts to overturn the basic laws of economics with ungrounded Keynesian policies will only lead us down the dangerous path of deficits, debt and debasement.

That we find ourselves once again traveling down the road of deficits, debt and debasement is not just a failure that can be pinned on new Keynesians who have failed to reject conclusions of Keynes's system that fail to pass basic microeconomic inspection. Economists who have failed to explicate the theoretical and historical failure of Keynesianism in a fashion that would be understood by the economic profession, politicians and the public are also to be blamed. The revival of recycled Keynesian ideas has not instigated a serious reformulation of the way in which basic economics is articulated and conveyed, but a simple duplication of arguments already rendered in the past. Both sides of the debate have suffered from a lack of intellectual creativity, as well as a failure to talk on the same terms.

Similar to the debate between Malthus and Ricardo (see Maclachlan, 1999), the debate between Keynesian proponents and opponents has not reached resolution primarily due to the lack of realization that they are using two fundamentally different styles of economic argument. While Keynes criticized the mathematization of economics and warned against the excessive reliance on econometrics, his aggregative formulas, which abstracted out of real essential elements in the economy, were highly translatable into mathematics and econometrics.

What is needed is a radical rethinking of the monetary institutions in society, and the binding rules on fiscal policies. Some of the foremost economic scholars of the twentieth century, Nobel Laureates F.A. Hayek, James M. Buchanan and Milton Friedman, all tried to seek creative ways to bind fiscal and monetary authorities, especially when these authorities act in concert, engendering fiscal profligacy and expansion of government. Each one, in his own way, ended up rejecting the possibility of controlling government spending. Hayek (1976) proposed allowing competitive money issue. Friedman (2007), in an interview published posthumously, advocated handing the responsibilities of the Federal Reserve over to a computer. Finally, Buchanan (1962: 172) suggests that our monetary institutions have so utterly failed us that a complete restricting and constitutionalization of our monetary institutions are needed, not just marginal adjustments. Market forces would then spontaneously work in order to adjust the price level. As the general price level rose, people would exchange currency for bricks, and as the general price level fell, people would exchange bricks for currency.

This kind of creative thinking has been carried forward by monetary theorists George Selgin and Larry White (1994), who wrote a summary of the major advances in free banking scholarship for the *Journal of Economic Literature*. Laurence Kotlikoff (2010) takes a novel approach in his book, *Jimmy Stewart is Dead*, as well, recognizing that loose monetary policy helped lead up to the financial crisis, and that fiscal profligacy is not a viable long-run remedy for it either.

Given the monetary mischief and fiscal irresponsibility that has characterized modern social democratic societies, the choice before us is how to get back on a policy path of sound money and fiscal responsibility. This is a choice over rules and institutional structures. We are confronted, as Gerald O'Driscoll has put it, with the choice of either free banking, narrow banking, or no banking. What we cannot do is continue down our current policy path. Creative thought among the best and brightest political economists of our age must be directed on finding that set of rules which effectively binds the hands of the fiscal authority, and finding the alternative institutional arrangements for money and finance which will eliminate the ability of the state to engage in monetary mischief. In this regard, as in some many others, we cannot simply point backwards to the work of Hayek, Friedman and Buchanan, but we must begin with their work and push it forward in time to address our problems in our time.

This lack of creativity on both sides cannot be ignored. We have pointed out why we believe Keynesian ideas are the wrong way to go but this does not change the fact that the supporters of these ideas, then and now, are extremely smart people. It is beyond the purpose of this chapter to explain why the ideas persist, but what we do want to stress is that if we want to convince them of the flaws in the Keynesian system then none of us can continue to make the same arguments that we have made in the past. We must push forward in new ways to strengthen our position.

The déjà vu we are currently living through is dangerous. Fortunately, but perhaps even more unnerving, is that it is also unnecessary. The lessons of the past should be learned before the same mistakes are made yet again. Political economy has the answers, if anyone is willing to listen.

NOTE

1. While Hayek published *Prices and Production* in 1931, and Keynes published *A Treatise on Money* in 1930 (some of the 'Keynesian' ideas can even be traced back further to 1919 in his *The Economic Consequences of the Peace*), both books that established their separate systems, they were not in contact during the publication of these books (Hicks, 1967). In 1936 John Maynard Keynes published *The General Theory of Employment, Interest and Money* (*General Theory*), a book that laid out the groundwork for the widespread acceptance of his ideas, jump-starting the 'Keynesian Revolution'. This was a revolution in macroeconomic thought that rejected the classical view that markets are inherently self-correcting, instead holding that markets are in a constant state of employment disequilibrium and that government intervention is necessary to allow free markets to work (Keynes, 1934). Established economists at the time simply rejected any such notion of a revolution. As Frank Knight (1937) mentioned in his review, 'I may as well state at the outset that the direct contention of the work seems to me quite unsubstantiated.' Even Keynes's intellectual opponent, F.A. Hayek, chose not to review the book, believing that it was just 'another tract for the time', and meant primarily for the 'momentary needs of policy' (Hayek, 1995 [1966]: 241). The older economists mostly rejected Keynes's ideas but the young took it and ran with it, making sure the debate continued throughout the century.

REFERENCES

Bajaj, Vikas and David Leonhardt (2008), 'Tax break may have helped cause housing bubble', *The New York Times*, 18 December available at: http://www.nytimes.com/2008/12/19/business/19tax.html, accessed 14 July 2010.

Barro, Robert (2009), 'Government spending is no free lunch: now the democrats are peddling voodoo economics', *The Wall Street Journal*, 22 January, available at: http://onlinewsj.com/article/SB123258618204604599.html, accessed 10 August 2010.

Beaulier, Scott and Peter J. Boettke (2009), 'Hiding debt just a juggling trick', *Independent Institute*, 16 November, available at: http://www.independent.org/newsroom/article.asp?id=2660, accessed 27 August 2010.

Bernanke, Ben S. (2007), 'GSE portfolios, systemic risk, and affordable housing', speech before the Independent Community Bankers of America's Annual Convention and Techworld, Honolulu, Hawaii, via satellite, available at: http://www.federalreserve.gov/newsevents/speech/bernanke20070306a.htm, accessed 11 August 2010.

Bernanke, Ben S. (2010), 'Monetary policy and housing bubble', *Annual Meeting of the American Economic Association*, 3 January, available at: http://www.federalreserve.gov/newsevents/speech/bernanke20100103a.htm, accessed 3 July 2010.

Besley, Tim, Christopher Pissarides Marcet, Danny Quah, Meghnad Desai, Andrew Turnbull, Orazio Attanasio, Costas Meghir, John Vickers, John Muellbauer, David Newbery, Hashem Pesaran, Ken Rogoff, Thomas Sargent, Anne Sibert, Michael Wickens, Roger Bootle and Bridget Rosewell (2010), *The Sunday Times*, 14 February, available at: http://www.timesonline.co.uk/tol/comment/letters/article7026234.ece, accessed 11 August 2010.

Block, Walter, Nicholas Snow and Edward Stringham (2008), 'Banks, insurance companies, and discrimination', *Business and Society Review*, **113**(3), 403–19.

Boettke, Peter J. (2009a), 'Paul Krugman and Scott Sumner – who is nominally misguided or speaking nominal nonsense?', *Coordination Problem*, 7 November, available at: http://austrianeconomists.typepad.com/weblog/2009/11/paul-krugman-and-scott-sumner-who-is-nominally-misguided-or-speaking-nominal-nonsense.html, accessed 27 August 2010.

Boettke, Peter J. (2009b), 'Jobless recovery: or why macroeconomics is bad for the brain', *Coordination Problem*, 18 December, available at: http://austrianeconomists.typepad.com/weblog/2009/12/jobless-recovery-or-why-macroeconomics-is-bad-for-the-brain.html, accessed 27 August 2010.

Boettke, Peter J. (2010), 'Simple economics is NOT necessarily simple-minded economics', *Coordination Problem*, 22 February, available at: http://www.coordinationproblem.org/2010/02/simple-economics-is-not-necessarily-simple minded-economics.html, accessed 11 August 2010.

Buchanan, James M. (1962), 'Probability: the criterion of monetary constitutions', in Leland B. Yeager (ed.), *In Search of a Monetary Constitution*, London: Oxford University Press, pp. 155–83.

Buchanan, James M. (2001 [1986]), 'Ideas, institutions and political economy', *The Collected Works of James M. Buchanan*, vol. 19, Indianapolis, IN: Liberty Fund Inc.

Buchanan, James M. and Richard E. Wagner (2000 [1977]), 'Democracy in deficit: the political legacy of Lord Keynes', *The Collected Works of James M. Buchanan*, vol. 8, Indianapolis, IN: Liberty Fund, Inc.

Buchanan, James M., John Burton and Richard E. Wagner (1978), *The Consequences of Mr. Keynes*, Hobart Paper 78, London: The Institute of Economic Affairs.

Cochrane, John (2009), 'Fiscal stimulus, fiscal inflation, or fiscal fallacies?', Working Paper, available at: http://faculty.chicagobooth.edu/john.cochrane/research/Papers/fiscal2.htm, accessed 10 August 2010.

Cowen, Tyler (2010), 'Why are corporations saving so much?', *Marginal Revolution*, 8 July, available at: http://www.marginalrevolution.com/marginalrevolution/2010/07/why-are-corporations-saving-so-much.html, accessed 8 August 2010.

de Rugy, Veronique (2010), 'Obama stimulus money goes where needed least', *Bloomberg*, 8 September, available at: http://www.bloomberg.com/news/2010-09-09/obama-stimulus-funds-go-where-need-is-low-commentary-by-veronique-de-rugy.html, accessed 10 September 2010.

Ebeling, Richard M. (2010), 'Still hearing defunct economists in the air: Krugman's misplaced attack on Hayek', *Think Markets*, 10 July, available at: http://

thinkmarkets.wordpress.com/2010/07/10/still-hearing-defunct-economists-in-the-air-krugmans-misplaced-attack-on-hayek/, accessed 11 August 2010.
Fama, Eugene (2009), 'Bailouts and stimulus plans', *Fama/French Forum*, 13 January, available at: http://www.dimensional.com/famafrench/2009/01/bailouts-and-stimulus-plans.html, accessed 10 August 2010.
Fannie Mae (1954), Fannie Mae Charter Act of 1954, 12, U.S.C., §1716.
Federal Home Loan Mortgage Corporation (1970), Federal Home Loan Mortgage Corporation Act of 1970, 12, U.S.C., §1451.
Ferguson, Niall (2009), 'Keynes can't help us now: governments cling to the delusion that a crisis of excess debt can be solved by creating more debt', *Los Angeles Times*, 6 February, available at: http://articles.latimes.com/2009/feb/06/opinion/oe-ferg6, accessed 12 July 2010.
Foster, J.D. (2009), 'Understanding the great global contagion and recession', *The Heritage Foundation*, 22 October, available at: http://www.heritage.org/Research/Reports/2009/10/Understanding-the-Great-Global-Contagion-and-Recession, accessed 3 July 2010.
Frame, Scott W. and Lawrence J. White (2005), 'Fusing and fuming over Fannie and Freddie: how much smoke, how much fire?', *Journal of Economic Perspectives*, **19**(2), 159–84.
Frank, Robert (2009), 'Don't let the stimulus lose its spark', *The New York Times*, 22 August, available at: http://www.nytimes.com/2009/08/23/business/economy/23view.html, accessed 11 August 2010.
FRED (2010), Federal Reserve Economic Data, Federal Reserve Bank of St Louis: Board of Governors of the Federal Reserve System, available at: http://research.stlouisfed.org/fred2/series/FEDFUNDS?cid=118, accessed 6 July 2010.
Freedman, Charles, Michael Kumhof, Douglas Laxton, Dirk Muir and Susanne Mursula (2010), 'Global effects of fiscal stimulus during the crisis', Working Paper, available at: http://www.stanford.edu/~johntayl/carnegie1march.pdf, accessed 10 August 2010.
Friedman, Jeffrey (2009), 'Bank pay and the financial crisis: G-20 accounting rules, not bank bonuses, put the system at risk', *The Wall Street Journal*, 19 September, available at: http://online.wsj.com/article/SB10001424052970204488304574429293838639418.html?mod=djemEditorialPage, accessed 13 July 2010.
Friedman, Milton (1966), 'Friedman and Keynes', Letters: *Time* magazine, 4 February, available at: http://www.time.com/time/magazine/article/0,9171,898916-2,00.html, accessed 6 August 2010.
Friedman, Milton (2007), 'Milton Friedman @ rest', *The Wall Street Journal*, 22 January, available at: http://online.wsj.com/public/article/SB116942792191783271-ZAcsMDZOCPy0yCR3ADsShGbx2vk_20070128.html?mod=blogs, accessed 13 August 2010.
Garrison, Roger W. (2001), *Time and Money: The Macroeconomics of Capital Structure*, New York: Routledge.
Gordon, R.J. (1990), 'What is New Keynesian Economics?', *Journal of Economic Literature*, **28**(3), 1115–71.
Greenspan, Alan (2010), *The Crisis*, Brookings Institute, available at: http://www.brookings.edu/~/media/Files/Programs/ES/BPEA/2010_spring_bpea_papers/spring2010_greenspan.pdf, accessed 3 July 2010.
Gregory, T.E., F.A. von Hayek, Arnold Plant and Lionel Robbins (1932), 'Spending and saving: public works from rates', *The Times*, 19 October,

available at: http://thinkmarkets.files.wordpress.com/2010/06/keynes-hayek-1932-cambridgelse.pdf, accessed 10 August 2010.

Hayek, Friedrich A. (1931), *Prices and Production*, New York: Augustus M. Kelley.

Hayek, Friedrich A. (1975 [1933]), *Monetary Theory and the Trade Cycle*, New York: Augustus M. Kelley.

Hayek, Friedrich A. (1941), *The Pure Theory of Capital*, Chicago, IL: The University of Chicago Press.

Hayek, Friedrich A. (1945), 'The use of knowledge in society', *American Economic Review*, **35**(4), 519–30.

Hayek, Friedrich A. (1995 [1966]), 'Personal recollections of Keynes and the "Keynesian Revolution"', *Contra Keynes and Cambridge: Essays, Correspondence*, The Collected Works of F.A. Hayek, ed. Bruce Caldwell, Chicago, IL: The University of Chicago Press.

Hayek, Friedrich A. (1974), 'The pretence of knowledge', *Nobel Prize Lecture*, available at: http://nobelprize.org/nobel_prizes/economics/laureates/1974/hayek-lecture.html, accessed 13 August 2010.

Hayek, Friedrich A. (1976), *Denationalisation of Money*, London: Institute of Economic Affairs.

Hazlitt, Henry (1979 [1946]), *Economics in One Lesson*, New York: Three Rivers Press.

Hazlitt, Henry (1959), *The Failure of the 'New Economics': an Analysis of the Keynesian Fallacies*, New Rochelle, NY: Arlington House.

Hazlitt, Henry (ed.) (1995 [1960]), *The Critics of Keynesian Economics*, Irvington-on-Hudson, NY: The Foundation for Economic Education.

Hicks, John (1967), *Critical Essays in Monetary Theory*, Oxford: Clarendon Press.

Higgs, Robert (1997), 'Regime uncertainty: why the Great Depression lasted so long and why prosperity resumed after the war', *The Independent Review*, **1**(4), 561–90.

Holtz-Eakin, Douglas (2010), 'The real arithmetic of health care reform', *The New York Times*, 20 March, available at: http://www.nytimes.com/2010/03/21/opinion/21holtz-eakin.html?_r=1&hp, accessed 13 July 2010.

Horwitz, Steven (1997), 'Understanding Say's Law of markets', *The Freeman: Ideas on Liberty*, **47**(1), available at: http://www.thefreemanonline.org/featured/understanding-says-law-of-markets/, accessed 12 August 2010.

Horwitz, Steven (2010a), 'The microeconomics of government stimulus spending and why Bastiat matters', *Coordination Problem*, 7 February, available at: http://www.coordinationproblem.org/2010/02/my-few-days-of-infamy.html, accessed 10 August 2010.

Horwitz, Steven (2010b), 'Krugman's way-too-simple model', *Coordination Problem*, 23 August, available at: http://www.coordinationproblem.org/2010/08/krugmans-waytoosimple-model.html, accessed 29 August 2010.

HUD (2008), 'Overview of the GSEs' housing goal performance, 2000–2007', *Housing and Urban Development*, available at http://www.huduser.org/Datasets/GSE/gse2007.pdf, accessed 14 July 2010.

Hutt, W.H. (1995 [1954]), 'The significance of price flexibility', *South African Journal of Economics*, March, pp. 40–51, reprinted in Henry Hazlitt (ed.), *The Critics of Keynesian Economics*, Irvington-on-Hudson: Foundation for Economic Education, pp. 386–403.

Kates, Steven (1998), *Say's Law and the Keynesian Revolution: How Macroeconomic*

Theory Lost its Way, Cheltenham, UK and Northampton, MA, USA: Edward Elgar Publishing.
Keynes, John M. (1971 [1919]), *The Economic Consequences of the Peace*, reprinted in Donald Moggridge (ed.), *The Collected Writings of John Maynard Keynes*, vol. II, New York: Macmillan, St Martin's Press.
Keynes, John M. (1971 [1930]), *A Treatise on Money*, vol. 1, *The Pure Theory of Money*, and vol. 2: *The Applied Theory of Money*, reprinted in Donald Moggridge (ed.), *The Collected Writings of John Maynard Keynes*, vols. V and VI, New York: Macmillan, St Martin's Press.
Keynes, John M. (1932), *Activities 1931–9: World Crises and Policies in Britain and America*, reprinted in Donald Moggridge (ed.), *The Collected Writings of John Maynard Keynes*, vol. XXI, New York: Macmillan, St Martin's Press.
Keynes, John M. (1934), 'Poverty in plenty: is the economic system self-adjusting?', *The Listener*, 21 November (Radio broadcast), reprinted in Donald Moggridge (ed.), *The Collected Works of John Maynard Keynes*, vol. 13, New York: Macmillan, St. Martin's Press, pp. 485–92.
Keynes, John M. (1957 [1936]), *The General Theory of Employment, Interest and Money*, London: Macmillan.
King Jr, Neil (2009), 'Politicians butt in at bailed-out GM', *The Wall Street Journal*, 30 October, available at: http://online.wsj.com/article/SB125677552001414699.html, accessed 13 July 2010.
Klein, Peter (2010), 'The era of laissez-faire?', *Organizations and Markets*, 28 January, available at: http://organizationsandmarkets.com/2010/01/28/the-era-of-laissez-faire/, accessed 6 August 2010.
Knight, Frank H. (1937), 'Unemployment: and Mr. Keynes's revolution in economic theory', *The Canadian Journal of Economics and Political Science*, **3**(1), 100–123.
Kotlikoff, Laurence J. (2010), *Jimmy Stewart is Dead: Ending the World's Ongoing Financial Plague with Limited Purpose Banking*, Hoboken, NJ: John Wiley & Sons.
Krugman, Paul (2009), 'Disaster and denial', *The New York Times*, 13 December, available at: http://www.nytimes.com/2009/12/14/opinion/14krugman.html, accessed 11 August 2010.
Krugman, Paul (2010a), 'Now and later', *The New York Times*, 20 June, available at: http://www.nytimes.com/2010/06/21/opinion/21krugman.html, accessed 7 July 2010.
Krugman, Paul (2010b), 'Making it up', *The New York Times*, 29 August, available at: http://krugman.blogs.nytimes.com/2010/08/23/making-it-up/, accessed 29 August 2010.
Lane, Patrick, Bradford DeLong and Luigi Zingales (2009), 'Economist debate', *Economist*, 10 March, available at: http://www.economist.com/debate/days/view/276, accessed 12 August 2010.
Leeson, Robert (1997), 'The eclipse of the goal of zero inflation', *History of Political Economy*, **29**(3), 445–96.
Leeson, Robert (1999), 'Keynes and the "Keynesian" Phillips Curve', *History of Political Economy*, **31**(3), 493–509.
Leijonhufvud, Axel (1968), *On Keynesian Economics and the Economics of Keynes*, London: Oxford University Press.
Levine, Ross (2010a), 'Financial innovation: this house believes that financial innovation boosts growth', *The Economist*, 23 February, available at: http://

www.economist.com/debate/days/view/471#pro_statement_anchor, accessed 6 July 2010.

Levine, Ross (2010b), 'An autopsy of the US financial system', *National Bureau of Economic Research*, Working Paper 15956.

Lucas, Robert E. Jr and Thomas J. Sargent (1978), 'After Keynesian macroeconomics', *Quarterly Review*, Federal Reserve Bank of Minneapolis.

MacGregor, D.H., A.C. Pigou, J.M. Keynes, Walter Layton, Arthur Salter and J.C. Stamp (1932), 'Private spending: money for productive investment', *The Times*, 17 October available at: http://thinkmarkets.files.wordpress com/2010/06/keynes-hayek-1932-cambridgelse.pdf, accessed 11 August 2010.

Maclachlan, F. Cameron (1999), 'The Ricardo–Malthus debate on underconsumption: a case study in economic conversation', *History of Political Economy*, **31**(3), 563–74.

Maddaloni, A. and J.-L. Peydro (2010), 'Bank risk-taking, securitization, supervision and low interest rates: evidence from the Euro area and the US lending standards', *ECB Working Paper*.

Meltzer, Alan (2010), 'Why Obamanomics has failed: uncertainty about future taxes and regulations is enemy No. 1 of economic growth', *The Wall Street Journal*, 30 June, available at: http://online.wsj.com/article/SB10001424052748704629 804575325233508651458.html?mod=WSJ_Opinion_LEADTop#printMode, accessed 14 July 2010.

Mises, Ludwig von (1948), 'Stones into bread, the Keynesian miracle', *Plain Talk*, **2**(6), 21–7.

Mises, Ludwig von (1949), *Human Action: A Treatise on Economics*, New Haven, CT: Yale University Press.

Mises, Ludwig von (1952), *Planning for Freedom: Let the Market System Work*, Indianapolis, IN: Liberty Fund.

Murphy, Robert (2008), 'Can the Feds save the housing market? Numerous government policies caused or exacerbated the crisis', *The Freeman*, **58**(5).

Newton-Small, Jay and Michael Scherer (2009), 'Does Obama have a double standard on earmarks?', *Time* [magazine], 26 February, available at: http://www.time.com/time/politics/article/0,8599,1881855,00.html#ixzz0tTvEfwg1, accessed 12 July 2010.

Norberg, Johan (2009), *Financial Fiasco: How America's Infatuation with Home Ownership and Easy Money Created the Economic Crisis*, Washington, DC: Cato Institute.

Ohanian, Lee (2009), 'The $787 billion mistake', *Forbes* magazine, 10 June, available at: http://www.forbes.com/2009/06/09/american-recovery-reinvestment-act-roosevelt-opinions-contributors-depression.html, accessed 10 August 2010.

Papola, John and Russell Roberts (2010), *Fear the Boom and Bust* [music video], available at: http://econstories.tv/home.html, accessed 6 August 2010.

Rajan, Raghuram (2010), 'Reviewing Krugman', *Fault Lines: Official Blog*, 14 September, available at: http://forums.chicagobooth.edu/faultlines?entry=24, accessed 18 September 2010.

Rizzo, Mario (2010a), 'Crowding out Brad DeLong', *ThinkMarkets*, 6 February, available at: http://thinkmarkets.wordpress.com/2010/02/06/crowding-out-brad-delong/, accessed 10 August 2010.

Rizzo, Mario (2010b), 'Jeffrey Sachs and the Keynesian conundrum', *ThinkMarkets*, available at: http://thinkmarkets.wordpress.com/2010/06/17/jeffrey-sachs-and-the-keynesian-conundrum/, accessed 10 August 2010.

Rizzo, Mario (2010c), 'Never let a crisis go to waste', *ThinkMarkets*, available at: http://thinkmarkets.wordpress.com/2010/08/10/%e2%80%9cnever-let-a-crisis-go-to-waste%e2%80%9d/, accessed 10 August 2010.

Rizzo, Mario (2010d), 'Functional finance fantasy', *ThinkMarkets*, 8 March, available at: http://thinkmarkets.wordpress.com/2010/03/08/functional-finance-fantasy/, accessed 10 August 2010.

Rizzo, Mario (2010e), 'The second Austrian moment', *ThinkMarkets*, 18 September, available at: http://thinkmarkets.wordpress.com/2010/09/18/the-second-austrian-moment/, accessed 18 September 2010.

Roberts, Russell (2010), 'Gambling with other people's money: how perverted incentives caused the financial crisis', The Mercatus Center.

Romer, Christina (2009a), 'So, is it working? An assessment of the American Recovery and Reinvestment Act at the five-month mark', 6 August, speech at The Economic Club of Washington DC available at: http://www.whitehouse.gov/assets/documents/DCEconClub.pdf, accessed 11 August 2010.

Romer, Christina (2009b), 'Lessons from the Great Depression for economic recovery in 2009', speech presented to the Brookings Institution, Washington DC, 9 March, available at: http://www.brookings.edu/~/media/Files/events/2009/0309_lessons/0309_lessons_romer.pdf, accessed 6 August 2010.

Rothbard, Murray (1962), *Man, Economy, and State*, 2 vols, Princeton, NJ: D. van Nostrand.

Samuelson, Paul A. (1955), *Economics*, 3rd edn, New York: McGraw-Hill.

Samuelson, Paul A. (1988), 'In the beginning', *Challenge*, **31**(4), 32–4.

Sargent, Thomas J. (1979), *Macroeconomic Theory*, New York: Academic Press.

Schram, Alan (2009), 'Stimulus plans don't work', *Huffington Post*, 20 January, available at: http://www.huffingtonpost.com/alan-schram/stimulus-plans-dont-work_b_159294.html, accessed 12 August 2010.

Selgin, George and Lawrence H. White (1994), 'How would the invisible hand handle money?', *Journal of Economic Literature*, **XXXII**(4), 1718–49.

Shackle, G.L.S. (1973), 'Keynes and today's establishment in economic theory: a view', *Journal of Economic Literature*, **11**(2), 516–19.

Shlaes, Amity (2010), 'FDR, Obama and "confidence"', *The Wall Street Journal*, 13 July, available at: http://online.wsj.com/article/NA_WSJ_PUB:SB10001424052748703636404575353431153327248.html, accessed 10 August 2010.

Skidelsky, Robert (2009), *Keynes: The Return of the Master*, New York: PublicAffairs.

Skidelsky, Robert, Marcus Miller, David Blanchflower, Kern Alexander, Martyn Andrews, David Bell, William Brown, Mustafa Caglayan, Victoria Chick, Christopher Cramer, Paul De Grauwe, Brad DeLong, Marina Della Giusta, Andy Dickerson, John Driffill, Ciaran Driver, Sheila Dow, Chris Edwards, Peter Elias, Bob Elliot, Jean-Paul Fitoussi, Giuseppe Fontana, Richard Freeman, Francis Green, G.C. Harcourt, Peter Hammond, Mark Hayes, David Held, Jerome de Henau, Susan Himmelweit, Geoffrey Hodgson, Jane Humphries, Grazia Ietto-Gillies, George Irvin, Geraint Johnes, Mary Kaldor, Alan Kirman, Dennis Leech, Robert MacCulloch, Stephen Machin, George Magnus, Alan Manning, Ron Martin, Simon Mohun, Phil Murphy, Robin Naylor, Alberto Paloni, Rick van der Ploeg, Lord Peston, Robert Rowthorn, Malcolm Sawyer, Richard Smith, Frances Stewart, Joseph Stiglitz, Andrew Trigg, John Van

Reenen, Roberto Veneziani and John Weeks (2010), *The Sunday Times*, 18 February, available at: http://www.skidelskyr.com/site/article/letter-to-the-financial-times-first-priority-must-be-to-restore-robust-grow/, accessed 11 August 2010.

Smith, Adam (1981 [1776]), *An Inquiry into the Nature and the Cause of The Wealth of Nations*, volume II, Indianapolis, IN: Liberty Fund.

Smith, Vernon L. (2007), 'The Clinton housing bubble', *The Wall Street Journal*, 18 December, available at: http://online.wsj.com/article/SB119794091743935595.html, accessed 14 July 2010.

Summers, Lawrence (2008), 'Obama's down payment: a stimulus must aim for long-term results', *The Washington Post*, 28 December, available at: http://www.washingtonpost.com/wpdyn/content/article/2008/12/26/AR2008122601299.html, accessed 7 July 2010.

Summers, Lawrence (2010), 'Larry Summers, Obama's top economic adviser, makes the case for another round of stimulus spending', *The Huffington Post*, 25 May, available at: http://www.huffingtonpost.com/2010/05/25/larry-summers-obamas-top_n_588787.html, accessed 14 July 2010.

Taylor, John B. (2009), *Getting off Track: How Government Actions and Interventions Caused, Prolonged, and Worsened the Financial Crisis*, Stanford, CA: Hoover Institute.

Time magazine (1965), 'The economy: we are all Keynesians now', *Time* magazine, Friday 31 December, available at http://www.time.com/time/magazine/article/0,9171,842353-1,00.html, accessed 6 August 2010.

White, Lawrence (2009), 'A brief history of credit rating agencies: how financial regulation entrenched this industry's role in the subprime mortgage debacle of 2007–2008', *Mercatus on Policy*, October, No. 59.

Wolf, Martin (2010), 'Why plans for early fiscal tightening carry global risks', *Financial Times*, 16 June, available at: http://www.ft.com/cms/s/fc8d1dd4-78b6-11df-a312-00144feabdc0,Authorised=false.html?_i_location=http%3A%2F%2Fwww.ft.com%2Fcms%2Fs%2F0%2Ffc8d1dd4-78b6-11df-a312-00144feabdc0.html&_i_referer=, accessed 11 August 2010.

Wright, David McCord (1958), 'Mr. Keynes and the "day of judgement"', *Science*, **128**(3334), 1258–62.

2. Traditional monetary economics vs Keynesianism, creditism and base-ism

Tim Congdon

How is the Great Recession to be explained from an intellectual standpoint? The argument here is that the heart of the problem is the lack of an agreed consensus among economists on answers to the questions, 'what are the key determinants of the equilibrium values of income and wealth *in nominal terms*?' and 'if income and wealth are not in equilibrium, how do these determinants restore their equilibrium levels?'. In the following I will argue that banking developments – particularly such developments when they affect the quantity of bank deposits – are critical in answering these questions. I should say at the outset that my argument is not universally shared among economists and that, in my opinion, the absence of a consensus has itself been largely to blame for the monetary and banking fiasco suffered since mid-2007. Although I regard my position as rooted in traditional monetary theory, I am well aware that central features of my analysis are – for the moment at least – deeply unfashionable. Moreover, my conclusion is distant from the current mainstream. I reject the notion that privately owned commercial banks have been to blame for the macroeconomic calamity of the last three years. These organizations patently do not control the recognized instruments of macroeconomic policy. On the contrary, the blame for the Great Recession lies with governments, central banks and regulators, particularly those in the English-speaking world. The bottom line is that, by punishing the banks, officialdom has punished everyone.

MONEY, WEALTH AND EXPENDITURE

I take it for granted that attempts to determine the equilibrium nominal values of income and wealth *separately* are a mistake. After all, wealth is merely the capitalization of some notion of income. I regard the dominant forms of wealth in a modern community as real estate, both residential and commercial, and corporate equity. Government bonds are not net wealth, and corporate bonds, while important, are not a dominant form of wealth.

In my view the equilibrium nominal values of income and wealth can be regarded as determined by the joint product of:

i. the quantity of money, and
ii. the desired ratios of money to income and wealth (and we can collapse this to 'the desired ratio of money to income' if the relationship between income and wealth is stable).

It follows that – if the desired ratio of money to income is also stable (as it is, pretty much) – the equilibrium nominal values of income and wealth can be interpreted as a function of the quantity of money. This may seem rather sweeping, but the logic is simple. The prices of all goods and services, and also of all assets, can vary. By contrast, the 'price' – in the sense of the nominal value – of money cannot vary, because the nominal value of the most basic type of money is fixed by law. So changes in the quantity of money cannot alter money's nominal value. Instead – if changes in the quantity of money rupture an existing general equilibrium – equilibrium can be restored only by changes in the nominal values of income and wealth. Is it so startling to propose that the total nominal value of all those things with variable nominal values depends on the quantity of that thing (money) which has a fixed nominal value?

I have argued in my work that the relevant 'quantity of money' must be an all-inclusive one, that is, one that embraces all assets, the nominal value of which is given.[1] Unfortunately, there is a serious ambiguity here, that modern economies have both a central bank and commercial banking system.[2] The liabilities of the central bank are 'the monetary base' and include notes/cash, where legislation states that their nominal value is enforceable in the courts and is therefore (more or less) 100 per cent certain. On the other hand, the nominal value of the deposit liabilities of commercial banks is not 100 per cent certain, as banks can 'go bust'. At any rate, institutional arrangements (a central bank plus banking regulation) are in place to ensure that bank deposits are always fully convertible into cash. For immediate purposes we can take it for granted that deposits, like cash, have the property of nominal value certainty.

My emphasis on the relevance of an all-inclusive (or broadly-defined) money measure arises largely from the kind of statement I am making, which is of course a theoretical statement about the general equilibrium of a modern economy. However, in my empirical work on macroeconomic data I have also found broad money to be the least untrustworthy guide in thinking about 'how money affects the economy'. Thus, the notion of drawing conclusions about asset prices from only one type of money asset (such as the base or sight deposits, M0 or M1), and excluding altogether time deposits (which are clearly a large part of portfolios), strikes me as bizarre.[3] If we are thinking in general equilibrium terms, we must embrace *all* assets with a given nominal value in our concept of 'money'.

Further, nowadays not only are the deposit liabilities of commercial banks a much more important kind of money than the note issue of the central bank, but also deposits dominate commercial banks' liabilities. Two points then follow:

i. changes in the rate of growth of nominal national income are likely to be closely related (although not identical) to changes in the rate of growth of the commercial banking system, and
ii. in episodes characterized by large fluctuations in the rate of growth of the banking system's balance sheet and so of broad money, the resulting macroeconomic disequilibrium is likely to have particularly obvious symptoms in the prices of assets, that is, real estate and corporate equity.

I am unsympathetic to the restriction of discussions of portfolio choice to the choice between money and bonds, as in Keynes's *General Theory* and much subsequent work. The relationship between money, on the one hand, and the prices of real estate and corporate equity, on the other, is crucial to the economy. By contrast, the relationship between money and the price of long-dated bonds (and so of bond yields and what Keynes called 'the rate of interest') is secondary. Attempts have been made by some economists to understand large-scale movements in *nominal* asset prices without reference to the dynamics of the banking system. If the Great Recession (like the Great Depression before it) has shown anything, it is that these attempts are misconceived, even ridiculous. If developments in the banking system are relevant to asset prices, they must also be of huge importance in the determination of national expenditure and income.

SOME IMPLICATIONS

The message of the above is surely clear, that public policy must be concerned

i. to maintain the full convertibility of deposits into cash (i.e., keeping the value of all types of money stable *in nominal terms*), and
ii. to ensure that the growth of the banking system's balance sheet, and particularly of its deposit liabilities (i.e., the quantity of money), is at a steady rate over time to avoid instability in asset prices and expenditure, and also at a steady rate which is appropriate (neither too high nor too low) for preserving the value of money *in real terms* (i.e., keeping the price level of goods and services fairly stable over time).

I know that a whole host of objections can be raised to the second of these points. All I would say is that my statement contains at least two strong and very plausible warnings:

i. that wide fluctuations in the rate of growth of the banking system are likely to be attended by macroeconomic instability, and
ii. that a large reduction in the size of the commercial banking system is likely to cause not a fall in the ratio of bank liabilities to national income, but a deflation of asset prices and the prices of goods and services.

Further, deflation will inevitably be associated with high unemployment and lost output.

PUBLIC POLICY IN THE LEADING NATIONS AT PRESENT

Given the above, it may seem astonishing that public policy in the leading nations could ever be intended to enforce a large reduction in the size of the commercial banking system. But that is exactly what was intended by the governments and leading regulatory agencies of North America, Europe and Japan in the early stages of the Great Recession. The President of the USA openly said that he wanted to see the banking system undergo 'shrinkage'. Large increases in banks' capital/asset ratios were mandated, with the undoubted purpose of limiting or even reducing banks' risk assets.

It is true that the deflationary impact of the shrinkage of banks' *risk* assets could be offset by the expansion of banks' *safe* assets (i.e. their cash and government securities), since the expansion of safe assets ought to be matched on the other side of the balance sheet by extra deposits (i.e. money). But only in the UK was this policy adopted in a deliberate fashion, with the Bank of England's programme of quantitative easing (QE). (I say 'deliberate', but I don't think the policy has been chosen with much enthusiasm or even understanding by most of the key relevant individuals in officialdom. It was adopted in February/March 2009 from despair that everything else was failing. [Note that this chapter was written in February 2010. In November 2010 the Federal Reserve announced a programme of purchases of government securities which was very similar to the Bank of England's March 2009 exercise in both structure and rationalization. It was labelled 'QE2' in financial markets. This label implied that the Fed had undertaken an earlier quantitative-easing operation. However, the Fed's previous asset purchases – notably those of commercial paper in late 2008 and of mortgage-backed securities in 2009 – were not intended to increase the quantity of money. They were instead supposed to 'ease credit conditions' and lower 'credit spreads'. Indeed, Bernanke specifically said that they should be characterized as 'credit easing'. They did in fact often boost the quantity of money, but this was one of their by-products, not their central purpose.][4]

Programmes with a similar impact to the Bank of England's QE have been undertaken in the USA, but not – in any substantive way – in Europe or Japan. However, in the USA the statements accompanying these programmes make no meaningful reference to the quantity of money and, in my view, do not reflect a well-structured and credible theoretical account of how the economy works. In the Eurozone the sensible conduct of policy has been obstructed by the wording of an international treaty. The founding document, the Maastricht Treaty, was written in the assumption that banks would always be able to expand their balance sheets by increasing loans to the private sector. The treaty therefore discouraged government borrowing from commercial banks and proscribed government borrowing from the central bank(s). Of course, in a period when bank lending to the private sector is on a falling trend, government borrowing from the banking system is the correct method of maintaining a positive rate of money growth. Indeed, if bank lending to the private sector is on a falling trend over several years, as may be the case in such countries as Spain and Ireland, government borrowing from the banking system must also be pursued over several years. Such government borrowing should not be viewed as a special or emergency response to a supposedly unique challenge in monetary management.

Even more alarming have been policy developments relating to

i. the size of budget deficits, and
ii. the financing pattern of such deficits.

Naive commentators have persuaded finance ministries to raise government spending and to increase budget deficits 'in order to boost demand', when the evidence for the effectiveness of fiscal policy is almost everywhere unconvincing. (The name of 'Keynes' is used as a slogan to justify these mistakes.) The long-run effects will be a higher ratio of government expenditure to GDP and larger public debts, while it is already clear that the short-run effects on *net* demand (i.e. private and government spending combined) have been disappointing.

If governments must run budget deficits, it is important in a deflationary context that the deficits be financed at the short end from the banking system, in order to expand the quantity of money. Indeed, monetary financing of deficits is a much simpler means of expanding the quantity of money than central bank purchases of assets from non-banks (i.e. than programmes such as QE). But, throughout the Great Recession, finance ministries have tended to finance budget deficits as far as possible at the long end from non-banks. They are doing so in the belief that they are acting responsibly and avoiding potential difficulties in rolling over debt in the next few years. (In the UK, policy decision-making in this area is still bedevilled by remnants of the 'full funding rule', which dates back to 1985. When introduced, this wholly misguided precept tried to prevent the financing pattern of the budget balance having any effect on broad money. Officialdom therefore dispensed with a valid means of influencing macroeconomic outcomes by adjusting the terms, instrument composition and maturity composition of public debt.)

The correct course of action is two- or three-fold:

i. to reduce budget deficits as soon as possible by as much as is politically feasible,
ii. to finance the remaining deficits (and to refinance maturing debt) at the short end from the banks in order to ensure that money growth is positive at a moderate rate, and
iii. if (ii) isn't sufficient, for the government to borrow from the banks in order to purchase its own long-dated debt from non-banks in order again to ensure that money growth is positive at a moderate rate.

Any future difficulty in rolling over debt as it matures is reduced if the size of the public debt is kept under control. It is deplorable that, across the industrial world, the topic of public debt management is currently viewed as distinct from that of monetary control. Part of the problem undoubtedly is an over-interpretation of the notion of 'central bank independence'. If the leading countries face a period of several years in which banks' claims on the private sector will be falling (as seems possible), central banks – whether 'independent' or not – must work with finance ministries to ensure that money growth remains positive. If that involves monetization of public debt, so be it. Let the Maastricht Treaty be damned.

THE INTELLECTUAL DRIVERS OF CURRENT MISTAKES IN PUBLIC POLICY

Ultimately, the current mess in policy-making arises because economists do not have an agreed theory for the determination of national income and wealth. I have sketched out above my own views about the correct theory. I will now refer – very quickly and briefly, and perhaps a little unfairly – to three alternative approaches. In my view all three are wrong, to a greater or lesser degree, for reasons I will explain.

1. Keynesianism: the central principle of Keynesianism is that output depends on expenditure and that expenditure can be viewed as a multiple of investment, including public investment, so that changes in public investment/'the budget deficit' boost demand and output. There are many mistakes here, but the most obvious is that the income–expenditure story overlooks that expenditure on current goods and services (i.e. expenditure that determines output) can be financed by the sale of assets and/or by running down a money balance. Agents' attitudes towards their wealth and portfolios, and the role of money in portfolio-balancing decisions, are fundamental. Ironically, Keynes himself regarded the integration of money into such portfolio-balancing decisions as essential to the understanding of macroeconomic fluctuations. I argued in my 2007 book on *Keynes, the Keynesians and Monetarism* (Congdon, 2007) that the Keynesians had betrayed Keynes's intellectual legacy.
2. Creditism: the main idea in creditism is that 'credit', and specifically bank lending to the private sector, has an important role in the determination of national expenditure and/or asset prices *independently of the quantity of money*. This idea had no place in traditional monetary theory. It has developed since the late 1980s, mostly in American East Coast universities, since academic articles were written by Bernanke, Benjamin Friedman (not Milton Friedman) and others about a supposed 'credit channel' in the monetary transmission mechanism. The thought behind creditism seems to be that the proceeds of a new bank loan enable an agent to spend above income and hence to boost aggregate demand. In fact, virtually all bank loans have the purpose of allowing the borrower to purchase an *existing* asset and do not have any first-round effect on the income–expenditure circular flow. The value of new bank loans to the private sector is a tiny fraction of the value of payments in a modern economy. (The value of such payments – nearly all mediated by money – is typically about 50 times national income.) Except through its effect on the quantity of money, new bank

lending to the private sector has no definite and necessary relationship with national expenditure.

3. Base-ism: the key notion in base-ism is that the relationship between the monetary base itself (i.e. the liabilities of the central bank) and the economy is the same as (or dominates) the relationship between the quantity of money and the economy. (By the 'quantity of money' I mean of course an aggregate mostly represented by bank deposits, that is, the liabilities of commercial banks.) An implication of pure base-ism – which is closely related to the school of New Classical Economics centred in American Mid-Western universities, including nowadays the University of Chicago – is that the banking industry is no more worthy of macroeconomic analysis than, say, the car industry or oil refining. According to base-ists, the central bank's decisions matter to the economy, but the rate of expansion or contraction of commercial bank deposits is of no relevance to macroeconomic outcomes. Both the Great Depression and the current Great Recession demonstrate that this claim is preposterous. A milder form of base-ism contends that changes in the level of bank deposits are regulated by changes in the monetary base. This milder form has been refuted in the last two years by the large rise in the monetary base made necessary by the breakdown since August 2007 of the international inter-bank market, which had much the same effect on banks' cash position as a run on their customer deposits. In accordance with principles that were clearly stated in Bagehot's 1873 *Lombard Street*, central banks should respond to such runs – when they are on solvent banks that have complied with regulations – by expanding the monetary base and ensuring that deposits remain convertible into cash. The ratio of money as a whole to the monetary base may change radically while the central bank is helping the commercial banks in this way.

It is very important, in interpreting the current mess, for non-economists to understand that most economists do not accept a single, shared theory on the determination of asset prices and national income. The majority of the profession – if economists can be said to constitute 'a profession' – is to be placed in one or another of the three schools just discussed. To be frank, the so-called 'discipline' is an extraordinary jumble. I believe that my own position – that the nominal levels of both asset prices and national income should be understood as a function of an all-inclusive quantity of money – is analytically correct, relatively easy to understand and corroborated by a great deal of evidence. But most economists do not agree with it.

The theoretical confusions lead to extraordinary divergences on policy. Roughly speaking, the Keynesians believe that the best antidotes to weak demand are increases in the budget deficit (or, at present when budget deficits are unsustainably large, by the postponement of actions to reduce them), while the creditists favour an increase in bank lending. Some creditists in the UK seem to think that more bank lending should be engineered by official arm-twisting to force banks to raise more capital or, in the extreme, by brute administrative fiat. (In late 2008 the Governor of the Bank of England pronounced, 'Lend more or we'll nationalize you'.) The Keynesians and the creditists virtually all agree that, at present (i.e. February 2010), the looming danger for the world economy is continued beneath-trend growth and more deflation. I agree with them on this, although not with their policy prescriptions.

By contrast, the base-ists now worry that the large increases in the monetary base in the USA, the Eurozone, the UK and so on will be inflationary, and are concerned to specify an early 'exit' from allegedly excessive monetary stimulus.

Many members of the three schools do not think that the quantity of money (i.e. as I keep on emphasizing, nowadays the quantity of bank deposits) is of any importance in macroeconomic analysis. They are indifferent if public policy has the effect of shrinking the banking system balance sheet and the quantity of money. In fact, they often assert the unimportance of the quantity of money in macroeconomic processes and refuse even to mention it in their analyses. If this seems incredible, may I mention the latest commentaries from the International Monetary Fund by its chief economist, Professor Olivier Blanchard, formerly of Harvard University? In these commentaries Blanchard uses the words 'liquidity' and 'credit' dozens of times, but not once does he mention 'money' or 'the quantity of money'. The contrast between the Blanchard commentary and the IMF database speaks volumes about the chaos in modern macroeconomics. As the IMF requires all its members to prepare data for different money aggregates, its database is in fact the best single internationally available source for long-run monetary statistics. But why should the IMF collect all these data if 'money' does not matter, as its chief economist clearly believes?

I have referred to Blanchard and the IMF partly because the IMF has been vocal in the last couple of years in issuing warnings about high levels of bad debts in the leading nations, alleging that banking systems are insolvent or nearly insolvent, and then urging banks to raise ever more capital. In my opinion the quality of the IMF's recent analyses has been unsatisfactory, with its analyses undermining national regulators' attempts to buttress confidence in their banking systems.

POLICY CONCLUSIONS

All being well, very low interest rates ought in due course to ensure that banking systems stabilize and start to grow again. But there is a possibility – certainly in the Eurozone – that the quantity of money will fall despite low interest rates. The falls in the quantity of money will be largely due to banks' shrinkage of risk assets, in response partly to genuine loan losses and inadequate capital, but mostly to foolish regulatory bullying. The bullying can in turn be attributed largely to the misunderstanding that, because banks are safer the more capital they have relative to their assets, any rise in banks' capital/asset ratios is socially desirable. This is not so. The more capital that banks have relative to their assets, the more they must charge for their loans in order to deliver a particular return on capital. In other words, the safer the banking system is in appearance (i.e. the higher its capital/assets ratio), the more expensive are the services it provides to non-bank customers. Of course the more that banks charge for their services, including their loan facilities, the lower is the equilibrium ratio of bank lending to national income. Paradoxically, the official drive for ever-higher ratios of bank capital to assets may be contributing to increases in the cost of bank services and motivating falls in bank lending. Officialdom may believe that its efforts are making banks safer, when in fact these efforts are to a significant extent responsible for the shrinkage of risk assets and the stagnation or contraction of the quantity of money.

I have two main policy recommendations to ensure that the quantity of money continues to grow despite the pressures from regulators, asset price weakness and so on. First, suppose that the contraction in banks' risk assets has a few years yet to run. Then the state – either the government or the central bank (or in fact both working together) – must conduct its own financial transactions so that increases in its borrowings from the banking system sustain banks' balance sheet totals. The UK's QE experiment is an example of what can be done, but the deliberate monetization of public debt by the government (i.e. with the initiative being taken in finance ministries) should also be considered. Secondly, decisions about financial regulation and the management of the public debt have monetary effects. Financial regulation and debt management therefore need to be integrated with monetary policy decision-making. Because of the inescapable interdependence of these aspects of public policy, the notion of 'central bank independence' can be over-interpreted. Central banks must work with finance ministries and regulatory agencies on public debt management and banking regulation, just as finance ministries and regulatory agencies must work with central banks on the monetary consequences of public debt management and banking regulation.

Unhappily, the politicians and officials now prominent in policy-making have little understanding of the relationship between money aggregates and macroeconomic variables. Further, many of their most senior economic advisers have an allergic reaction even to the mention of phrase 'the quantity of money'. (The IMF's Blanchard is a good example of this problem.) In November 2008 Queen Elizabeth II asked on a visit to the London School of Economics, 'why did no one see the crisis coming?' A few months later a seminar at the British Academy tried to provide an answer, but apparently did not agree on one that satisfied any of its attendees. Non-economists need to appreciate that economics – or, at any rate, the macroeconomic component of the subject that calls itself economics – is an intellectual shambles. The Great Recession is to be blamed not on inherent weaknesses of liberal capitalist economies, but on economists' failure to agree on how liberal capitalism works.

NOTES

1. See, for example, the final two essays in Congdon (2007), particularly pp. 301–7 and footnote 33 on p. 314.
2. In a recent paper, 'Monetary policy at the zero bound' (Congdon, 2010), I explained that, because modern economies have two types of monetary asset (i.e., bank deposits in 'the quantity of money', as usually understood, and the monetary base), macroeconomic analysis ought to recognize (at least) two concepts of 'liquidity trap': one relating to a deposit-dominated money concept and the other to the base. Modern economists – like Keynes in *The General Theory* – have overlooked this ambiguity.
3. The argument is developed in, for example, Congdon (2005). See, particularly, pp. 133–4.
4. I advocated 'quantitative easing' in a February 2009 pamphlet for the London-based Centre for the Study of Financial Innovation, *How to Stop the Recession* (Congdon, 2009). The pamphlet was jointly financed by the CSFI and Lombard Street Research.

REFERENCES

Congdon, T. (2005), *Money and Asset Prices in Boom and Bust*, London: Institute of Economic Affairs.

Congdon, T. (2007), *Keynes, the Keynesians and Monetarism*, Cheltenham, UK and Northampton, MA, USA: Edward Elgar Publishing.

Congdon, T. (2009). *How to Stop the Recession*, London: Centre for the Study of Financial Innovation.

Congdon, T. (2010), 'Monetary policy at the zero bound', *World Economies*, **11**(1), 11–46.

3. Can a progressive capital gains tax help avoid the next crisis? Public sector governance in a comprehensive neo-Schumpeterian system

Horst Hanusch and Florian Wackermann

1 INTRODUCTORY REMARKS

As we seem to exit from the deep crisis, we have to deal with many subjects which are of highest current interest and which make these days appear to be so special and unique, only comparable to the period at the end of the 1920s and the beginning of the 1930s. Back then, however, there existed more or less only one real problem for society and politics, namely the economic crisis which began to spread in a dramatic way to become a worldwide crisis of nations and cultures.

Today, we also have to consider other developments which will significantly influence and limit our lives and our future besides the consequences of the economic crisis. The climate change and the ecological effects which will apparently derive from it for us and the next generations are an enormous source of danger opening up in a parallel way to the economic crisis (see for example IPCC, 2007). Questions concerning the exploitation and the use of energy and the sustainable management of our natural resources shape another field of concern of growing significance for the existence and the form of our life on this planet Earth (see for example Baumann, 2008). The same is true for the threatening developments stemming from an ageing population in societies in highly developed economies which we cannot afford to lose sight of in times when almost all crisis comments focus on the financial and economic sector (see for example Balestra and Dottori, 2009).

However, it is not our ambition here to deal with all of these unpleasant developments from a neo-Schumpeterian perspective. We will only try to address the recent global crisis and present some thoughts which may help to avoid a comparable downturn in the future. Only one short comment should be allowed: this crisis does not only carry risks and dangers with it, it also offers the great opportunity to link economic policy to other goals such as a sustainable climate and environmental policy. The slogan should be to make economic policy not at the expense of climate and environmental concerns, but to understand economic policy also as a kind of climate policy. The next wave of innovations in the world will certainly be based on climate-aware and resource-protecting technologies.

Nevertheless, we will focus our contribution on the present economic and financial problems and will link it to a school of thought which can be best illustrated by the name of the great economist, Joseph A. Schumpeter.

The chapter therefore begins with an analysis of the current crisis, which we believe to be a Schumpeterian crisis. Therefore, we introduce the neo-Schumpeterian economics approach, which is mainly focused on the real side of the economy. However, in order to meet the complexity of economies in developed industrialized countries, it is important to broaden the analysis and to include the financial and public sectors as additional key actors. This is found in our third section, where we introduce the concept of comprehensive neo-Schumpeterian economics (CNSE). From this idea, we can derive in Section 4 the dynamic idea of the neo-Schumpeterian corridor, which serves as a heuristic to illustrate a dynamically appropriate development of an innovation-focused economy which is sustainable and future-oriented. Section 5 builds on those ideas and proposes a progressive capital gains tax scheme designed to avoid large exaggerations, uncontrolled excesses or even financial bubbles which could then cause economic crises like the one we have just suffered. We conclude in Section 6.

So, let's begin with a postulate, which we would like to propose:

2 IT'S A SCHUMPETERIAN CRISIS

The current crisis can be characterized as a typically Schumpeterian crisis. In any case, it is not a malicious development in the Keynesian sense, which would be based on price and allocation processes related to and determined by rigidities in a market economy or on a mismatch of aggregate supply and aggregate demand. Furthermore, we cannot recognize any classical or neo-classical market failures as triggers – failures in the supply of collective services or market imperfections connected with misleading competition. No, the current crisis is hardly reducible to exogenous errors or shortcomings of such kind in the market economy or the capitalistic system. It is much more the result and product of an excessive and exaggerated success of this system. One of the first economists who recognized this correlation was Joseph Schumpeter (see Schumpeter, 1975). His interpretation shows a strong opposition to the common, Anglo-Saxon-influenced neoclassical approach of economics.

According to Schumpeter, the capitalistic system is defined in its dynamics and its development in a prominent way by forces largely ignored in the neo-classical theory. This includes creative entrepreneurs and bankers ready to assume risks, whose actions are future-oriented and aimed at replacing old forms of doing business by creating new ones, which means by 'creative destruction' (see Schumpeter, 1975).

Thus defined, capitalism becomes a system which is to a high degree linked to uncertainty and insecurity, both in a positive and negative sense. Basically, everything can and will happen if the system is allowed to develop freely. It is capable of generating the most impressive performances and also of causing most painful collapses. It is, therefore, not a system of balance and harmony as neo-classics supposes, but one which flutters between possible extremes of the highest success and the most deplorable decay. This is true for companies as well as regions, nations and global economic areas. Basically, it oscillates in a Schumpeterian cycle of 'Boom and Bust'.

It is this cyclical up and down which also holds much of the responsibility for the crisis we currently suffer. The true base of today's global financial crisis lies in the USA and in the enormous economic boom that started there about twenty years ago and which was spurred by the coincidence of several economic factors that may be called Schumpeterian: the innovative key or general-purpose base technology in the IT sector which spread like wildfire; the readiness of creative entrepreneurs and the availability of sufficient risk capital that could be used to finance a future-oriented extraordinarily strong expansion. In addition, governments provided the necessary framework by choosing a policy of low taxes and deregulation of economic processes. This expansion period proved to be so tremendously successful that it burst all scales of evaluation of companies – not only in the IT sector –and it carried with it many other economic sectors to unseen heights.

Around the year 2000, the boom stumbled over its own hubris and the limitless optimism of the involved actors. But the central banks also held their share of responsibility. They suddenly focused on a tight monetary policy by raising the interest rates in order to fight a perceived inflation in consumer markets. In the run-up to the emerging crisis, however, they had carelessly ignored the inflation in assets that had been developing in the stock markets. However, it is this inflation in assets which is in a Schumpeterian context an essential cause for distortion and crises (Hayek,

1937). The eventual bursting of the inflated bubble preceded the deep slump of the New Economy and the Dot-Net-World.

The central banks had no other option but to react almost in panic, this time by lowering interest rates and therefore by adding even more new liquidity into the economic circular flow. The new money searched for new fields of investment, and this is the point at which we find the shift from the firm sector to the households' real estate sector. Here the same unregulated interdependence of greed, short-term focus and exaggerated optimism surfaced. A new, incredibly large bubble formed, which crashed about three years ago in the US (see for example Welfens, 2008).

From there, international spillover effects occurred worldwide and spread into the financial sector. And here the bubble burst on a worldwide scale with a more and more audible noise. The central banks were part of the trigger of this outpouring due to their policy of rapid increases in the interest rate designed to tame the enormous volumes of liquidity. This culminated in a shambles, a global financial and economic crisis, which should consequently rather be called a 'Schumpeterian crisis'.

So, what can we do in such a crisis? Which tasks are reserved for the market and which ones are bound to the government as a knight in shining armor?

We think Schumpeter and also Austrian economics would take the easy way out of this argument (Paul, 2009). They would probably reason that we should leave the capitalistic system alone. There are enough self-healing forces within it that will make sure that after a certain period of global downturn, we would return to a phase of common growth, meaning that it would start a development which will once again lead through a powerful, maybe technological incitation from a bust towards a boom situation. But, can and may we consider this option justifiable in economic or political terms after the terrible experiences during the first world economic crisis and, in the subsequent years, in the devastating consequences of the Second World War? No, the political dangers that would arise are far too unforeseeable and dramatic for such a strategy to be tested under any circumstances because of consequences such as an increasing nationalism, social riots and possibly even wars. Therefore, the crisis needs the government and the central banks with their policies.

So, it does not seem controversial that successful capitalistic economies cannot exist without a certain amount of regulation if we want them to generate an economic development which is sustainable and less erratic than the unregulated invisible hand could achieve. The government as a political actor can, and should, of course, make a contribution so that ups and downs in the development process of an economy are more moderate and steady, and so that a smoother evolution can be attained. In this context, we propose a concept as an analytical framework which we have introduced earlier as comprehensive neo-Schumpeterian economics (CNSE) (Hanusch and Pyka, 2007a).

3 COMPREHENSIVE NEO-SCHUMPETERIAN ECONOMICS (CNSE)

CNSE is based on neo-Schumpeterian economics. In that context the central actors under investigation are entrepreneurs and entrepreneurial firms, the most important process to be analyzed is innovation and the underlying knowledge creation and diffusion processes. Here, in sharp contrast to neo-classical economics, the notion of innovation focuses on the removal and overcoming of limiting constraints and the setting of new ones.

However, neo-Schumpeterian economics, in its present shape, is still far from offering an integral theory of economic development. Most of the research of the last decades has primarily concentrated on the real sphere of an economy. Technological innovations propelling industry dynamics and economic growth obviously are a major source of economic development. But technological innovations are not the only source, nor can industry development occur in a vacuum. Instead, development is accompanied and influenced by the monetary realms of an economy as well as the public sector. The degree of maturity which the neo-Schumpeterian approach has meanwhile reached in the field of industrial dynamics admittedly does not hold when it is aiming at the future orientation of financial markets and the developments of the public sector (cf. Fagerberg et al., 2005).

Undoubtedly, the neo-Schumpeterian approach has to be set on a broader conceptual basis. And for this purpose we suggest comprehensive neo-Schumpeterian economics (CNSE) as a theory composed of three pillars: one for the real side of the economy, one for its monetary side and one for the public sector (see Figure 3.1). Economic development then takes place in a co-evolutionary manner, pushed, hindered or even eliminated within these three pillars.

In order to understand the crucial co-evolutionary relationship, one must explore the bracket accompanying all three pillars, namely their orientation towards the future which introduces uncertainty into the analysis. The fundamental importance of true uncertainty (cf. Knight, 1921) has to be seen as a characteristic concerning the single pillars as well as a phenomenon shaping the relationships between the three pillars causing a high degree of complexity.

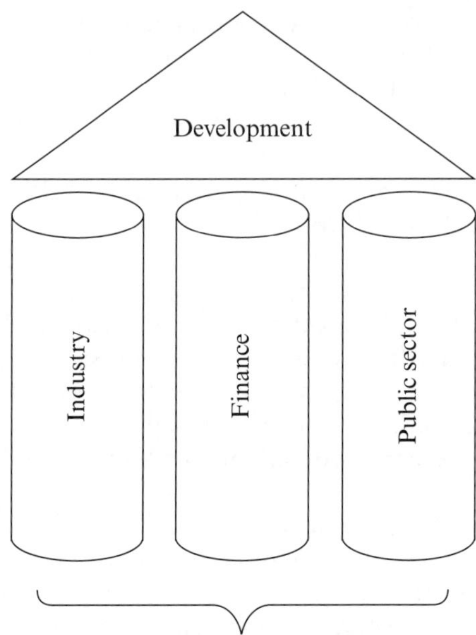

Figure 3.1 The three pillars of CNSE

Such a CNSE approach, however, focusing on innovation-driven qualitative development, should not only look at the co-evolutionary aspects of economic life. It should also analyze the various issues of each of these pillars and work out their proper role in a theoretical and political context, because each of the three sectors has to serve the future design of society and economy and assumes a corresponding role.

In such a concept, the task of the real economy will be to foster at all times, through innovation and parallel investments, the knowledge-oriented progress and the resulting wealth of a country or a region. To accomplish this task, it needs certain freedoms and the active support of the government, for example through a growth and progress-oriented tax system on the revenue side of the public budget or investments in education and research on its expenditure side (Barroso, 2008).

The financial economy has an even closer, almost symbiotic relationship with the real economy. Its task is not – as it just happened – a short-term decoupling from the real economy spurred by speculation, but quite the opposite, the medium- and long-term-oriented sustainable financial accompaniment and encouragement of innovative and successful companies and sectors (Trichet, 2009).

The governmental and political responsibility lies, as we just mentioned, in the monitoring of the future-oriented, long-term symbiosis of the real and the financial economies as well as their co-evolutionary development. For that purpose it has to install an adequate intelligence and control system. But monitoring and controlling is only one side of the coin.

If necessary, the government also has to support the co-evolutionary development of the system through specific budgetary and institutional instruments. On the revenue side of the budget, for instance, a growth and progress-oriented tax system may be an effective instrument; on the expenditure side investments in education and research seem to be adequate measures and on the institutional side means such as standardization patterns and property rights as well as regulatory activities can be recommended.

All these measures, however, should be guided by a two-sided countercyclical strategy: on the one hand the concern to avoid trends of exaggerating or overheating in time and on the other hand the responsibility and effectiveness to overcome a possible period of stagnation as quickly as possible.

We certainly do not need to point out specifically that fulfilling these goals is an extremely complex and difficult political challenge with respect to the intelligence as well as the instruments required.

As substantial as this challenge may be, there are a few rough and avoidable mistakes in politics which we can already point to today. The political framework should by all means not be limited to singular, not deeply thought-through, reactive measures such as those that have been discussed largely in Europe and worldwide for the financial and other sectors of the economy.

Due to the prevailing mind of the important makers and shakers in academia and politics, who consider the government to be a sort of repair garage of last resort, the people in charge are skating on thin ice and risk overreacting. They think that they have recognized some faults in the market system and are trying to eliminate them by very strong public involvement. Apparently, this provides the government with a role and responsibility that far exceeds every dimension accepted so far. The currently discussed inventory of possible measures is an exhaustive representation of the whole spectrum of public activity: intervention, regulation, control and nationalization are the most frequently cited terms when it comes to using governmental help to cope with both the financial crisis and the developing economic crisis. This can be an extremely risky attitude, especially when it leads to a policy of partial 'piecemeal engineering' (see for example Irzik, 1985) and when the overall context that characterizes modern economies in the era of the knowledge societies is not respected.

From a comprehensive neo-Schumpeterian perspective the focus should be much more on the dynamic overall performance of a modern, capitalistic economy which is on the brink of transforming from an industrial into a knowledge-based system. This evolution is driven by the three most important pillars of its economic and social regime, which are the sectors of the real economy, the financial sector and the public sector. All three have to serve the future design of society and the economy and assume a corresponding role.

4 THE NEO-SCHUMPETERIAN CORRIDOR: THEORETICAL AND POLITICAL ASPECTS

An improved understanding of development processes in modern societies and effective public policy governance which should build on that, can only be expected when the co-evolutionary dimensions and the proper role of the three pillars are taken into account. This can be illustrated within a concept that we introduced earlier as the neo-Schumpeterian corridor (cf. Hanusch and Pyka, 2007b and Hanusch and Wackermann, 2009) (see Figure 3.2).

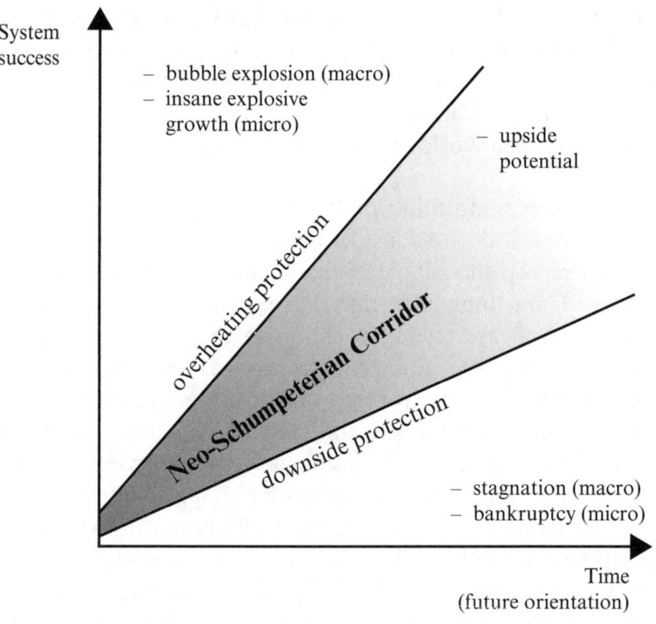

Figure 3.2 Neo-Schumpeterian corridor

Such a corridor is designed in a future-oriented way and represents an open space for development which runs acute-angled between two axes representing time and economic success, and in which the innovation- and firm-driven dynamics of modern economies can be modeled. Within this corridor, economic entities, companies as well as economies, can move freely and can choose a success-based and promising position dependent on their specific preconditions. In this sense, the corridor also serves as an outline for possible developments that political actors in their governance have to respect as well.

The idea of such a corridor presupposes that the political sphere can actively decide on the framework and take the appropriate measures that can effectively and opportunely tame and dominate those forces in a capitalistic system which continuously try to go through the roof and risk exiting the corridor towards an excessive growth path. On the other hand, politicians have to make sure that an economy will not fall out of the corridor, and that it will not have to cope with economic stagnation. Probably the greatest challenge for academics and politicians in the coming years will be to bring this neo-Schumpeterian corridor to life by providing the economic and political content of implementing the right strategies for public sector governance.

So, what we can do today in that respect is just to give some ideas and to make a few suggestions regarding how such a policy could or should look. However, before one can consider concrete proposals, it is necessary, in a first step, to know and determine the actual position characterizing an economy in the neo-Schumpeterian corridor. In principle, there are three system states possible: within, below and above the corridor.

Empirical findings and the economic history show that, in general, two spheres of economic activity are responsible for determining the state and the position of an economic body in the corridor. The causal factors are in the real sector in the first part and to a large degree in the financial sector of an economy in the succeeding part (Bernanke, 1995).

Let us start with the case of an economy that is too successful and attains growth rates far above average, rates which may be neither sustained nor stabilized; that is, with a situation above the corridor. The great success may very well create the positive and optimistic basic attitude in the economic agents necessary for future-oriented operations. But rapid growth is also always linked to an accelerated process of change in the structures of an economy. There are sectors which are readily expanding and others that do not grow as dynamically and so cannot keep up with the very swift pace of development pushed upon them by the fast-growing domains. The real development in such an economic system will then be determined by two velocities. The forces that impose and can bear high speed will be found in the innovative and strongly growing sectors and companies, while the sluggish variables fall into the sectors of low growth. As long as the latter serve as a natural brake for an exuberant economic dynamics, the economy will continue to position itself within the corridor and quite possibly even at its upper boundary. From a theoretical point of view, this is the best and economically the most successful situation for an economy (cf. Saviotti and Pyka, 2008). Admittedly, this case will empirically only occur in the rarest cases for a longer period of time.

The structural conflict between the fast and the slowly developing industries in an economy can – even if it were limited to the real sector and would therefore seem to follow the Schumpeterian idea of 'creative destruction' – lead to the complete breakdown of the entire system, because the inert sectors can no longer support the high pace of growth of the dynamic industries. This may happen when, for example, the infrastructure, the training of employees or the adaptation to customers' wants or suppliers' conditions cannot be altered and harmonized rapidly and flexibly enough, and will then work as a scotch block for all sectors (see for example Wong, 1999).

Moreover, history shows that dynamic industries, such as the IT sector in the 1990s, will attract the attention and interest of all those economic actors who desire to participate in the boom in fast-growing domains as financial investors, and who will also want to enjoy the high returns achievable. The technology-driven expansion in the dynamic part of the industrial sector will then be spurred and artificially inflated in the asset part of the financial sector and might even be triggered to a boom by the greed and short-term focus of the financial investors (see for example Minsky, 1990).

It is this finance-based overheating that can topple the whole economy into a severe crisis. This will always happen when we observe a situation where the market is full of fear of inflation and where the monetary policy is quickly shifted from an expansion to a contraction strategy. Just as we can see in the examples of Japan and the USA, this will lead in most cases to a panicking reaction of private investors in the financial markets. They suddenly see their return opportunities going down the drain and try to save all they can. Financial bubbles that had been built up in the time leading to this point will burst, and in their wake the industrial part of the economy will be torn down. The more significantly and faster a technology-induced expansion develops into a financial boom and the more interconnected an economy is in the global economic sphere, the more global and dramatic the consequences and crises will appear (Perez, 2002).

Too little growth on the other side, which means a situation below the corridor, cannot establish an advancing dynamics, and the standard of living in an economic area would have to suffer. The increase in investments would be insufficient both in the private and the public sector as well as with respect to physical, human, intellectual and social capital. The people will then adopt a negative view on the future development and, therefore, oppose and block the creative access to innovations and risk propensity. These two elements, however, sum up the driving forces of development in a capitalistic economy. At the end of a period of insufficient growth, the living conditions will inevitably decline on an absolute and relative basis. This recession may even be aggravated, if other regions, nations or economies suffer the same decreasing standard of living.

The only sensible path for a future-integrated, continuous and sustainable development of an economy or of an economic system is, in our opinion, a political strategy of having monitored, moderate overall growth with a corresponding rate of development (see for example McCraw, 2008). Only then can all structures, both in the real and the financial sectors, advance within the neo-Schumpeterian corridor in a 'healthy', co-evolutionary way. So, it is the government and the central banks that bear the responsibility to generate an almost natural balancing between 'Fast' and 'Slow', between 'Dynamics' and 'Statics', between 'New' and 'Old'. The fast-growing industries must have the possibility to expand without the risk of having their dynamics devitalized by the more sluggish sectors. On the other hand, the latter are supposed to form a natural brake that prevents the development of an excessive dynamics, both in the industrial and in the financial sector.

What does that mean for public sector governance, looking at concrete strategies and measures? In this chapter we will focus on the financial sector's role, and propose a tax scheme which might be able to support such a neo-Schumpeterian development in the spirit of the CNSE approach.

5 A PROGRESSIVE CAPITAL GAINS TAX AS A POSSIBLE CURE FOR FINANCIAL OVERHEATING

The most dangerous situation for an economy is when an exaggerated development in the real sector is coupled with an over-optimistic attitude in the financial market leading to herd behavior among the investors and the aforementioned bubble creation. In those situations, the possible rent seems to be far more interesting than the linked risk and many investors will ignore the looming danger of a burst bubble.

The quest for economists will be to come up with a *system of incentives* which will not limit the positive effects generated with this behavior but which may help reduce the negative consequences that are inevitably linked to a system that is allowed to develop freely. Furthermore, the proposed set of measures has to be politically feasible.

Some authors have argued extensively for a higher equity ratio for banks, which will increase the actual risk which remains at the bank and consequently reduce their willingness to take risks (cf. for example, Sinn, 2010). The new Basel III regulations, with their focus on the capital ratio of banks, do address major shortcomings which have surfaced during the last crisis, such as the pro-cyclicality of reserves and the leverage ratio (cf. for example, Blundell-Wignall and Atkinson, 2010). Nevertheless, there are still many aspects where banks may have the opportunity to try to reach greater returns by taking higher risks which may not be backed by sufficient equity. Consequently, there still is a risk of a renewed development of systemic risks endangering the entire economy.

Other proposals include the introduction of the Tobin tax, which will increase the cost of trading, focusing particularly on high-frequency traders (Tobin, 2003). The major drawback of such a system, however, is that there is always an escape possibility for financial actors if not all the countries in the world participate in it. Consequently, there is a great opportunity for smaller states to attract financial investors and traders for whom the transaction cost of moving their business is lower than the expected tax payment. Since it seems difficult to actually implement such a system on a truly global scale, it might not be possible to set it up in such a way that it affects the target group of highly speculative investors without making them leave. While some economists argue that serious companies will not move their shares to a country which does not abide by those then 'global rules', and that therefore the exodus of capital would not be dramatic, a high risk remains that such a drain of capital would nevertheless result and may have fairly detrimental effects on those countries from where the investment potential is withdrawn.

In order to look for a neo-Schumpeterian proposal, we should find a measure which can both limit and reduce the overwhelming dynamics in boom times as well as attract and incite investors in dull times of low growth. Such a system could then work as an *automatic stabilizer* which brings the economy back within the neo-Schumpeterian corridor both from below and from above and, consequently, supports a future-oriented sustainable development. While we should be careful not to over-regulate the market, such a measure could very well help retain the financial sector on a path where it supports the developments in the real sector and enables innovative processes with a lower risk of generating bubbles.

From our point of view, such a measure has to start at the *behavior* of the market actors and should incite them to invest in a more sustainable way. The tax system is always a standard means which the public sector may use to influence its citizens in certain ways and to increase the attractiveness of some options against others. Our proposal therefore centers on *capital gains tax*, and suggests using it as an automatic stabilizer to investment behavior, reducing exaggerated risk-taking in boom times while making investments more attractive in times of low returns.

The progressive income tax used in many countries is designed to collect a higher percentage of income from those who earn more. Consequently, those who generate a higher financial return from their use of time during one year, pay a higher amount of taxes. While the justification in the income tax scheme is different, the mechanism can just as well be used for capital gains tax. Investors who generate a higher return on their investments could pay a higher percentage of capital gains tax. This could, for example, mean that an investor who earned 100 euros interest from an investment of 100 000 euros will pay less tax on this amount than an investor who earned 100 euros from an investment of 1000 euros.

Most capital gains tax schemes in the world today tax returns either at a flat rate, irrespective of the amount, meaning that a return of 100 euros and of 1000 euros generates the same percentage of tax debt independent from the amount invested. Alternatively, in other countries, the capital gains tax is linked to the income tax, and the tax rate increases with the amount earned from the investment. Consequently, a return of 100 euros will be taxed at a lower rate than a return of 1000 euros, once again without looking at the amount invested.

The tax scheme we propose would lead to a situation where returns will be taxed progressively depending on the rate of return generated. Therefore, a low return will be taxed at a low rate and a high return will be taxed higher. While this concept does not yet include specific figures, we could create an example where the tax bracket ranges from 10 per cent to 50 per cent. Then a low return of 1 per cent would only require a 10 per cent tax payment, while a return of, say, 100 per cent would face a 50 per cent tax rate. In economic models, we would have to make the tax rate on capital gains a function of the generated return, $\tau_c(r_i)$, where τ_c corresponds to the capital gains tax rate and r_i is the rate of return earned on investment i.

The great advantage of such a taxation scheme is that it would favor investors who are taking low risks through a low tax rate and would penalize those who take high risks. Overall, we would see a shift in the behavior away from highly speculative investments promising a high rate of return, because some investors will lose interest because of the increased tax burden. In a situation where the economy finds itself above the corridor, fewer people will join the bandwagon, and the dangerous bubble formation might evolve at a slower speed. This would give the system the chance to slow down on its own or integrate the highly dynamic sectors in such a way as to widen bottlenecks before a looming breakdown.

In times when the economy is stagnating and below the neo-Schumpeterian corridor, the low tax rates incite investors to leave their money in the capital market and support a sustainable development. Compared to today's scheme, where the tax rate is constant independently of the rate of return, the incentive effects of such a progressive capital gains tax would work in favor of a neo-Schumpeterian development and would help keep the economy within the neo-Schumpeterian corridor.

Furthermore, the government would increase its tax receipts above average in boom times due to the rising tax rates and could, theoretically, use that money to support the economy in times when it nevertheless falls through the corridor. Even though it is not always clear that the public budget is maintained in a counter-cyclical way for political reasons, the proposed means certainly make such a behavior possible.

Additionally, the progressiveness of the tax rate could be designed in such a way that it will lead to similar tax receipts while the economy is within the neo-Schumpeterian corridor. Consequently, the threat of overheating is reduced because investors will shift to less risky and consequently less rewarding returns.

The greatest disadvantage that most political measures applied to the financial markets share is that they can be easily avoided by moving the funds abroad, resulting in detrimental effects on the home economy. Therefore, it is important to either work in a concerted manner on a worldwide scale including all tax havens, or to use means which will avoid capital flight. When introducing a system as we have proposed above, it is more favorable for those actors investing in low-risk/low-return sectors to be taxed than it was before. Consequently, a country using such a progressive tax rate will attract capital in those fields which are more sustainable and do not risk an overheating of the system. Nevertheless, the increased funding in those less dynamic branches might make it easier for companies within those sectors to invest in future-oriented projects. In the current system it is very difficult for them to attract the funds necessary to finance an innovative idea in sectors that are not among the fastest developing.

On the other hand, investors who prefer high-risk/high-return assets and who find themselves penalized by the new system may opt to invest their money differently or to withdraw it from that country. This may seem to be a disadvantage of the proposed tax scheme, since innovative sectors are in need of large amounts of money. One can argue, however, that the start-up phase of a sector or a company is often not linked to high returns. Only when a company or a sector has proven to be successful and when it is able to generate high surpluses will the run and hype from the financial sector start. It is at that point when the proposed system would show its specific advantages by punishing the herd behavior of mere speculation.

From an international point of view, it would therefore not be detrimental for a country to introduce such a tax scheme and it may even lead to a less erratic course for the economy, since the system contains automatic stabilizers, making investments in sectors promising a high-return in the short run less attractive and therefore limiting the herd behavior in boom times. On the other hand, it increases the incentive for investors to stay active in times of low return, because it is possible to keep a comparatively large share of the return.

Such a system could also be joined with one that encourages investors to hold their investments for a longer period of time, meaning that the tax rate decreases with the amount of years that an asset is held. For instance, a rent of 100 euros might then lead to a 25 per cent tax rate if a bond or a share had been sold within the first year, and to a tax rate of 15 per cent if the investor had kept it for more than 12 months.[1] It is generally possible to design such a system with many different steps, rewarding a long-term investment in potentially innovative firms or projects. This will also spur long-term investment strategies and reduce the short-sighted run for possible high rents in speculative financial positions. Consequently, financing truly innovative projects will not be punished merely due to their high returns.

There is also an anti-cyclicality built into this measure because once the returns rise, the tax rates rise as well; therefore less money will be invested and the system keeps from overheating. As returns decrease, the tax rates decrease as well, which might stabilize the investment behavior of the economic actors. Furthermore, the public sector can use the tax returns to support this anti-cyclical trend by investing money in times of stagnation and by keeping the receipts in boom times.

We find a similar picture concerning the monetary policy of the central banks. Whenever they try to slow investment activity by increasing the interest rate, the money supply of investors rises due to the higher returns. A progressive capital gains tax would work against this development, thus supporting the central bank's contractive policy goal. On the other hand, it would again support the central bank's intention when the interest rate is lowered in order to incite economic activity in an expansive way. Even though the returns for financial investments are falling, the incentive to leave the money in the system does not fall as sharply as it does in the current system. Since the goal of the central bank is to spur economic activity through lower interest rates, it is important that the money supply stays up. A tax scheme which supports this tendency seems to be favorable.

From a practical point of view, introducing such a capital gains tax scheme would not be linked to higher costs or organizational difficulties than most systems that are already in place. Compared with the current system in Germany, where banks deduct the taxable amount right away and the taxpayer can request a recalculation with his/her income tax return, such a system could work on the same basis. The financial institutions would withhold the taxes from the amount which is paid out and the taxpayer could file his/her overall statement at the end of the year. Besides, it seems politically feasible to introduce such a system and it is not detrimental if it is initially applied only in one country.

Besides, such a tax scheme would have incentive effects on the companies. Whenever a firm is looking for money, the financial market will judge its prospects and the actual development path. A firm in difficulties will have to offer a higher return than a firm which is in good shape. Under our new system, a firm in distress would have to offer an even higher return since the progressive tax rates have to be added to the offered rent. Consequently, it will be more difficult for a company to get money if it is already in bad condition. Financial stability will therefore increase in the private sectors since some companies might fear not being able to attract sufficient funds. This may once again lower returns, but the aim is to avoid a bubble formation comparable to the one we just experienced.

6 CONCLUDING REMARKS

Even though a progressive capital gains tax scheme may not be able to solve all problems in the financial market, and it certainly does have its disadvantages, it seems that it could well support the goal of keeping the economy from constantly creating more and more dangerous bubbles. The tendency for the financial market to even increase an unsupportable dynamics in the real sector would be limited. On the other hand, this system increases the willingness of investors to keep their money in the financial market in times of low returns.

It is certainly not a disadvantage to have a neo-Schumpeterian solution in order to avoid a new Schumpeterian crisis. The progressive tax scheme introduced in this chapter opens the discussion for a more integral approach which will keep positive incentives and help to limit exaggerating behavior as well as supporting an economy that is growing too slowly. It is therefore designed to stabilize an erratic economy.

NOTE

1. Such a system existed in Germany until 2008.

REFERENCES

Balestra, C. and D. Dottori (2009), 'Aging society, health and the environment', CORE discussion paper 2009/37, May.

Barroso, J.M. (2008), 'European economic recovery plan', European Commission, 26 November.

Baumann, F. (2008), 'Energy security as multidimensional concept', CAP Policy Analysis, No. 1.

Bernanke, B. (1995), 'The macroeconomics of the Great Depression: a comparative approach', *Journal of Money, Credit and Banking*, **27**(1), 1–28.

Blundell-Wignall, A. and P. Atkinson (2010), 'Thinking beyond Basel III: necessary solutions for capital and liquidity', *OECD Journal: Financial Market Trends*, **2010**(1).

Fagerberg, J., D. Mowery and R. Nelson (2005) (eds), *The Oxford Handbook of Innovation*, Oxford, New York: Oxford University Press.

Hanusch, H. and A. Pyka (eds) (2007a), *Elgar Companion to Neo-Schumpeterian Economics*, Cheltenham UK and Northampton, MA, USA: Edward Elgar Publishing.

Hanusch, H. and A. Pyka (2007b), 'Manifesto for comprehensive neo-Schumpeterian economics', *History of Economic Ideas*, **15**(1), 23–42.

Hanusch, H. and F. Wackermann (2009), 'Global Financial Crisis: causes and lessons – a neo-Schumpeterian perspective', *Volkswirtschaftliche Diskussionsreihe*, No. 303, University of Augsburg.

Hayek, F.A. von (1937 [1989]), *Monetary Nationalism and International Stability*, Fairfield, NJ: Augustus M. Kelley.

IPCC, Intergovernmental Panel on Climate Change, R.K. Pachauri and A. Reisinger (eds) (2007), *Climate Change 2007: Synthesis Report*, Geneva, Switzerland: IPCC.

Irzik, G. (1985), 'Popper's piecemeal engineering: what is good for science is not always good for society', *British Journal for the Philosophy of Science*, **36**(1985), 1–10.

Knight, F.H. (1921 [1965]), *Risk, Uncertainty and Profit*, Chicago/New York: Harper and Row.

McCraw, T. (2008), *Joseph A. Schumpeter*, Hamburg: Murmann Verlag.

Minsky, H. (1990), 'Schumpeter: finance and evolution', in A. Heertje and M. Perlman (eds), *Evolving Technology and Market Structure: Studies in Schumpeterian Economics*, Ann Arbor, MI: The University of Michigan Press, pp. 51–74.

Paul, R. (2009), *End the Fed*, New York: Grand Central Publishing.

Perez, C. (2002), *Technological Revolutions and Financial Capital: The Dynamics of Bubbles and Golden Ages*, Cheltenham, UK and Northampton, MA, USA: Edward Elgar Publishing.

Saviotti, P.P. and A. Pyka (2008), 'Product variety, competition and economic growth', *Journal of Evolutionary Economics*, **18**(3–4), 323–47.

Schumpeter, J. (1975), *Capitalism, Socialism and Democracy*, Harper Torchbooks, vol. 3, New York: Harper and Row.
Sinn, H.W. (2010), 'Kasino-Kapitalismus: wie es zur Finanzkrise kam und was jetzt zu tun ist', *Polis*, no. 1/2010, April, 9–12.
Tobin, J. (2003), *World Finance and Economic Stability: Selected Essays of James Tobin*, Cheltenham, UK and Northampton, MA, USA: Edward Elgar Publishing.
Trichet, J.-C. (2009), 'Lessons from the Financial Crisis', Keynote Address at the 'Wirtschaftstag 2009', organized by the Volksbanken and Raiffeisenbanken, Frankfurt-am-Main, 15 October 2009, available at http://www.ecb.int/press/key/date/2009/html/sp091015.en.html.
Welfens, J.J. (2008), 'Banking crisis and prudential supervision: a European perspective', *International Economics and Economic Policy*, **4**(4), 347–56.
Wong, Y.C.R. (1999), 'Lessons from the Asian financial crisis', *Cato Journal*, **18**(3), 391–8.

4. The Great Recession and its aftermath from a monetary equilibrium theory perspective*

Steven G. Horwitz and William J. Luther

Modern macroeconomists in the Austrian tradition can be divided into two groups: Rothbardians and monetary equilibrium (ME) theorists. The name for the latter is somewhat misleading, however, as both groups argue that monetary equilibrium is ultimately achieved where the quantity of money supplied equals the quantity of money demanded. The difference between these two approaches concerns what *should* adjust so that equilibrium is obtained. Rothbardians argue that '*any* supply of money is optimal', provided only that it is above some trivial minimum necessary to conduct transactions (Rothbard, 1988: 180).[1] Because Rothbard's proposal for 100 per cent gold reserves ties the money supply rigidly to the supply of gold, Rothbardians effectively hold the money supply constant in the short run and thereby rely on price adjustments to bring about monetary equilibrium in the face of changes in the demand for money.

In contrast, monetary equilibrium theorists argue that an ideal monetary system would expand or contract the supply of money to prevent changes in the demand to hold money from affecting its current value. Whereas price changes are typically desirable to clear markets for goods and services, ME theorists note that money is unique in that it has no price of its own. Because money is one half of every exchange, changing 'the price of money' to clear the money market requires changing *all* prices. The economy-wide price changes needed if the price level is to bear the burden of adjustment disrupt the process of economic coordination and lead to macroeconomic instability and either a deflationary recession or inflation and a potential boom–bust cycle. These significant costs of changing all prices to reflect a change in the demand for money are not offset by a corresponding benefit. ME theorists therefore hold that a system under which the supply of money could be reliably counted on to respond to changes in the demand to hold money would be much preferred over a system where the price level bears the burden of adjustment.

The monetary equilibrium approach should not be confused with the standard neo-classical position of price level stability. Both the Rothbardian and ME approaches recognize that prices – and, as a result, the aggregate price level – should fall in response to increases in productivity. Similarly, if goods become more scarce on average – as a result of a natural disaster, for example – the aggregate price level should increase to reflect this. ME theorists do not advocate stabilizing an aggregate price level. Rather, they suggest that the appropriate approach is to change the money supply to offset changes in money demand and to allow the price level to move inversely to changes in productivity. One can characterize this as a desire to keep the MV side of the quantity equation constant, and allow P to move inversely to Y. It is from this perspective that we consider the events of the last few years and offer policy recommendations for the present and future.

Our approach finds its roots in the work of Knut Wicksell, Ludwig von Mises and Friedrich A. Hayek.[2] These authors claimed that a shift in the supply or demand for money may cause the market rate of interest – that is, the rate that banks charge on loans – to diverge sharply from the unobservable Wicksellian natural rate of interest – the rate that equilibrates the supply and demand for the real resources available for investment.[3] Entrepreneurs react to these faulty price signals by altering their investments, lengthening or shortening the production process in line with the prevailing interest rate. The resulting malinvestments – to use the Austrian term – are fundamentally at odds with the underlying time preferences of individuals and will eventually reveal themselves as mistakes, leading to the process of self-correction that is the recession that follows the boom.

We argue that the primary source of business fluctuation observed over the last decade is monetary disequilibrium. Additionally, we claim that unnecessary intervention in the banking sector distorted incentives, nearly resulting in the collapse of the financial system, and that policies enacted to remedy the recession and financial instability have probably made things worse. Finally, we offer our own prescriptions to reduce the likelihood that such a scenario occurs again. Those come in two stages. First we suggest some changes to the way monetary policy and banking regulation are conducted under the assumption that we continue to have a central bank in more or less the form that the Federal Reserve System takes in the US. We conclude by offering a more radical solution that involves a change in the monetary regime, specifically a move toward a truly competitive free banking system.

BANKING GONE AWRY

The origins of the Great Recession in the housing market have been well documented. Austrian economists have consistently argued that excessively expansionary monetary policy generated a credit boom while a series of regulatory and institutional interventions encouraged the resulting malinvestment to concentrate in the real estate sector of the economy.[4] Policy errors – not a market gone mad – created a bubble that eventually had to burst.

Virtually no one denies that Congress aggressively sought to promote homeownership. The Federal National Mortgage Association (Fannie Mae) and the Federal Home Loan Mortgage Corporation (Freddie Mac) were instructed by Congress to increase the number of mortgage loans extended to low-income families under both Clinton and Bush administrations (Schwartz, 2009: 20). Furthermore, government agencies dominated the mortgage securitization market, increasing the number of securitized mortgages at a rate much greater than non-government agencies in the first half of the decade (Horwitz and Boettke, 2009: 8). But these facts merely explain why errors clustered *where* they did. The underlying reason for these errors, regardless of *where* they would turn up, was too-easy monetary policy.[5]

Although the Fed let interest rates fall below recommended Taylor-rule levels, especially from 2002 to 2004, it is difficult to demonstrate convincingly that monetary policy was too easy or too tight, because the natural rate of interest is not directly observable (Taylor, 2009a: 2). Beckworth and Selgin (2010: 5) provide a 'crude estimate' of the natural rate. Assuming that population growth and household time preference rates are constant, they estimate the natural rate of interest as the long-run average real rate plus the difference between the currently forecasted and mean total factor productivity (TFP) growth rates. The measure created by Beckworth and Selgin (2010: 13) 'suggests that monetary policy was excessively easy in the aftermath of the dot.com collapse, and that it was so to an extent unmatched since the inflationary 1970s'. Specifically, they show that the estimated natural and actual real federal funds rate began diverging in 2001 and, in 2004, the actual real federal funds rate was five percentage points lower than the estimated natural real federal funds rate (Beckworth and Selgin, 2010: 6). While their measure of the natural rate is admittedly imperfect, the magnitude of the difference leaves little doubt that monetary policy was excessively expansionary over the period.

Although there is a growing consensus that the Federal Reserve held interest rates too low for too long, some continue to argue to the contrary. Hummel and Henderson (2008: 2) reject the Austrian account, denying that monetary policy under Greenspan was too loose. They claim a central bank's ability to affect interest rates 'is increasingly diminished, even for a major central bank like the Fed, as globalization integrates global financial markets' (2008: 3). Low interest rates, according to Hummel and Henderson, merely reflect a rapid increase in the supply of loanable funds brought about by savings from developing Asian economies.[6]

The Hummel–Henderson hypothesis is plausible, but empirical evidence suggests it is incorrect. As Taylor (2009b: 348) notes, 'a good fraction' of the European Central Bank's 'interest rate decisions can be explained by the influence of the Fed's interest rate decisions'. Hence, the evidence suggests that central banks around the world look to the Fed as the authority on optimal monetary policy. And while one central bank may play but a small role, several banks acting erroneously in concert could have a destabilizing effect. Furthermore, global savings as a share of GDP was lower in the 2002 to 2004 period than the thirty-year average from 1970 to 2000 (Taylor, 2009b: 345–6). And the fact that global savings was less than investment for the period suggests a shortage – one we contend was brought about by monetary expansion – rather than a glut.

L.H. White (2008) provides even more evidence in conflict with the Hummel–Henderson hypothesis. If monetary expansion under Greenspan was not excessive, changes in the stock of money would have merely offset changes in velocity and, according to the equation of exchange, nominal spending would have been stable. Using the growth rate for final sales of domestic goods, White (2008: 117) shows that nominal spending increased rapidly from a compounded rate per annum of 3.6 per cent between 2001 and 2003 to 7.1 per cent between 2004 and 2006. As a result, Selgin (2008) remarks that, 'whatever M was up to during the housing boom, it was not simply adjusting so as to offset opposite changes in V'.

Although the Fed may be wholly to blame for creating the bubble, it is not entirely responsible for the widespread bank failures and the financial meltdown that was purportedly staved off in 2008. The housing bubble merely strained an already weak and fragile banking system crippled by perverse incentives. Specifically, we argue that federal deposit insurance and an implicit promise to bail out financial firms plagued the banking sector with moral hazard.

The Federal Deposit Insurance Corporation (FDIC) was created by the Banking Act of 1933 (Glass–Steagall). The economic argument for deposit insurance is relatively straightforward. In a fractional reserve system, lack of confidence can cause depositors to run on a bank. If this lack of confidence is unfounded, a solvent bank could be rendered insolvent through no fault of its own. Guaranteeing deposits provides depositors with the confidence necessary to prevent bank runs. However, it also discourages depositors from rewarding a prudent bank by accepting a lower rate of return. Since risky banks are then able to draw in insured deposits without paying the risk premium they would have to pay if depositors were still risk-sensitive, deposit insurance effectively amounts to a subsidy for bank risk-taking.

In order to mitigate this problem, Glass–Steagall placed restrictions on banks receiving deposit insurance. Although investment banks would not be subject to the additional restrictions, deposits at investment banks would not be federally insured and, hence, individuals with deposits at investment banks would have to keep a close eye on their balance sheets. Commercial banks, on the other hand, would receive deposit insurance. And since individuals no longer have an incentive to monitor the bank once their deposits are insured, FDIC was charged with the task of ensuring that these banks were run prudently. Gorton (2010) argues that the geographic restrictions on banks in place until the 1990s created local monopoly power that enhanced the value of a bank charter, creating incentives for banks to avoid the risky behavior we would normally expect with deposit insurance. In addition to the FDIC attempts at monitoring, the complex set of government regulations actually interacted in a way that solved the principal–agent problem, though not without other costs to consumers and economic efficiency thanks to the geographic restrictions and other regulations.

The Riegle–Neal Act of 1994 effectively ended many of the geographic restrictions on banks. As the monopoly profits associated with bank charters fell, the incentive for banks to avoid excessive risk declined as well. To make matters worse, Congress tore down the wall between investment and commercial banks in 1999 by passing the Financial Services Modernization Act (Gramm–Leach–Bliley). Gramm–Leach–Bliley allowed commercial and investment banks to merge. FDIC would still insure commercial deposits, but they would no longer prevent banks holding commercial deposits from taking on excessive risk. Without monopoly profits, bankers were no longer encouraged to act prudently under this system. Depositors with insured accounts had no incentive to watch the banks. Regulators were no longer concerned with moral hazard. And taxpayers – who would ultimately be on the hook if the Deposit Insurance Fund[7] fell into the red – were in the dark. Unsurprisingly, banks leveraged up.

To make matters worse, historical experience had revealed to banks that the federal government would bail them out if they got into trouble. Direct bailouts first became a policy option in the US with the Federal Deposit Insurance Act of 1950, which allowed the FDIC to provide emergency assistance to banks deemed 'essential to provide adequate banking service in its community'. It used this authority for the first time in 1971 by bailing out Unity Bank in Boston (Hetzel, 1991: 5). In 1984, it demonstrated the extent of its support by infusing an unprecedented $4.5 billion into the failing Continental Illinois National Bank and Trust Company. Then, in 1999, the Fed reaffirmed the federal government's commitment to backing insolvent institutions by orchestrating a bailout for Long-Term Capital Management.[8] These actions gave banks an implicit guarantee that, should they find themselves in a pinch, the government would cover the losses. With risk effectively subsidized and gains privatized, these financial institutions took risks they otherwise would have avoided.

The US government had made it quite clear it would cover the costs if major banks were in trouble – a promise it largely kept. And banks responded accordingly. Too-big-to-fail and too-many-to-fail doctrines encouraged banks to consolidate and employ similar strategies.[9] Government backing – in terms of deposit insurance and an implicit guarantee to bail out banks – meant that the American taxpayer would ultimately foot the bill if losses were incurred. It was as if we sent the CEOs of the world's largest financial firms to Las Vegas with Uncle Sam's credit card to cover their losses and told them they could keep their winnings. Predictably, they made very risky bets that would make them unbelievably wealthy in the improbable event that they panned out. But those bets did not pan out.

IT ALL CAME CRUMBLING DOWN

In 2004, the federal funds rate began to converge toward the natural rate as estimated by Beckworth and Selgin (2010: 6) and the bubble began to burst. Housing prices – having been bid up in the boom – reached their peak in 2005 and started to fall. Mortgage defaults increased. By the end of the second quarter of 2006, foreclosures sat 50 per cent higher than in 2002. Financial giants like Bear Sterns and Lehman Brothers watched as the value of their assets collapsed. Investing heavily in mortgage-backed securities had been lucrative for a while, but ultimately turned out to be a losing strategy. On 17 October 2007 then-Treasury Secretary Henry Paulson declared that the housing decline was 'the most significant current risk to our economy'. And everyone seemed to be asking the same question: what can we do about it? Virtually no one wondered if we had done too much already, or whether the best solution was to allow prices to get themselves in line with the underlying variables.

Fearing a repeat of the deflation of the early 1930s, the Fed rapidly expanded the monetary base to offset what appeared to be a collapse in the money multiplier.[10] From September 2008 to May 2010, the monetary base increased by 138 per cent, from $843 billion to $2007 billion. Although increasing the monetary base would be necessary to maintain monetary equilibrium if the money multiplier were falling, simultaneous changes in other variables like velocity complicate the situation. As noted above, it is difficult to know for sure whether the money supply is too big or too small under central banking. It is true that nominal GDP growth, which averaged 5.7 per cent a year from 1986 to 2006, began falling in 2007 and turned negative in late 2008, suggesting that monetary policy was too tight. But if the last decade was marked by monetary expansion (as we argue above), the 5.7 per cent benchmark overstates the sustainable long-run GDP growth rate. As such, the fall in nominal GDP growth might very well indicate the inevitable return to the sustainable long-run trend. Whether the decline in nominal GDP growth is evidence of monetary disequilibrium is harder to discern given that the prior years of growth took place in an inflationary environment, but the magnitude of the decline suggests that some increase in the monetary base over the past two years was probably the appropriate response. Even if the Fed acted in the right direction, it is not at all clear whether this expansion was too big or too small.

Any good the Fed's monetary policy might have done has arguably been more than offset by a plethora of policy errors. Acting in concert with the Treasury, the Fed increased uncertainty by hosting secret meetings with key players in the banking system and Washington, DC. The political nature of these meetings made it difficult for entrepreneurs to assess their options accurately. And the tone of fear established by top Fed and Treasury officials decreased confidence among consumers and investors.[11] Ironically, this frenzied response may have caused the very panic the Fed and Treasury aimed to prevent.

Even though increasing uncertainty and perpetuating a climate of fear has almost certainly had an impact on present conditions, other policy errors have the potential to do significant damage over the long haul by amplifying the extent of moral hazard already present in the system. For starters, the maximum deposit balance insured by FDIC was increased from $100 000 to $250 000 in 2008, reducing the incentive for those with deposits in excess of $100 000 to monitor banks even further. Similarly, the Treasury extended deposit insurance to cover money market mutual funds.

Although both of these programs were initially purported to be temporary, whether or not they will actually be rolled back remains to be seen.[12] And, at the very least, they reaffirm a dangerous precedent capable of increasing risk regardless of whether these particular programs are officially terminated in the next few years.

The increase in moral hazard from deposit insurance is likely to pale in comparison to that resulting from the bailouts offered over the last few years. When Bear Stearns approached the brink in March 2008, the Fed lived up to expectations established in dealing with Long-Term Capital Management. In exchange for purchasing Bear Stearns for $2 per share – down from $93 in February 2008 – the Fed extended a $30 billion non-recourse loan to JP Morgan. Having accepted Bear Stearns' mortgage debt as collateral, the Fed would have no recourse (i.e., it cannot seize any other assets from JP Morgan) should the value of these so-called 'toxic assets' fall below the value of the loan. In other words, the Fed – and ultimately the taxpayer – bears the risk associated with the bad loans while JP Morgan receives the benefits if things work out.

Unfortunately, deals like this abound. Congress set aside $700 billion for the Treasury to dole out through the Troubled Asset Relief Program (TARP). By January 2009, the US government had become a major shareholder in the banking system by purchasing $178 billion worth of bank equity shares through the Capital Purchase Program;[13] $25 billion more was spent on preferred stock of Citigroup and GMAC. Another $40 billion was used to buy up a large chunk of AIG. Tack on the $19.4 billion spent to bail out the auto industry and $25 billion to backstop the Fed and guarantee loans for Citigroup and – as Everett Dirksen might say – pretty soon you're talking real money.

Although most of the money spent thus far has been to acquire stock (which can eventually be resold) or issue loans (much of which has already been repaid), these expenditures might still add to the growing government debt. The Congressional Budget Office estimates that the subsidy cost of the $247 billion spent from October 2008 to January 2009 amounts to roughly $64 billion (CBO, 2009: 1). Worst of all, as Lawrence Kotlikoff (2010: 92) argues, 'bailouts are teaching corporate America a very bad lesson about looking to the government in times of trouble'. If Kotlikoff is correct – and if the government does nothing to remedy the situation – moral hazard will be an even bigger problem in the future.

WHERE DO WE GO FROM HERE?

The desire to end the recession as quickly as possible has prompted the Bush and Obama administrations to cut taxes and increase government spending. Unfortunately, the best medicine for ending a recession is time. It takes time for capital to be retooled and reallocated. It takes time for labor to learn new skills and relocate. And only in time will entrepreneurs have enough information to feel comfortable pursuing new plans. Efforts to jump-start the economy prematurely by providing fiscal stimulus merely interrupt and postpone the inevitable adjustment process. However, one thing policy-makers can do is ensure that, when enough time has passed, market participants will return to an institutional environment conducive to the market process. This requires addressing two major problems moving forward: monetary instability and moral hazard.

In our view, monetary stability means continuously adjusting the supply of money to offset changes in velocity.[14] Given the current monetary regime, where such adjustments are in the hands of the central bank, they should be made as mechanical as possible. Discretionary monetary policy unnecessarily introduces instability into the system with little or no offsetting benefit. Instead, the Fed should commit to a policy rule. Given our monetary equilibrium view, we hold that the Fed should adopt a nominal income target. Although nominal income targeting would require price adjustments in response to changes in aggregate supply, these particular price changes convey important information about relative scarcity over time and would be much less costly than requiring all other prices to change, as would be the case under a price-level targeting regime (Selgin, 1997: 23–9). Under a nominal income targeting regime, monetary policy would have the best chance to maintain our goal of monetary equilibrium, at least to the extent that central bankers can accurately estimate and commit to follow an aggregate measure of output. As imperfect as this solution would be, we believe it is superior to the alternatives available in the world of the second best, and certainly an improvement over the status quo of the Fed's pure discretion in monetary policy and beyond.

A monetary regime that stayed closer to monetary equilibrium would have probably prevented the housing bubble and subsequent recession. However, it is also important to weed out the moral hazard problem perpetuated – and recently exacerbated – by nearly a century of policy errors. Among other things, this means ending federal deposit insurance and credibly committing not to offer any more bailouts. The political consequences of such a policy are admittedly unclear. And the feasibility of credibly committing to refrain from stepping in should a similar situation result, having just exemplified a willingness to do precisely the opposite, does not look promising. Nonetheless, we contend that ending the moral hazard problem is essential to long-run economic growth free of damaging macroeconomic fluctuations.

The absolute worst solution in terms of dealing with moral hazard would be to abolish these programs officially without credibly committing to refrain from re-establishing them in the future. If market participants expect the government will bail them out when they get into trouble, they will act accordingly. The difference, however, would be that the Deposit Insurance Fund – having been abolished – would be empty and the full cost of bailing out depositors would fall on taxpayers in general. If bailouts and deposit insurance are going to be offered in the future, those likely to take advantage of them should be required to pay into respective funds to be used when the occasion arises. Ideally, payouts would be limited to the size of the fund. But given that a lack of credibility is the only acceptable reason to perpetuate these programs, their continuance suggests that the resulting government would be unable to tie its hands in this capacity as well.

We end our policy recommendations within the current monetary regime by emphasizing our reluctance to keep FDIC or establish an official bailout fund. These suggestions are clearly made in a world of the second best, where the government is incapable of choosing our preferred alternative. In such a world, we argue that the combination of the FDIC and a Deposit Insurance Fund drawn from the banks is preferred to no official deposit insurance program and an implicit guarantee to be funded by taxpayers in general when the need arises, with all the dangers of the political process defining 'need' that such a situation would bring. Similarly, we would prefer explicit promises to bail out financial institutions via deposit insurance, and a corresponding fund to provide the resources, to the implicit promises existing in our current system, provided that the government is incapable of denying bailouts *ex post* regardless of their position *ex ante*. Unfortunately, as Mises (1996: 8) pointed out, interventions typically have unintended consequences that run counter to their desired goals; and '[i]f government is not inclined to alleviate the situation through removing its limited intervention [. . .] its first step must be followed by others'. The interventions we might reluctantly accept here are no different.

Mitigating the moral hazard associated with continuing federal deposit insurance and establishing an official bailout fund would probably require raising capital requirements and overseeing financial services to an even greater extent in the future. With the prospect of regulatory capture at one end and a bureaucratic banking system at the other, this is obviously the least desirable of the potential alternatives we outline. In the world of the second best, a deposit insurance system sufficiently funded by the banks might be better than perpetuating a system that fully socializes costs while privatizing gains, as a greater share of the costs of bailing out failed banks are borne by banks and depositors rather than taxpayers broadly. These dilemmas of the second-best world further emphasize that the ultimate solution to the problems of the Great Recession is to remove the whole panoply of government interventions that caused it, with the Federal Reserve System being first and foremost among them. In the final section we explore what the free banking alternative might look like and why it offers a first best solution.

THE FREE BANKING ALTERNATIVE

Normally, the only alternative to central banking that receives real consideration is some kind of commodity standard, not unlike the classical gold standard of the nineteenth century. There was much to recommend about that system, but in practice, it never gave the full play to market forces that are required to minimize deviations from monetary equilibrium. Under a commodity standard, the supply of money expands and contracts more or less the way monetary equilibrium theorists claim is desirable. Consider the automatic response under a gold standard to a sudden increase in the demand to hold money.[15] The increase in demand puts upward pressure on the purchasing power of gold. As a result, some individuals currently using gold in other, non-monetary capacities (e.g., jewelry, candelabra) will choose to melt and mint, unintentionally increasing the quantity of money in circulation. Furthermore, mine owners are encouraged to increase their production of gold. With more gold being produced, the money supply expands until the purchasing power of gold is restored to its original level.

The advantage of such a system is that the supply of the commodity serving as money responds to offset changes in money demand. Unfortunately, it does not do so very rapidly. The process of converting the commodity from non-monetary sources and mining is very time-consuming. Although precise estimates are not available, the adjustment process of the historical gold standard, White (1999: 38) claims, 'probably required a decade or more on average'. With changes in the money supply delayed by a decade or more, changes in velocity make aggregate demand unstable. As a result, prices and output fluctuate and generalized economic discoordination abounds.

An alternative monetary regime, normally referred to as 'free banking', has the potential to adjust more rapidly. Under free banking, private banks create money, both in deposit and currency form. Both forms of bank liabilities would be redeemable in some outside money, most likely a commodity such as gold. Prior to the creation of central banks, this was the typical way in which both deposits and currency were produced. In the more successful of these systems (e.g. Canada and Scotland), banks were left free to produce their liabilities to the best of their judgment. In other systems, such as the US, other forms of government regulation (e.g. limits on branch banking and requirements to hold federal government bonds as collateral against currency issues) prevented banks from making the appropriate adjustments in the money supply. In a truly free banking system, banks would be left to determine the quantity of money (in the form of bank liabilities) they create, based on their calculations of profit maximization. Free banking theorists argue that a free banking system will lead profit maximizing banks to produce the quantity of bank liabilities that is equal to the demand to hold those liabilities at the current price level. In other words, profit maximizing banks will maintain monetary equilibrium.[16]

The key to that result is the calculation banks make about their holdings of reserves. Free banks would determine their reserve holdings at the clearinghouse and in their vaults by balancing the risk of being illiquid in the face of demands for redemption against the opportunity cost of forgone interest from the loans those reserves could support. If such a bank creates more liabilities than the public wish to hold in their money balances, those excess liabilities will be spent and eventually come back to the issuing bank for redemption. Whether that redemption is 'over the counter' for the outside money commodity or, more likely, through the clearing system by other banks, it will reduce the issuing bank's holding of reserves. If we assume the bank was maximizing profits before the over-issue, then this loss in reserves means a loss in profits, and the bank will have both the signal (in the form of reduced reserves) and the incentive (in the form of lost profits) to reduce its liabilities back to that amount the public wish to hold. Conversely, should it issue too few liabilities compared to demand, it will see reserves piling up as redemptions fall. Those excess reserves reflect an opportunity cost in terms of forgone interest on loans that could be made with them, just as is true in banking systems today. The profit maximizing free bank would see that signal and recognize the incentive to increase its liability issuance to provide the amount the public wish to hold. Profit maximization produces monetary equilibrium.

What is true of the free bank misjudging the quantity of money its customers want to hold is equally true of how it will respond to a change in consumer demand for its liabilities. Bank customers express their new demand to hold money by spending less. As a result, fewer notes are redeemed directly and through the clearinghouse system, just as we saw above when the bank issued too few liabilities in the face of a constant demand for money. Assuming that banks were optimizing subject to consumer preferences prior to the change in demand, they now find that their reserves are in excess of that amount required to maintain liquidity and that the bank is forgoing interest returns it could safely be earning. The profit motive directs each individual bank to expand the number of loans and securities it holds until reserves are reduced to the new equilibrium level. In the aggregate, the money supply is expanding to match the increase in money demand. And since individual banks need only to print up more of their notes or credit electronic accounts, the supply of money can adjust much more rapidly in comparison to a strict commodity standard.

Absent a free market in money and banking, the supply of money must be consciously adjusted by a central bank if monetary equilibrium is to be maintained. Compared to free banking, central banks face at least three problems in conducting optimal monetary policy. First, they do not have access to the information that is readily available in the form of market prices to gold miners and bankers in the two regimes discussed above. Instead, the central bank must rely on costly aggregate data sets that arguably hold less informational content in comparison to prices. That these data sets become available to the central bank with a significant lag is also problematic, as it means they often do not know an adjustment is necessary until the very events the adjustment might have prevented begin to materialize. Relying on changes in macroeconomic aggregates to signal the need to change the money supply to prevent changes in those very aggregates seems an unsolvable problem.

In addition to the information problem, central banks do not face the same incentives as private participants. Under free banking, for example, an over-issuing bank would suffer reserve losses when adverse clearings manifest at the clearinghouse. Although a similar incentive might exist if politicians lose votes for continually appointing highly inflationary central bankers, this incentive appears to be much weaker than those faced by market participants in alternative regimes.[17] After all, the US public debt currently exceeds $13 trillion. As the world's largest debtor, the US government stands to gain from a little unexpected inflation.

Finally, the monopoly status of central banks amplifies errors. Under a competitive free banking system, where an individual bank might maintain only 20 per cent of the total circulation, any single bank's over-issuing by 10 per cent would only result in a 2 per cent over-issue in the aggregate. Furthermore, this error could potentially be offset by the under-issuing of another bank. Central banking, on the other hand, assigns the entire task of getting it right to a single central planner.[18] There is no possibility of offsetting errors, and a 10 per cent over-issue by the single bank is a 10 per cent over-issue by the banking system.

The early history of the central bank illustrates its potential for blunders. While productivity soared in the 1920s, for example, the Fed over-expanded the money supply, resulting in a relatively constant price level.[19] It would be the error at the end of the decade, however, that would stand out in the twentieth century. As Friedman and Schwartz (1963: 299–407) detail, the money supply contracted by roughly a third from 1929 to 1933 because the Fed did not respond as it should have.[20] Had the Fed maintained monetary equilibrium, the period now known as the Great Depression might have turned out to be a garden variety recession, along the lines of, though perhaps somewhat more severe than, the 1920–21 recession. Instead it became the worst economic crisis in US history.

Because central bankers fear nothing more than being seen as responsible for another Great Depression, they have erred in the opposite direction of the deflationary mistakes made in the early 1930s. Beckworth and Selgin (2010: 1) show that – as was the case in the 1920s – the Fed's 'occasional, unintentional exacerbation of the business cycle is largely attributable to its failure to respond appropriately to persistent changes in the growth rate of total factor productivity'. Specifically, when factor productivity growth is high and monetary equilibrium theory would require a falling price level, the Fed expands the money supply to prevent prices from falling. In doing so, the Fed pushes the federal funds rate below the natural rate and leads entrepreneurs to generate malinvestment. Fearing deflation, the Fed consistently over-expands the money supply with little regard for the ill effects.

One other explanation for the inflationary bias of the Fed is that the costs of inflation are far more subtle and long-run than those associated with deflation. The ways in which inflation plays havoc with prices and disrupts microeconomic coordination and entrepreneurship are widespread and hard to connect directly to the inflationary activities of the central bank (Horwitz, 2003). In contrast, deflation usually makes itself known quickly, as the shortage of money begins to reduce the number of mutually beneficial exchanges that take place, which, in combination with prices not falling, immediately leads to surpluses of goods and labor. The shortage of money is felt acutely and its effects can be tied back to that cause. Not only does inflation benefit governments by reducing the real burden of their debt, it is politically less costly to the central bank directly, as its consequences cannot easily be connected with its cause.

The Fed's fixation with deflation was perhaps best exemplified in a November 2002 speech by then-Governor Ben Bernanke. Honoring Milton Friedman on his ninetieth birthday, Bernanke (2002) made it clear that those at the Fed understood the lesson of the Great Depression. He ended his talk by 'abusing slightly' his 'status as an official representative of the Federal Reserve' to address Friedman and co-author Anna Schwartz directly with the following words:

> Regarding the Great Depression. You're right, we did it. We're very sorry. But thanks to you, we won't do it again.

Since being appointed Chairman of the Fed in 2006, Bernanke has made good his promise. Unfortunately, he has followed many of his predecessors in making precisely the opposite error, setting the stage for the current recession and financial market instability.

The structure of a free banking system not only eliminates these destructive incentive and information problems, it replaces both with market signals that provide the needed information wrapped in the necessary incentives, with the result that the banks' incentives are aligned with the goal of maintaining monetary equilibrium. Although such a dramatic change in monetary regimes may not be politically feasible in the near future, especially because central banks are very useful for governments that are trillions in debt, the increasing public scrutiny that the Fed and other central banks are under is one reason to continue to argue for a fundamental change in regimes. As we have argued, central banks, along with other forms of government intervention, have given us the Great Recession. It seems only fair that all of the parties responsible for the current mess be subject to equal critical scrutiny and that those who wish to avoid further damage to the world economy be willing to put on the table every proposal they believe will help, regardless of whether it is currently politically possible. Serious economic problems require the courage of radical, and potentially unpopular, solutions.

NOTES

* The authors thank the Mercatus Center at George Mason University for generously supporting this research.

1. Rothbard (1988: 181) makes his position quite clear: 'There is never any social benefit to increasing the quantity of money, for the increase only dilutes the "objective exchange value", or purchasing power, of the money unit. Monetary calculations and contracts are distorted, and the early recipients of the new money, as well as debtors, gain income and wealth at the expense of later recipients and of creditors. In short, increasing the quantity of the money is only a device to benefit some groups in society at the expense of others'.
2. Intellectual predecessors also include American economists Harry G. Brown, Herbert J. Davenport and Clark Warburton, the English economist Dennis H. Robertson, and the South African economist William H. Hutt.
3. As Horwitz (2000: 77) explains, 'the inflationary disequilibrium theory that emerged from Wicksell's work was the Austrian theory of the business cycle in the hands of Mises and Hayek'.
4. Essays from Austrian economists on the Great Recession include Boettke and Luther (2009); Horwitz and Boettke (2009); Horwitz (2009a, 2009b), White (2008, 2009), among others. See also the historian Tom Woods's (2009) book, which makes use of Austrian school theory.
5. In a recent interview with Brian Carney (2008), Anna Schwartz implicitly endorsed the Austrian theory of the trade cycle: 'If you investigate individually the manias that the market has so dubbed over the years, in every case, it was expansive monetary policy that generated the boom in an asset. The particular asset varied from one boom to another. But the basic underlying propagator was too-easy monetary policy and too-low interest rates that induced ordinary people to say, well, it's so cheap to acquire whatever is the object of desire in an asset boom, and go ahead and acquire that object. And then of course if monetary policy tightens, the boom collapses'.

6. This position is consistent with Greenspan's (2007: 385–8 and 2008) own claim that emerging economies created a savings glut.
7. From 1989 to 2006, FDIC managed two funds: the Bank Insurance Fund (BIF) and the Savings Association Insurance Fund (SAIF). These funds were merged in 2006 to create the Deposit Insurance Fund (DIF) when President Bush signed the Federal Deposit Insurance Reform Act of 2005 (FDIRA) into law.
8. Dowd (1999) discusses the failure and rescue of LTCM.
9. Stern and Feldman (2004) provide a comprehensive analysis of the too-big-to-fail doctrine. Acharya and Yorulmazer (2007) show that the too-many-to-fail results in herding, particularly among smaller banks.
10. Recall that in a fractional reserve banking system, $M = Bm$, where M is the money supply, B is base money, and m is the money multiplier. We return to the issue of central bank fear of deflation in a later section.
11. At a White House meeting held in September 2008, for example, then-Treasury Secretary Henry Paulson literally got down on one knee to beg House Speaker Nancy Pelosi to pass the Troubled Asset Relief Program (Herszenhorn et al., 2008).
12. The temporary increase in FDIC insurance coverage from \$100 000 to \$250 000 per depositor as established in the Emergency Economic Stabilization Act of 2008 was originally scheduled to expire on 31 December 2009, at which point coverage levels would return to \$100 000. It was then rescheduled to last until 31 December 2013. The increase was made permanent with the signing of the Dodd–Frank Wall Street Reform and Consumer Protection Act on 21 July 2010.
13. The Capital Purchase Program is a component of TARP allowing the Treasury to purchase preferred stock and equity warrants.
14. As we shall discuss in the next section, we believe that a fundamental change in monetary regimes in the form of adopting a free banking system is the first best way to achieve this end. Unfortunately, 'a combination of governmental desire to manipulate money and economic theory favoring central banking led governments to replace competitive issue of notes (paper money) by commercial banks with monopoly issue by central banks' in the period since the start of WWI (Schuler, 2001: 453). Given that these forces are still in play, abolishing the Fed and establishing a system of competitive note issue, though ideal, is probably out of the question, at least in the short run. This necessarily leaves us in a world of the second best.
15. White (1999: 28–37) graphically details the automatic mechanism underlying the classical gold standard.
16. Selgin and White (1994) detail the mechanics of free banking in much greater detail. The interested reader should also consult the sources referenced there.
17. The implicit promise by free banks to maintain monetary equilibrium is self-enforcing via profit and loss, while any explicit promise by central banks to do so lacks the incentive compatibility necessary to enforce such a promise.
18. If equating central banking to central planning seems unwarranted, recall that former Fed Chairman Alan Greenspan was affectionately called 'The Maestro'.
19. The Board of Governors of the Federal Reserve System (1937: 827–8) ultimately admitted to this error in describing monetary policy objectives: 'No matter what price index may be adopted as a guide, unstable economic conditions may develop, as they did in the 1920's, while the price level remains stable; business activity can change in one direction or the other and acquire considerable momentum before changes are reflected in the index of prices. There are situations in which changes in the price level work toward maintenance of stability; declining prices resulting from technological improvements, for example, may contribute to stability by increasing consumption'.
20. The Fed's inaction was a result of the combination of (1) not quite understanding the dimensions of the problem; (2) holding to an incorrect monetary theory, in the form of the Real Bills Doctrine, which led many members to recommend a wrong cure; and (3) to the extent other voices had it right, their recommended actions were too little, too late.

REFERENCES

Acharya, Viral V. and Tanjo Yorulmazer (2007), 'Too many to fail – an analysis of time-inconsistency in bank closure policies', Bank of England Working Paper no. 319.

Beckworth, David and George Selgin (2010), 'Where the Fed goes wrong: the "productivity gap" and monetary policy', manuscript, 20 April, available online at: http://econfaculty.gmu.edu/pboettke/workshop/Spring2010/Beckworth2.pdf.

Bernanke, Ben S. (2002), 'On Milton Friedman's ninetieth birthday', conference to honor Milton Friedman, University of Chicago, 8 November, available online at: http://www.federalreserve.gov/BOARDDOCS/SPEECHES/2002/20021108/default.htm.

Board of Governors of the Federal Reserve System (1937), 'Objectives on monetary policy', *Federal Reserve Bulletin*, **23**(9), 827–8.

Boettke, Peter J. and William J. Luther (2009), 'The ordinary economics of an extraordinary crisis', in Steven Kates (ed.), *Macroeconomic Theory and its Failings: Alternative Perspectives on the Global Financial Crisis*, Cheltenham, UK and Northampton, MA, USA: Edward Elgar Publishing, pp. 14–25.

Carney, Brian (2008), 'Bernanke is fighting the last war', *Wall Street Journal*, 18 October , available online at: http://online.wsj.com/article/SB122428279231046053.html.

Congressional Budget Office (2009), 'The troubled asset relief program: report on transactions through December 31, 2008', CBO Report, Washington, DC: CBO, available online at: http://www.cbo.gov/ftpdocs/99xx/doc9961/01-16-TARP.pdf.

Dowd, Kevin (1999), 'Too big to fail? Long-term capital management and the Federal Reserve', Cato Briefing Paper, 23 September.

Friedman, Milton and Anna J. Schwartz (1963), *A Monetary History of the United States, 1867–1960*, Princeton: Princeton University Press.

Gorton, Gary B. (2010), *Slapped by the Invisible Hand: The Panic of 2007*, New York: Oxford University Press.

Greenspan, Allan (2007), *The Age of Turbulence: Adventures in a New World*, New York: Penguin Press.

Greenspan, Allan (2008), 'A response to my critics', *Financial Times*, 6 April.

Herszenhorn, David M., Carl Hulse, Sheryl Gay Stolberg and Elisabeth Bumiller (2008), 'Day of chaos grips Washington; fate of bailout plan unresolved', *New York Times*, 26 September, A1.

Hetzel, Robert L. (1991), 'Too big to fail: origins, consequences, and outlook', *Federal Reserve Bank of Richmond Economic Review*, November, pp. 3–15.

Horwitz, Steven (2000), *Microfoundations and Macroeconomics: An Austrian Perspective*, London: Routledge.

Horwitz, Steven (2003), 'The costs of inflation revisited', *Review of Austrian Economics*, **16**, 77–95.

Horwitz, Steven (2009a), 'The microeconomic foundation of macroeconomic disorder: an Austrian perspective on the Great Recession of 2008', in Steven Kates (ed.), *Macroeconomic Theory and its Failings: Alternative Perspectives on the Global Financial Crisis*, Cheltenham, UK and Northampton, MA, USA: Edward Elgar, pp. 96–111.

Horwitz, Steven (2009b), 'The "Great Recession" as the institutional and ideological residue of the Great Depression', manuscript, available online at: http://myslu.stlawu.edu/~shorwitz/gsutalk.htm.

Horwitz, Steven and Peter J. Boettke (2009), *The House that Uncle Sam Built: the Untold Story of the Great Recession of 2008*, Lawrence W. Reed (ed.), Irvington, NY: Foundation for Economic Education.

Hummel, Jeffrey R. and David R. Henderson (2008), 'Greenspan's monetary policy in retrospect: discretion or rules?', Cato Briefing Paper, 109, 3 November.

Kotlikoff, Lawrence J. (2010), *Jimmy Stewart is Dead: Ending the World's Ongoing Financial Plague with Limited Purpose Banking*, Hoboken: Wiley.

Mises, Ludwig (1996), *Critique of Interventionism*, revised edn, Irvington-on-Hudson: Foundation for Economic Education.

Paulson, Henry M. (2007), 'Current housing and mortgage market developments', Georgetown University Law Center, 16 October, available online at: http://www.ustreas.gov/press/releases/hp612.htm.

Rothbard, Murray N. (1988), 'Timberlake on the Austrian theory of money: a comment', *Review of Austrian Economics*, **2**(1), 179–87.

Schuler, Kurt (2001), 'Note issue by banks: a step toward free banking in the United States?', *Cato Journal*, **20**(3), 453–65.

Schwartz, Anna J. (2009), 'Origins of the financial market crisis of 2008', *Cato Journal*, **29**(1), 19–23.

Selgin, George A. (1997), *Less than Zero The Case for a Falling Price Level in a Growing Economy*, London: Institute of Economic Affairs.

Selgin, George A. (2008), 'Guilty as Charged', *Mises Daily*, 7 November.

Selgin, George and Lawrence H. White (1994), 'How would the invisible hand handle money?', *Journal of Economic Literature*, **32**(4), 1718–49.

Stern, Gary H. and Ron J. Feldman (2004), *Too Big to Fail: Hazards and Bank Bailouts*, Washington, DC: Brookings Institution Press.

Taylor, John B. (2009a), *Getting Off Track: How Government Actions and Interventions Caused, Prolonged, and Worsened the Financial Crisis*, Stanford, CA: Hoover Institution.

Taylor, John B. (2009b), 'The financial crisis and the policy responses: an empirical analysis of what went wrong', *Critical Review*, **21**(2), 341–64.

White, Lawrence H. (1999), *The Theory of Monetary Institutions*, Oxford, UK: Blackwell.

White, Lawrence H. (2008), 'How did we get into this financial mess?', Cato Briefing Paper, 18 November.

White, Lawrence H. (2009), 'Federal Reserve policy and the housing bubble', *Cato Journal*, **29**(1): 115–25.

Woods, Thomas E. (2009), *Meltdown: A Free-Market Look at Why the Stock Market Collapsed, the Economy Tanked, and Government Bailouts Will Make Things Worse*, Washington, DC: Regnery Publishing.

5. Policy in the absence of theory: the coming world of political economy without Keynes

Steven Kates

Although not yet translated into our economic texts, the one lesson we appear to have learned during the Global Financial Crisis and the recession that followed is that Keynesian policies do not work. We have learned that increased public spending during recessions does not lead to recovery. We have learned that it instead leads to large increases in public sector deficits, massive increases in debt and stagnation in the private sector. Nor have these policies been accompanied by much, if any, recovery in the labour market whose improvement had been their main justification. And so, even while unemployment remains high, public policy has now moved towards cutting the level of public spending and attempting to return national budgets towards surplus, the exact reverse of the policies of the first two years following the GFC.

Yet so far as the mainstream of economic theory is concerned, everything is as it was before. Nothing has changed. We still teach that amongst the most useful measures to take when unemployment is high are those that will increase the level of aggregate demand with particular emphasis on increasing the level of public spending. But after only two years of the stimulus, virtually no one in a policy-making role any longer believes a word of this. In reversing the policies of the first two years of recession, where high levels of public spending were almost universally adopted, economic policy has now moved sharply away from the only macroeconomic theory most economists have ever known. We are now in a new world where the actions that governments take to deal with recession are directly opposite to the theories found in our major economic texts.

But as it happens, there already are theories of the cycle on which such policies can be based. These were the theories accepted by virtually every economist right up until the publication of Keynes's *General Theory* in 1936. Although today's policy-makers are almost completely unaware of the parallels, the actions that circumstances have forced them to take are the policies that almost every economist prior to 1936 would have recommended as measures to deal with the downturn when it came.

In following modern theory we have tried to induce faster growth by increasing the level of public sector demand. Classical economists would have recommended policies that encourage the private sector through reductions in rates of interest, reduced levels of taxation and even through lower levels of unproductive forms of public expenditure. It is in this direction that policy is heading, guided by the common sense response to the failures that Keynesian policies have clearly caused.

Nor have classical policies been absent even up until now. At the very start of the GFC, the approach every government applied in dealing with the immediate problems in their financial markets was to adopt a series of essentially classical measures that were well known and well understood to the extent anything can be well known and well understood during such an unprecedented catastrophe. These measures worked more or less as they were intended. The panic came almost immediately to an end in every economy in which such measures were introduced.

But then, when the dust had settled, the policies adopted to revive our economies were largely Keynesian in nature, not classical, and designed to restore aggregate demand to previous levels. It is these Keynesian policies which have left a trail of further devastation in their wake. They have almost certainly done more harm than the original GFC, and the debilitating effects of these policies will be with us for many years to come.

This chapter looks at the measures taken during the financial crisis itself and then at the policies used to deal with the subsequent downturn. What will be discussed is the almost complete absence of insight into the downturn provided by the standard textbook Keynesian macroeconomic model and the consequences of having adopted Keynesian policies to generate recovery after financial markets had finally been calmed. The need for a root and branch rejection of such Keynesian models and a restoration of the pre-Keynesian theory of the cycle based on an acceptance of Say's Law is the central conclusion of this discussion. Until and unless this is done, we will live in a twilight zone between theory and policy where economists learn a theory no government will apply in practice.

WHO SAW IT COMING?

The inadequacies of modern theory were evident even before the GFC began. It is fair to say that none of the major economic forecasting agencies, either national or international, saw the devastation that was to come. There had certainly been greater pessimism across the world from the end of 2007 and into the start of 2008. A slowdown was expected, even a quite severe downturn, but the depth and extent of the devastation when it finally revealed itself was unexpected. Certainly amongst market analysts there was a profound pessimism in many quarters, but amongst economists there were few, if any, forecasting the meltdown to come. The possibility of a collapse in the world's entire financial structure was not on the horizon for any major economic forecaster in the world.

But what is more to the point is to recognize that the mainstream neoclassical synthesis model, built on a Keynesian framework, was incapable of even registering the problem. Built as it is on the components of demand, and using a failure of aggregate demand as the main element in its theory of recession, the actual concepts needed to make sense of the problems that were growing in size were largely unavailable. Using the standard Keynesian framework left these problems virtually invisible so far as standard theory was concerned.

Missing within the standard framework are detailed considerations of the operation of money markets and the role of debt. Also missing was a theoretical perspective that looked at the interlocking nature of production in an economy characterized by division of labour, where most purchase and sale takes place between producers of inputs (such as the production and sale of iron ore for use in the making of steel, neither one of which is a consumer good). While these are theoretical considerations at the fringes of the mainstream, they are not part of the mainstream itself. In this, economics today is very different from its pre-Keynesian past.

PHASE ONE: THE FINANCIAL CRISIS

The near collapse of the financial system was unprecedented in its scale but this was by no means the first time such an event had taken place. Indeed, central banking had evolved in the way it had because of the need to deal with credit crises in the past. Dealing with previous sets of similar upheavals had made the general contours of what needed to be done reasonably well known. Since each crisis is unique, and almost invariably comes without warning, there is always a sense of mass confusion at the time, which is why such events are typically referred to as 'panics'. But that there was a need for positive action to stabilize financial markets was well recognized, even though there might be wide differences in the specifics of what in particular ought to have been done.

Money and finance are odd products. Money values are an abstract measure of a quantum of goods and services. Money and credit in the modern world can, moreover, be created at the touch of a keyboard.

Keeping the growth in the nominal amount of expenditure at or near the growth in the quantum of goods and services available for purchase is one of the most difficult, but crucially important issues for the management of an economy. If the amount of money, credit and finance increases more rapidly than the quantum of goods and services, the effect is a rise in the price level. If, on the other hand, these increase more slowly than the flow of goods and services is increasing, there is a potential for prices to fall and for the economy to slow.

But in the situation of a typical panic, there is an actual fall in the flow of money, credit and finance in comparison with the past. And if the sense of danger increases, so that no one any longer trusts the banking and financial system as a repository for their savings, and a large proportion of savers seek to liberate their savings and convert these into cash as rapidly as possible, the collapse in the system of credit creation can pull the entire economy down. Without credit to mediate transactions between buyers and sellers, the real economy will invariably go into reverse.

What is therefore required during such panics is that those responsible for the management of the financial system find a means to quell such fears and inject credit back into the economic system. Money and credit can be instantaneously created by central banks and that is what needed to be done. Nor are these new ideas. More than a century ago, these were spelled out in Walter Bagehot's *Lombard Street: a Description of the Money Market*, first published in 1873. It is a book no one interested in the nature of the cycle or the world of finance should be without.

Lombard Street

If there is a lesson to be learned from reading *Lombard Street* it is that so far as reckless money market behaviour is concerned, we have been through it all before. The desire for wealth and the willingness for some to take enormous risks that end up in failure seems to be embedded in the DNA. The following excerpts from Bagehot – long-time editor of *The Economist* (1860–77) – should be a reminder that so far as financial folly is concerned, there is nothing new under the sun. The passages below come from Bagehot's discussion of the business cycle in his chapter, 'Why Lombard Street is often very dull, and sometimes extremely excited'. This was as mainstream a text as could be found in the English-speaking world, and represented the consensus view of economists of his own time and of economists right up until the publication of the *General Theory* in 1936. It is a perfectly lucid standard classical statement on the causes of the business cycle where downturns were seen as a natural, although highly unfortunate part of the process of economic expansion. How applicable, for example, would the following words from 1873 be to the circumstances of 2008? I apologise in advance for this somewhat quaint nineteenth-century language, but the points are crystal clear.

> Every great crisis reveals the excessive speculations of many houses which no one before suspected. . . . [Savers] speculate with [their capital] in bubble companies and in worthless shares. . . . At the very beginning of adversity, the counters in the gambling mania, the shares in the companies created to feed the mania, are discovered to be worthless; down they all go, and with them much of credit. (Bagehot, [1873] 1915: 150–51)

To add to the problems there are all those opportunities for what Bagehot called 'ingenious mendacity' which are not carefully examined due to a misplaced optimism. The words are ancient, but the condition is as modern as today. Human nature is a constant. Bagehot again:

> The good times too of high price almost always engender much fraud. All people are most credulous when they are most happy; and when much money has just been made, when some people are really making it, when most people think they are making it, there is a happy opportunity for ingenious mendacity. Almost everything will be believed for a little while, and long before discovery the worst and most adroit deceivers are geographically or legally beyond the reach of punishment. (Ibid.: 151)

The financial system, by its very nature, will on occasion be driven towards major dislocation by an unexpected unfolding of events. The future is never perfectly foreseen and financial disasters must be an expectation that an economic system must make contingencies for. Bagehot makes clear that there must therefore be a financial authority who has both the responsibility and capability to keep the financial system intact during periods of great stress. Bagehot stresses how crucial it is that those with responsibility for the financial system act: 'The Bank of England is bound, according to our system, not only to keep a good reserve against a time of panic, but to use that reserve effectually when that time of panic comes.'

This advice, written in 1873, remains valid for those who were dealing with the circumstances of the GFC. In an article titled 'Bagehot on the Financial Crisis of 1825 . . . and 2008', Richard Anderson, a Vice President of the Federal Reserve Bank of St Louis, wrote: 'Bagehot's principal message is that the first task of a central bank during a financial panic is to end the panic.' (Anderson, 2009: 1)

Financial authorities must stop the rot as best they can. But in saying this, Anderson emphasized an all-important additional consideration, that 'sustaining the banking firms does not preclude imposing losses on the firms' owners and debtors – indeed, so doing is essential if banks are to exercise prudence *after* the panic' (ibid.: 2). But the need for financial authorities to take action during financial panics should not be in doubt.

A successful free market economy is not one in which the government disappears and does nothing in the face of major financial dislocation. It is one in which those in government understand how a market economy works and take appropriate steps when necessary to ensure that the financial system will continue to function when it is in danger of collapse. Governments are not in this way running the economy, they should be seen as managing it.

PHASE TWO: THE KEYNESIAN STIMULUS

But whatever one might believe about the specific actions that were taken to calm financial markets during the GFC, and there is a great deal that is open to criticism,[1] they did bring the financial side of the financial crisis to an end. And in so doing, they followed the classical model in choosing the actions they took. But then, with recessionary conditions having settled in, the question was what actions should be taken to hasten our economies' return to full employment and rapid rates of growth. It was at this moment that the global economy saw a return to Keynesian economics and policies based on stimulation of demand through higher levels of public spending financed by increased levels of public debt.

For reasons that are almost incomprehensible, there was a widely held view amongst a large proportion of the economics community that Keynesian economics had for all practical purposes disappeared, that Keynesian theory has been transcended by a new and improved understanding of the structure of an economy, and that Keynes and Keynesian theory and policy were no longer mainstream.

And a very important part of the reason this view is held is that a very large proportion of the economics community does not actually know what it means that a model is Keynesian and has little, if any, idea of the theories of the cycle that had existed prior to the publication of the *General Theory*. Economists consequently have little comprehension of the theories that had existed before Keynes wrote and the policies that were derived based on their guidance.

WHAT MAKES A POLICY KEYNESIAN?

To understand what makes a policy Keynesian, it is therefore imperative to understand what Keynes's aim was in writing the *General Theory*. And this was stated as explicitly as it is possible to state anything by Keynes himself in one of the early and most lucid passages of the book. There he wrote:

> The idea that we can safely neglect the aggregate demand function is fundamental to the Ricardian economics, which underlie what we have been taught for more than a century. Malthus, indeed, had vehemently opposed Ricardo's doctrine that it was impossible for effective demand to be deficient; but vainly. For, since Malthus was unable to explain clearly (apart from an appeal to the facts of common observation) how and why effective demand could be deficient or excessive, he failed to furnish an alternative construction; and Ricardo conquered England as completely as the Holy Inquisition conquered Spain. Not only was his theory accepted by the city, by statesmen and by the academic world. But controversy ceased; the other point of view completely disappeared; it ceased to be discussed. The great puzzle of Effective Demand with which Malthus had wrestled vanished from economic literature. (Keynes, [1936] 1973: 32)

And then a page later he further amplified this same point:

> The celebrated *optimism* of traditional economic theory, which has led to economists being looked upon as Candides, who, having left this world for the cultivation of their gardens, teach that all is for the best in the best of all possible worlds provided we will let well alone, is also to be traced, I think, to their having neglected to take account of the drag on prosperity which can be exercised by an insufficiency of effective demand. (Ibid.: 33)

If a model of the economy used to explain fluctuations in output and employment is based on deficient aggregate demand, then that model is Keynesian. It is this that Keynes introduced to economic theory in 1936 and it was this theory that was the basis for policy formation across the world in the aftermath of the GFC.

More specifically, a Keynesian policy is one that attempts to restore momentum to an economy through increased levels of public spending and in which concerns about public debt and budget deficits are largely suppressed. It does not refer to tax cuts or reductions in rates of interest which are attempts to encourage growth through higher levels of private sector activity. A Keynesian policy is one in which the size of the public sector is increased with the specific aim of replacing the fall in private sector expenditure with higher levels of spending by governments.

THE KEYNESIAN MODEL IS UNIVERSAL

It is hard to imagine a student of economics, whether intending to become a professional economist or taking only a course or two as part of some other discipline, not coming into contact with the standard Keynesian model. It is the universal framework of the introductory course and comes in a variety of forms. There is the basic $C+I+G+(X-M)$ model in which the level of output, and therefore the level of employment, is determined, as the letters of this expression indicate, by the amount of expenditure on consumption (C), investment (I), government spending (G) and net exports (being exports minus imports, $X-M$). The higher the level of any of these components, the higher the level of aggregate demand and therefore, according to the theory, the higher output and employment are expected to be. This model has been the staple of the classroom almost since it was first devised and introduced into economics by Paul Samuelson in 1939, only three years after the publication of the *General Theory* (Schneider, 2010).

There is then the slightly more sophisticated AS–AD model. To aggregate demand (AD) was added aggregate supply (AS). The production side of the economy was duly recognized and the price level brought into the equation as well. So far as actually explaining the fall in output, reductions in aggregate demand were seen as of paramount importance, although the occasional 'supply shock' might also, on occasion, have to be taken into account. But in thinking about a restoration of growth, other than in the longer term only a shift on the demand side can cause an economy to grow.

Then, thirdly, there is what is known as the IS–LM model. Published in 1937, it attempted to explain in simplified terms the meaning of the *General Theory* that had been published only the year before. The model has remained embedded within almost all teaching of macroeconomics beyond the introductory level. The model attempts to explain shifts in the level of GDP by locating the effects of interest rates on production via investment and savings on the one hand (shown by the 'IS' curve) and the money market on the other (shown by the 'LM' curve). It is a model that is entirely based on the demand side of the economy.

What is particularly notable about this model is that its publication only a year after the publication of the *General Theory* in many ways fixed the meaning of the Keynesian Revolution. What especially made it such a landmark paper is that its very title, 'Mr Keynes and the Classics', caused the model presented to be seen as a short-form means to understand both Keynesian theory and the classical theory that had come before. It therefore created the belief amongst economists, a belief that has never gone away, that even pre-Keynesian economics could be comprehended using this framework. Milton Friedman, for example, used the IS–LM model to compare his version of monetarism with Keynesian theory. It is a model that has a lot to answer for, but the certainty is that no economist will graduate without learning how this model works.

Nor are any of these taught as historical relics that have been superseded by more modern ways of thought. These are the theoretical models that are to this day given to students as representations of reality. And in each of these models, an increase in government spending will unambiguously lead to an increase in production. And while there is the additional concept of the 'potential' level of production, which is the level of production that an economy should not try to exceed because of the inflationary strains it may create, so far as an economy at less than full employment is concerned, that is, in so far as an economy is at a level of production below its potential, there is no question, according to such models, that the way forward is to increase the level of aggregate demand through an increase in the level of government spending.

The idea, therefore, that somehow Keynesian economics had been expurgated from our economic texts and was no longer part of the conceptual apparatus of economists is straightforwardly wrong. Rather, Keynesian economic theory, and the associated policy of government spending during recession, is taught to every student of economics. It is the one conclusion from economic theory that virtually every student of economics will have had drilled into them during their time of study.

There may be various schools of thought where Keynes is criticized and there is a rejection of some body of thought that is given the name 'Keynesian'. But Keynes and Keynesianism is a brand that no longer has any specific meaning and it is not usually recognized for its introduction of aggregate demand into economic theory. What is therefore found virtually nowhere is an absolute denial of the role that aggregate demand is said to play in propelling growth. Demand deficiency and a recovery in the level of demand are in one way or another seen as crucial to the revival of an economy in recession.

DEMAND IN MODERN AND CLASSICAL THEORY

This is very different from how things were before the *General Theory* was published. Economic theory had almost from its first days rejected the notion of demand deficiency as a cause of recession. As Keynes correctly noted, prior to 1936 the 'doctrine that it was impossible for effective demand to be deficient' was accepted universally across the mainstream of the profession, with only very few exceptions. Demand was based on production, on the production of goods and services that could be sold at prices and volumes that allowed for the recovery of all of the production costs involved. There was, in fact, no other basis for demand other than the production of something someone else would buy, which is what turned demand into effective demand.

So far as classical economic theory was concerned, you might as well expect an economy to be revived by an increased spread of counterfeit money as be dependent on an increase in non-value-adding public spending. Government outlays not backed by the production of goods and services that could find for themselves a profitable market could never add to the sum total of saleable product nor could they stimulate the real volume of sales and output, other than in the short term in the same way that counterfeit money might do.

It is this conception of demand that has disappeared. Any spending at all will do. So far as Keynesian theory is concerned, and therefore so far as any version of today's mainstream model is concerned, it is irrelevant what that spending is on. Whatever it may be, whether productive or unproductive, such spending can be expected to pull an economy forward. Keynes stressed this point in the *General Theory* itself:

> In so far as millionaires find their satisfaction in building mighty mansions to contain their bodies when alive and pyramids to shelter them after death, or, repenting of their sins, erect cathedrals and endow monasteries or foreign missions, the day when abundance of capital will interfere with abundance of output may be postponed. 'To dig holes in the ground,' paid for out of savings, will increase, not only employment, but the real national dividend of useful goods and services. (Keynes, [1936] 1973: 220)

Digging and refilling the same holes would, in Keynes's view, cause an economy to grow. It is this belief that has become the mainstream. Such expenditure will be shown as creating growth in all modern models of the economy and will even be recorded as growth in GDP statistics. It is expenditure alone that matters, and whatever may have been bought with that money, the multiplier effects will guarantee that all subsequent rounds of that initial spending will be productive and growth enhancing. Those who accept this as a valid statement of how economies work are Keynesians. It is this that separates modern economics from what came before.

THE CLASSICAL THEORY OF THE CYCLE

A modern recession is seen in terms of a deficiency of aggregate demand. The GFC, from a mainstream macroeconomic perspective, was the result of a fall in demand. Add in as much detail as you like about why that was, it all comes to the same thing. People were buying less. The cure was therefore an increase in public spending to restore the demand that had for one reason or another been lost.

From a mainstream macroeconomic perspective, the issue is the *level* of demand. From the perspective of a classical model, the problem is the *structure* of demand. Since from the classical perspective, demand is made up of the earnings from the sale of one's own products, demand will disappear if the value of the products being produced cannot be sold at prices that cover their costs.

Demand in aggregate is not something separate from supply in aggregate. It *is* supply in aggregate. It is comprised of all of the goods and services that had been produced and which have an exchangeable value. And how do we know they have an exchangeable value? We know this because others who had produced and earned incomes themselves are willing to part with the money they have earned in order to possess those goods and services produced by others.

Thinking in terms of aggregate demand leaves out everything that matters if one is to understand what is actually taking place in an exchange economy during an economic downturn. It is structural dislocation that is the cause of recession, not a failure of aggregate demand. Misdirected credit has a large part to play in this recessionary process, but it is the direction of expenditure, and not its level, that is the critical issue. Not a single one of the standard macroeconomic textbook models will explain any of this.

KEYNESIAN POLICY AND CLASSICAL RECESSIONS

The GFC was in every way a textbook example of a recession best interpreted using classical ideas. Massive misdirected investment coupled with misdirected credit expansion created the conditions for a major downturn. Ultimately firms could no longer meet their debt repayments, the housing industry found itself with buyers who could not afford the mortgages they had taken out, financial institutions discovered that their borrowers were unable to repay, holders of securitized debts found their paper wealth had evaporated while insurance companies who had covered these debts became insolvent.

The underlying structure of the American economy in particular, but a substantial part of the world economy as well, suddenly found that businesses were failing. With trade credit disappearing at the same time, production levels fell and unemployment rose. To describe this as 'a fall in aggregate demand' is to hide every detail of interest. Nevertheless, the recessionary conditions that revealed themselves in every major industrialized economy were conceptualized in Keynesian aggregate demand terms. The solutions that were therefore adopted were based on this mainstream theory and designed to increase the level of aggregate demand through major increases in public spending. They added to expenditure without creating an additional flow of exchangeable product.

Although from a classical perspective these policies could never succeed, since they tried to increase demand without increasing value-adding supply, these were, for all that, the direct conclusions from the Keynesian framework found in textbooks across the world, and were acted upon. The *C+I+G* aggregate demand equation was the basis for policy because there was nothing else. That is all anyone knew. So far as the mainstream is concerned, there was virtually no other frame of reference one could turn to. To varying degrees this framework was used to craft policies across the world with little, if any, opposition from within the mainstream.

THE KEYNESIAN POLICY FAILURE

And yet in spite of that virtual unanimity within the economics profession, what can no longer be denied is that the policy has been an absolute failure. In not a single instance has this Keynesian stimulus worked and, in the United States and the UK in particular, this policy has been a spectacular disaster. Other economies which have experienced a meltdown following increased public spending have included Greece, Spain, Portugal and Ireland. Rising public expenditure has not led to a return to better times.

Instead, despite confident expectations that such 'stimulus' packages would cut short the time required to return to normal growth rates and low unemployment, the effect has been exactly the reverse. The most closely examined such failing has been in the United States. In spite of near-trillion dollar expenditures and the largest deficit in US history, unemployment has stayed above 9 per cent with no reason to think it might not go higher. Two years after the introduction of the stimulus, the American labour market has refused to budge, while private sector activity remains dormant.

Figure 5.1 was much reproduced during the early years of the stimulus package. This is the story as at November 2010. The dotted line was the projection of what would happen if there had been no stimulus package. Unemployment would then reach a peak of around 9 per cent in early 2010. The solid line shows the projections made by the new American administration. With the recovery plan in place, a maximum unemployment rate of 8 per cent would be reached in early 2009, after which unemployment would continue to fall. The dots show the actual unemployment rate in each month with the rate continuously above the projection with or without the recovery plan.

These projections were supplanted by a second set of projections that

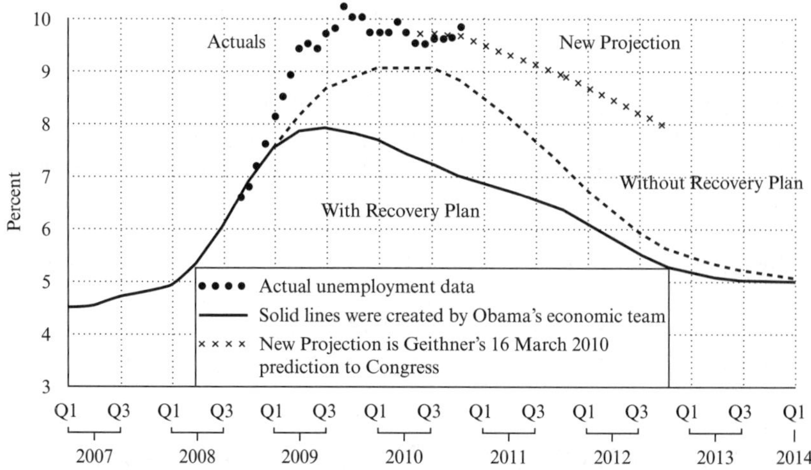

Source: From Ace of Spades website, http://ace.mu.nu.

Figure 5.1 Unemployment rate with and without the recovery plan

were released in March 2010 and they, too, are shown on the chart as crosses. They may or may not be more realistic, but they are structured around the much higher unemployment rate whose existence and persistence could no longer be evaded. As policy has also shifted away from introducing more fiscal stimulus and instead to lower taxes, the period of Keynesian stimulus has now been brought to an end in the US just as it has been everywhere else. Whatever may be the fate of the textbook theory, the Keynesian model as a guide to policy is now, for all practical purposes, dead. Even if their economic advisors keep recommending more expenditure, no government will any longer take such advice seriously.

WHAT DOES IT TAKE TO DISCREDIT A MODEL?

In a more rational world, these figures would be the death knell of the mainstream macroeconomic model based as it is on Keynesian principles. How to survive failure such as this ought to be inconceivable. The model did not predict the downturn; it is incapable of explaining the GFC in anything other than in the vaguest terms, and the policies it promoted have been unquestionable failures.

All of this is a repetition on a global scale of the 'lost decade' of the Japanese recovery following the use of Keynesian policies in the early

1990s. The Japanese economy, once amongst the strongest in the world, has remained subdued ever since. It has never recovered its former strength.

The deficits and the debt have become a deadweight loss. Unlike private sector debt taken on to fund various forms of capital investment, public sector deficits are not self-financing. The expenditures are not used to produce forms of capital which will themselves contribute to a flow of income that will cover their costs.

From those with a mainstream Keynesian perspective, the only answer has been that the stimulus had not been large enough. The problem was that it had been too paltry; the deficits had been too low. These are hollow arguments that carry less and less weight with each passing day.

KEYNESIAN POLICIES ARE DEAD: WHAT ABOUT KEYNESIAN THEORY?

As is now becoming more evident, there is nothing in the standard mainstream Keynesian macroeconomic model that can be used to provide guidance. Policy will no longer follow a Keynesian mainstream path. Keynesian models and the advice they offer will be systematically ignored as governments cut spending and pull deficits down even with unemployment as high as it is. These are the policies being pursued in the US, the UK and elsewhere. Even though there is not a single mainstream model that tells governments to take these steps, the massive problems we now have are so unmistakably related to the stimulus packages that preceded them, there is no option but to adopt these very unKeynesian policies, these being the very policies that were at the core of the classical model and its theory of the cycle.

These steps are being taken, not because economic theory makes these the only steps that are consistent with recovery. They are being taken because the opposite has been tried and the results have been disastrous. It is political self-preservation that is guiding the hands of policy-makers, not an articulated theory of economic management. Governments are doing not what modern textbooks instruct them to do, but what classical economic policy would have told them to do had there been any classical economists around to offer advice.[2]

The business cycle, it should not be forgotten, is cyclical. Had governments done nothing other than stabilize their financial systems and taken steps to improve the cash flow of private sector firms, the recovery would already have been well and truly established. The dismal part is that these Keynesian policies have actually made matters worse. The world's economies are performing less well because we have applied these non-solutions than they would have if no measures to hasten growth had been applied at all. The massive levels of debt have become a new impediment that had not existed in 2008, or at least not to anything like the extent that they subsequently did after the stimulus packages were applied.

In time recovery will come. With less regulation, with less take-up of resources by the public sector, with public sector deficits being wound back, there will be recovery, even though each of the actions taken will appear to be contrary to what is needed, at least according to what is said by existing mainstream economic theory.

Keynesian theory must now be discarded. Aggregate demand must be included amongst the many other discredited economic ideas of the past which have been considered, tried and rejected. To achieve recovery a different approach to policy is needed, an approach that emphasizes value-adding activity, a much greater role for decentralized entrepreneurial decision-making and a smaller role for government. And along with these policy shifts, what is also now needed is an accompanying theory that provides an understanding of why these kinds of policies work.

That is what is required. The danger is, however, that economic theory and policy will simply diverge. There will be economists with their primitive and discredited models. And at the same time there will be policies devised around an appreciation of value-adding private sector-driven production. In such a world, the views of economists will become less and less relevant because they will be recognized as providing less and less assistance in the policy debates.

The danger of turning economics into an irrelevant science offering impractical advice on many of the most important policy questions is very real. Unless economists learn from this Keynesian debacle, that is the fate economic theory will face.

A MARKER IN THE SAND

Missing in economic theory is what is now known as Say's Law. And in understanding Say's Law, it is important to appreciate this. That all of the public spending that has gone on may not have led to a net addition of even a single job across the entire world's economy. There has been some attempt to argue that things would have been worse had such spending not occurred, but so far as job creation goes, it has failed at every test. And even assuming there has been net job creation, something for which there is all too little evidence, the cost has been insanely high.

Nor is this just the wisdom of hindsight. I wrote the following in March 2009 when the Global Financial Crisis was at its most intense:

> The world's economies are not suffering from a lack of demand and the right policy response is not a demand stimulus. Increased public sector spending will only add to the market confusions that already exist. What is potentially catastrophic would be to try to spend our way to recovery. The recession that will follow will be deep, prolonged and potentially take years to overcome. (Kates, 2009)

I repeated this same point at greater length in a paper which was published in January 2010. These words were obviously written well before then, sometime in 2009:

> A marker in the sand must be established now. There has been an absolutely undeniable use of Keynesian economic theory to bring this downturn to an end. If it does not work, it will not be because we have not seen Keynesian theory in action.
>
> We have seen the real thing and then some. If it fails to deliver the strong robust upturn as promised, if recovery is slow and minimal, if real wages stagnate and debt remains an enduring problem, then Keynesian economics should go the way of all crank theories.
>
> If the policies that have been used to hasten recovery are eventually recognised as having prolonged the downturn and delayed the return to better times, no one should be allowed to walk away from ownership of what may well be an unparalleled economic disaster.
>
> And these are not the political consequences. They will take care of themselves. What is being referred to are the consequences for the teaching of macroeconomic theory and the future use of the Keynesian macroeconomic model in the formation of policy. If our economies end up in something like a lost decade, the entire theoretical apparatus that has led us down this path should be discarded for being the misleading and useless nonsense that it will have proven itself to be. (Kates, 2010: 125)

And if you go back to either article you will see that the problem was not that we would add to our levels of debt, although it was patently clear that we would. The problem was that you cannot create demand without first creating value-adding supply. Demand can only be increased by first increasing the level of productive output. If you want the level of purchases to rise, you must first increase the amount of goods and services others wish to purchase.

SAY'S LAW: ECONOMIC THEORY'S LAW OF GRAVITY

These are all different ways of trying to state the same thing. And what they are attempts to restate is the classical principle now referred to as Say's Law. It is Say's Law that has disappeared from the entire discourse amongst economists where I would suspect not one economist in a hundred has any idea what these words mean. Because of the way in which macroeconomics is taught, economists therefore have little understanding why the stimulus packages did not and could not work.

Say's Law is economic theory's law of gravity. It is the theory without which it is impossible to understand how an economy at the macro-economic level works. Keynesian economics has been an attempt to repeal Say's Law but, as with the law of gravity, it cannot be repealed, but can only be ignored. And to ignore Say's Law will cause an economy to fall to earth in the same way that attempts to ignore the law of gravity in the physical world will cause objects to fall to earth.

Keynesian economics tries to defy gravity by arguing that employment can be increased through higher demand without there having been a prior increase in value-adding production. It argues that intrinsically useless forms of government-financed expenditures, such as digging holes and filling them in again, can create economic growth and higher employment. It makes it appear that governments just wasting money is in some sense equivalent to the patient and exceedingly difficult entrepreneurial task of finding profitable ways to employ a community's labour and capital.

Macroeconomics because of Keynes has become a pseudo-science, a crackpot theory. It has become unable to explain the simplest things and can offer no useful advice to governments in trying to find their way out of the problems of recession, low rates of growth and high unemployment. It guides economic policy in directions that lower living standards and diminish our productive potential.

Understanding Say's Law makes it plain that unless an outlay in producing some good or service creates more value than the resources that were used up in its production, it has not added to demand and has not caused an economy to expand. There may be reasons for such outlays, but they should never be seen as part of the process in which economic growth is encouraged. They should instead be recognized as a form of welfare that uses up our productivity rather than increasing it.

Say's Law may well have been the single most important macro-economic principle that economic theory had ever developed. And it was a true insight since its meaning is far from intuitive. But understanding what it meant ensured that the relationship between production and demand was never lost sight of. Understanding Say's Law meant that economic policies were designed in ways that actually encouraged real economic growth because it encouraged the production of goods and services that other people wanted to buy. It made plain why leaving things to the market was the only way in which economies could be made to grow and was the only way by which living standards could be made to rise.

We have ignored Say's Law for three-quarters of a century and it has now led the world's economies into the greatest fiscal catastrophe in the planet's history. Undoing the damage of the Keynesian policies that have been followed will take many years to achieve. What needs to be recognized is that Say's Law is the essential bedrock principle in the design of economic policies. Understanding this principle and what it means is the absolutely necessary first step to returning our economies to the non-inflationary growth paths that are the only means to maintain rising living standards within an economy in which everyone who wishes to be employed can find a job.

NOTES

1. It is not my intention to deal at length with the various national programmes to restore stability and calm to domestic financial markets, but I will note that the absence of any real pain experienced by financial institutions that were at the centre of these problems may have merely stored up problems for the future. Few lessons have really been learned, so the moral hazards are even greater than they were.
2. These were also the policies that were successfully used in the United Kingdom and Australia to pull themselves out of the Great Depression.

REFERENCES

Anderson, Richard G. (2009), 'Bagehot on the Financial Crises of 1925 . . . and 2008', St Louis, MO: Federal Reserve Bank of St Louis.

Bagehot, Walter ([1873] 1915), *Lombard Street: a Description of the Money Market*, with an introduction by Hartley Withers, London: Smith, Elder and Co.

Kates, Steven (1998), *Say's Law and the Keynesian Revolution: How Macroeconomic Theory Lost its Way*, Cheltenham, UK and Northampton, MA, USA: Edward Elgar Publishing.

Kates, Steven (2009), 'The dangerous return of Keynesian economics', *Quadrant*, no. 454, **LIII** (3).

Kates, Steven (2010), 'The crisis in economic theory: the dead end of Keynesian economics', in Steven Kates (ed.), *Macroeconomic Theory and its Failings: Alternative Perspectives on the Global Financial Crisis*, Cheltenham, UK and Northampton, MA, USA: Edward Elgar Publishing.

Keynes, John Maynard ([1936] 1973), *The General Theory of Employment, Interest and Money*, London: Macmillan.

Schneider, Michael (2010), 'Keynesian income determination diagrams', in M. Blaug and Peter Lloyd (eds), *Famous Figures and Diagrams in Economics*, Cheltenham, UK and Northampton, MA, USA: Edward Elgar Publishing.

Smith, Adam ([1776] 1976), *An Inquiry into the Nature and Causes of the Wealth of Nations*, edited by Edwin Cannan, Chicago, IL: University of Chicago Press.

6. Hindsight on the origins of the global financial crisis?

Steve Keen

As one of the handful of economists who anticipated the crisis (Bezemer, 2009; Fullbrook, 2010), my hindsight explanation of the crisis is the same as my foresight prediction of it in December 2005: it was a copybook manifestation of the final debt-deflationary stage in Hyman Minsky's 'Financial instability hypothesis'.

Our real world economy is essential monetary, innately cyclical, and subject to fundamental uncertainty – unlike the mythical world of neoclassical 'rational expectations' macroeconomics, in which the economy is essentially 'real' or barter in nature, varies stochastically around its long-run equilibrium, and is inhabited by agents who can accurately predict the future.[1]

Given that investors must make decisions despite uncertainty about the future, they do so in the manner captured by Keynes: they act on the basis of the convention of 'assuming that the existing state of affairs will continue indefinitely, except in so far as we have specific reasons to expect a change' (Keynes, 1936: 152). Minsky extended this insight to assert that, given the inherently cyclical nature of economy, a period of economic tranquillity after a financial crisis – like the bursting of the dot.com bubble in 2001 – will lead to rising expectations by both borrowers and lenders. The economy will then pass from a period of tranquility into one of euphoria, in which 'Financial institutions . . . accept liability structures – their own and those of borrowers – that, in a more sober expectational climate, they would have rejected' (Minsky, 1982: 122–3).

This euphoric period drives the debt to income level up and precipitates another crisis, especially since much of the borrowing finances 'Ponzi investment', which drives up asset prices without adding to the productive capacity of the economy. The euphoria evaporates in yet another debt-induced crisis, and the cycle continues – but from a higher level of debt than before, since the process of taking on debt during a boom, and then repaying it during a slump, gives the debt to GDP ratio a tendency to 'ratchet up' over time. Ultimately, the amount of debt taken on exceeds the debt servicing capacity of the economy, leading to a Depression.

I first modeled this process in 1995 and generated a pattern of declining instability, followed by increased instability and an eventual Depression (see Keen, 1995, Figure 9, p. 625). I observed in my conclusion that:

> From the perspective of economic theory and policy, this vision of a capitalist economy with finance requires us to go beyond that habit of mind which Keynes described so well, the excessive reliance on the (stable) recent past as a guide to the future. The chaotic dynamics explored in this paper should warn us against accepting a period of relative tranquility in a capitalist economy as anything other than a lull before the storm. (Keen, 1995: 634)

Unfortunately, the neo-classical economists in charge of US economic policy followed the habit Keynes warned against, and saw not a 'lull before the storm', but 'The Great Moderation', which they attributed to their 'improved control of inflation' (Bernanke, 2004). They were oblivious to the dangers of rising private debt, and largely remain so after the crisis – though they no longer speak of 'The Great Moderation'.

My 1995 Minsky model lacked price dynamics. I have since extended it to include an explicit monetary sector and price dynamics, and this model generates a 'Great Moderation' followed by a 'Great Recession', with cyclically falling unemployment and inflation giving way to rising unemployment and deflation as the debt to GDP ratio rises (Keen, 2011). Though the model has not been empirically fitted to the US data, there is a strong qualitative correspondence between the model (Figure 6.1) and the data (Figure 6.2).

A focus on inflation and unemployment alone – something that has become institutionalized in neo-classical economic policy by the so-called Taylor Rule (Davig and Leeper, 2007) – conveyed a false sense of declining volatility: a 'Great Moderation'. But the dampening of these cycles was driven by rising private debt – a phenomenon that neo-classical economics ignored (Bernanke, 2000: 24). Ultimately the dampened cycles in unemployment and inflation gave way to runaway unemployment and deflation as investment collapsed, since the rising debt level overwhelmed capitalists' capacity to service the debt.

Even as the GFC was at its height in early 2009, I anticipated that the US debt to GDP ratio (which was still rising in the December 2008 data that was available at the time of publication) would start to fall under the impact of deliberate de-leveraging by the private sector and bankruptcies (a factor that my model does not yet include). That is now strongly evident: the private debt to GDP ratio peaked at 298 per cent of GDP in February 2009, and by June 2010 had fallen to 268 per cent (see debt ratio

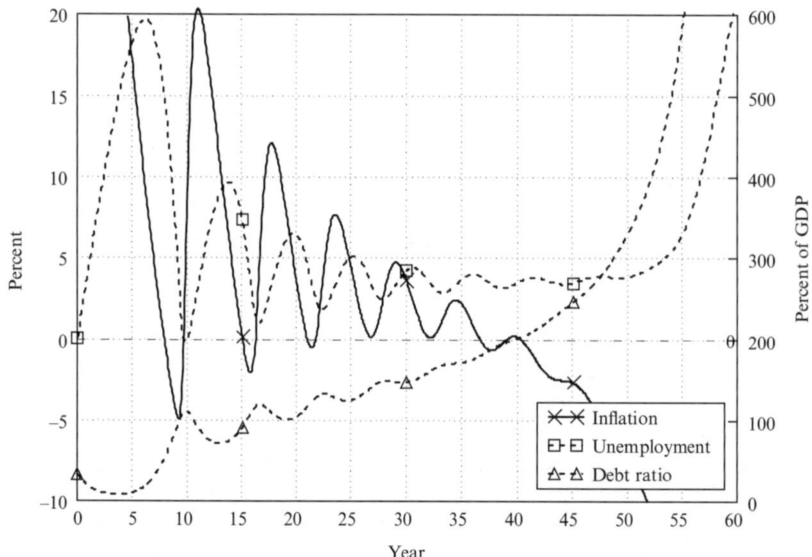

Figure 6.1 Inflation, unemployment and debt in a monetary Minsky model

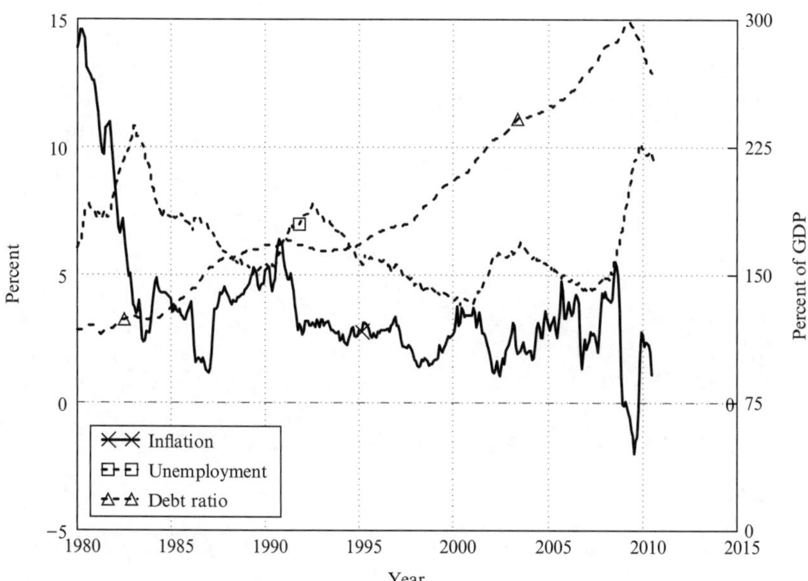

Figure 6.2 Inflation, unemployment and debt in the USA

in Figures 6.2 and 6.5). This extreme de-leveraging is what turned the preceding debt-financed boom into the most severe economic crisis since the Great Depression.

However, it was not the level of debt itself, but the rate of change of debt and its acceleration (and deceleration) that turned boom into crisis – which is why the crisis itself pre-dated the reversal in the growth of the debt to GDP ratio. Here I have formalized insights from Minsky and Schumpeter about the role of credit in expanding aggregate demand beyond what is generated from the sale of commodities (Schumpeter, 1934; Minsky, 1982),[2] to define aggregate demand as the sum of GDP *plus the change in debt*.

This aggregate demand is expended upon all markets – both commodity and assets – and it is possible for aggregate demand to fall even when debt is still rising if the rate of growth of debt declines. This is precisely what happened at the beginning of 2008, when the trend for private debt to grow abruptly ceased. The decline in the rate of growth of private debt was enough to reduce aggregate demand and precipitate the crisis (see Figure 6.3). Having peaked at $18.7 trillion in January 2008 (when both private and government debt are considered), it then started to fall – despite the fact that private debt was still rising – until

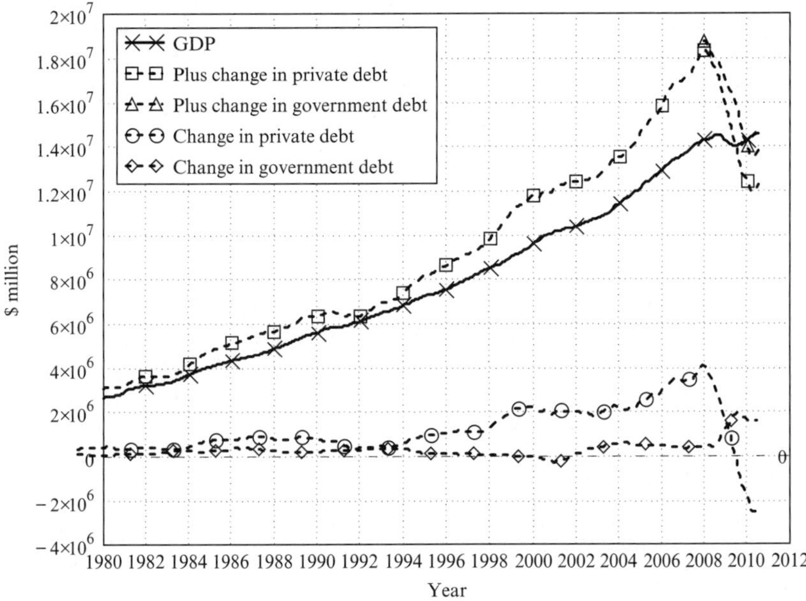

Figure 6.3 Aggregate demand as GDP plus the change in debt

it hit a low of $13.4 trillion in February 2010. It has since risen slightly because the rate of private sector de-leveraging has declined slightly – which brings us to the next topic: what has caused the recent apparent stabilization?

WHAT, IN YOUR VIEW, CAUSED THE WORLD'S ECONOMIES TO STABILIZE?

There is no doubt that the massive government stimulus packages across the OECD – including direct handouts to household, firms and banks, dramatic cuts in interest rates, and huge increases in government deficits and debt – drove the stabilization. However, a major transmission channel by which this stimulus worked was a temporary reversal of the private debt dynamic that caused the crisis in the first place.

Just as aggregate demand is the sum of GDP plus the change in debt, the change in aggregate demand is the sum of the change in GDP plus the acceleration (or deceleration) in debt. Meyer, Biggs and Pick coined the term 'credit impulse' for the second differential of debt divided by GDP, and they point out that this can mean that the change in aggregate demand can be positive even when de-leveraging is occurring, if the rate of de-leveraging is slowing down (Biggs et al., 2010: 3).

This second order effect – a slowing down in the rate of de-leveraging causing an increase in the rate of growth of aggregate demand – is the key factor that has caused the recent stabilization. Though the private sector is still de-leveraging, the rate of de-leveraging has slowed recently – largely under the impact of government policy that has encouraged Americans to return to borrowing – and this deceleration in the rate of de-leveraging has actually boosted aggregate demand and thus reduced the rate of growth of unemployment (Figure 6.4).

This boost to aggregate demand from debt has occurred even though the aggregate level of private debt is still falling. This is emphasized by Table 6.1, which shows the change and acceleration of private debt on a quarterly basis versus unemployment and the quarterly rate of change of unemployment since 2008, when the crisis began. Unemployment rose in 2008–09 even though the rate of change of debt was still positive, because its acceleration was negative. Then in 2010 unemployment fell, even though the rate of change of debt was now negative, because the rate of decline of debt dropped so that its acceleration was positive.

However, there are good reasons to expect that this stabilization will not be maintained, and the US economy will fall back into recession:

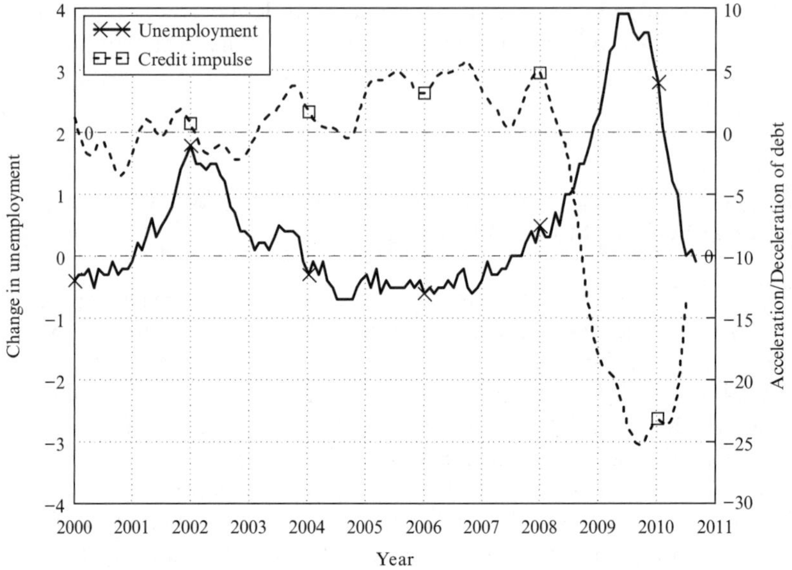

Figure 6.4 Annual change in unemployment and debt acceleration

Table 6.1 Change and acceleration of private debt versus unemployment and the rate of change of unemployment

Quarter	Private debt per quarter		Unemployment	
	Change (%)	Acceleration (%)	Rate (%)	Quarterly percentage change
2008	6.5	−1.9	4.9	4.3
2008.25	3.3	−3.2	5.1	4.1
2008.5	3.2	0.0	5.6	9.8
2008.75	2.8	−0.4	6.2	10.7
2009	0.8	−2.1	7.2	16.1
2009.25	−1.2	−2.0	8.5	18.1
2009.5	−4.4	−3.2	9.5	11.8
2009.75	−4.3	0.1	9.8	3.2
2010	−3.3	0.9	10.0	2.0
2010.25	−5.9	−2.7	9.7	−3.0
2010.5	−2.2	3.7	9.5	−2.1

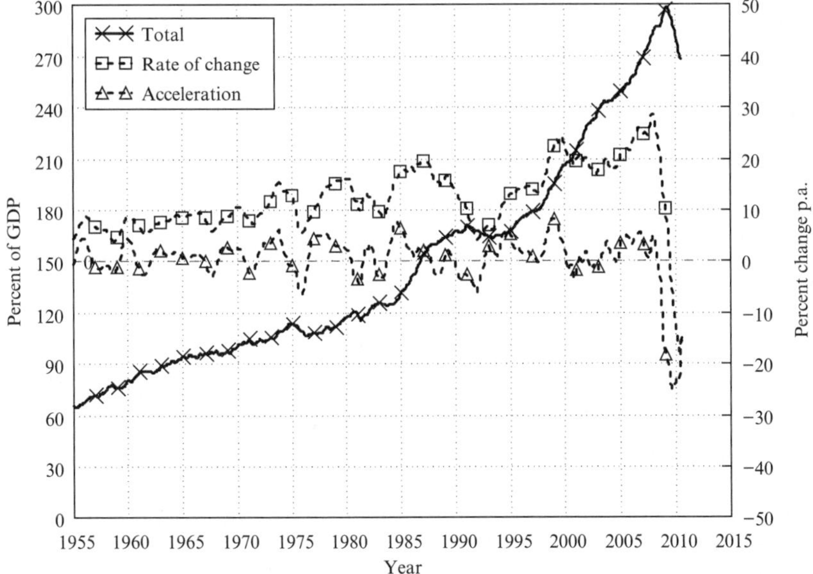

Figure 6.5 US private debt to GDP: ratio, change and acceleration

though the credit impulse determines changes in aggregate demand (and hence employment), the rate of change and level of debt still matter. First, as Figure 6.5 emphasizes, the USA has never before experienced this level of private debt. Secondly, this is the first time since the Great Depression that the rate of change of private debt has been negative (and the rate of change of the debt to GDP ratio has been even more negative).

For the deceleration in de-leveraging to continue giving a positive boost to aggregate demand, deceleration of de-leveraging would have to lead to rising debt, and ultimately a rising ratio of debt to GDP. This is very unlikely to occur when all sectors of American society – except non-financial business[3] – are carrying unprecedented levels of debt (see Table 6.2), and the odds of enticing the business sector into further debt now are rather low.

The current deceleration of de-leveraging is therefore highly likely to end, so that the contribution to change in aggregate demand from debt acceleration will at best cease, and at worst will turn negative once more as deleveraging continues – leading to a debt-induced 'double dip'.

Table 6.2 Debt to GDP ratio (percent)

Sector/Year	December 1930	March 1932	March 2009	June 2010
All private	177	237	298	268
Financial	24	23	121	101
Business	111	157	80	75
Household	42	57	97	92
Government	34	68	65	76

WHICH POLICY MEASURES TAKEN BY GOVERNMENTS HAVE PROVIDED THE GREATEST CONTRIBUTION TO STABILIZATION AND IN WHAT WAY HAVE THEY CONTRIBUTED?

There is no doubt that the enormous stimulus expenditure by governments around the world made the decline in employment far less severe than it would have been otherwise. Similarly reductions in interest rates reduced the servicing cost of debt, and prevented a chain reaction of bankruptcies in otherwise solvent firms.

In our mixed fiat/credit money world, the rapid increase in base money as part of 'Quantitative Easing' has gone some way to restoring the balance between fiat and credit money, which had become badly unbalanced as the obsession with running government surpluses minimized the growth of fiat money while debt-based money creation ran amok.

However, I do not believe – as do the post-Keynesians who describe themselves as Chartalists – that government deficit spending alone can end the crisis. Nor is quantitative easing alone sufficient to give us a balanced monetary system for the future.

IN CONTRAST, HAVE ANY OF THE MEASURES TAKEN BY GOVERNMENTS ADDED TO THE ECONOMIC PROBLEMS THAT MUST NOW BE DEALT WITH AND, IF SO, WHICH POLICIES WERE THESE AND WHAT HAVE BEEN THEIR HARMFUL EFFECTS?

I have argued elsewhere that the US economy in particular, and the OECD in general, has been a Ponzi economy since Alan Greenspan's rescue of Wall Street in 1987 prevented what should have been a mini-depression (Keen,

2009a: 9). The rescues worked by enabling Ponzi finance behavior to move to another locus for asset price speculation – from Wall Street in general in 1987, to residential and commercial real estate in the savings and loans scandal, to telecommunications and Internet in the dot.com bubble, though that bubble at least had its Schumpeterian aspects (Schumpeter, 1934: 110–32) – and finally to the sub-prime scam. A terminal crisis has been postponed every time by renewing the speculative frenzy that caused the crisis.

This rescue has been very similar, all the more so because the US predominantly rescued the banks and the shadow banking sector directly. As I have shown, such a rescue is far less effective at stimulating the economy than funding debtors (Keen, 2009b: 24–6), so that the primary impact of the rescue was to directly resuscitate financial sector speculation rather than turnover in the physical economy.

Ultimately, the successful delaying of a terminal Minsky cycle has meant that the private debt to GDP level has grown well beyond what it would have been without these rescues, so that the scale of potential de-leveraging is far greater now than it would have been without them. The size of the parasitic component of the financial sector – the proportion of it devoted to funding speculation on asset prices rather than actual investment or working capital for industrial firms – has also expanded dramatically, making the physical adjustment needed in the future far greater.

The government-supported growth of the financial sector has gone hand in hand with a relocation of physical production to developing nations. In the aftermath (whenever that begins) to the crisis, when debt-financed expenditure will no longer mask the reduced incomes of the working and middle classes, the USA in particular will face a difficult task in rebuilding productive capacity.

Finally, the case of the most successful government intervention during the crisis – Australia's – needs to be considered. Part of the success arose from the Australian government's decision to target households in its stimulus packages, rather than bank reserves (Keen, 2009b: 24–6). However, a major factor was also the 'First Home Owners Boost', which reignited the Australian house price bubble by turning what was on track to be a 3 per cent decline in mortgage debt (compared to GDP) into a 6 per cent increase – a reversal in de-leveraging equivalent to a more than A$100 billion boost to this A$1.3 trillion economy.

This huge boost in household debt stopped Australia's de-leveraging in its tracks, as Figure 6.6 illustrates: changing private debt never reduced aggregate demand in Australia, and by mid-2010 it was still adding 3.5 per cent to demand, with government debt adding a further 0.5 per cent. In contrast, falling private debt reduced aggregate demand in the USA by 15 per cent, with government debt reducing that to a 'mere' 5 per cent reduction.

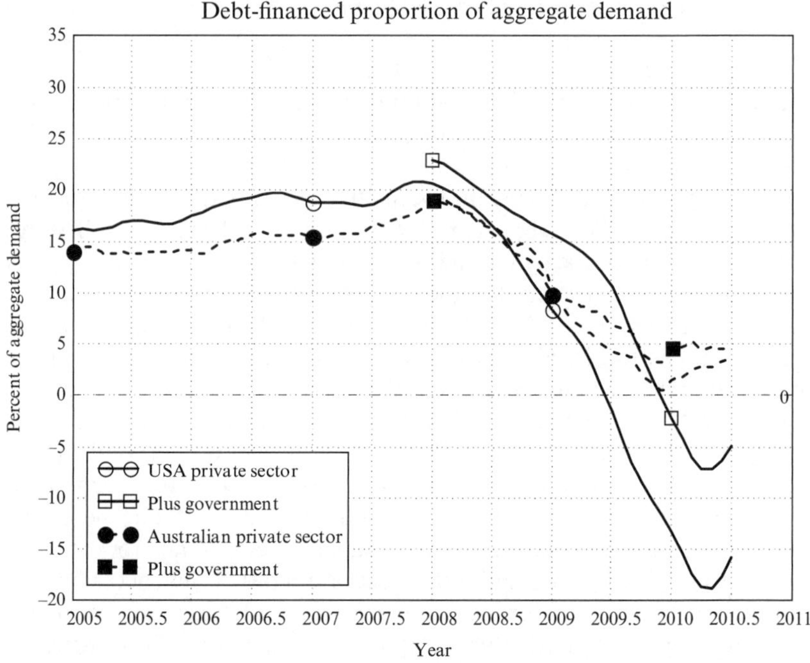

Figure 6.6 US versus Australian debt-financed demand

Australia's success has therefore to some degree been won by recreating the conditions that caused the crisis in the first place: rising private debt financing a speculative bubble. It remains to be seen what the outcome will be for Australia when this bubble bursts, but the fact that government policy involves extending Ponzi schemes is a reason to reject rather than champion government intervention in the marketplace.

WHAT LESSONS HAVE WE LEARNED ABOUT ECONOMIC MANAGEMENT AND STABILIZATION POLICIES DURING THE GFC?

An undoubted benefit of the GFC is that it has permanently given the empirical lie to a once popular neo-classical assertion, the 'policy ineffectiveness proposition' (Sargent and Wallace, 1976) that government policy cannot affect the real level of output.[4] Government policy clearly does have real and monetary effects on the economy, though whether those policies address the core problem of speculative finance is a moot point.

Apart from that, the lessons to date are limited, not because the GFC has not given economists much to learn, but because the conceptual framework that economists still employ is incapable of taking those lessons on board. The main benefit of the GFC for economics would be if it helped economists abandon the neo-classical methodology they developed to forget the lessons of the last great economic crisis, the Great Depression. Keynes's observation that 'The difficulty lies, not in the new ideas, but in escaping from the old ones, which ramify, for those brought up as most of us have been, into every corner of our minds' (Keynes, 1936: viii), is even more true today than it was in 1936.

GIVEN YOUR OWN THEORETICAL PERSPECTIVE, WHAT SHOULD POLICY-MAKERS NOW DO TO ASSIST IN THE RECOVERY PROCESS?

The policies needed to finally end this crisis – rather than to temper it and convert a potentially short, deep crisis into a longer, shallower one – are pithily summarized in Michael Hudson's phrase: 'Debts that can't be repaid, won't be repaid'.

The enormous increase in debt since 1987, and especially the increase in household debt during the sub-prime scam, represented irresponsible lending that should never have occurred in the first place. Debtors should not wear the opprobrium for this debt. Though they were of course complicit to some degree, they did not have economists advising them that this lending was sound, nor physicists to design complex financial instruments to disguise the risk, nor did they earn the enormous salaries that witting or unwitting Ponzi merchants in the finance sector garnered.

This debt should therefore be honored only in its abolition. In a manner that avoids discriminating against non-borrowers, the debt should be written off, and the lenders put into receivership, while lending for productive purposes – essentially providing working capital for firms, a task that the banking sector has largely neglected in the last two decades – should be maintained.

At the same time, governments should make up for the decline in private-debt-financed expenditure by expanding government deficits without covering these deficits by bond issues. In a sense this is undertaking two wrongs to achieve a right: there is a sound reason for governments to run unfunded deficits proportionate to the level of GDP in growing economies, and the failure to do this is one reason why debt-financed money has expanded so much compared to fiat money in the last 20 years.

DO YOU BELIEVE REGULATORY CHANGES ARE NEEDED AND, IF SO, WHAT KIND OF REGULATORY CHANGES SHOULD BE INTRODUCED?

For the reasons outlined above, I don't believe that regulatory changes would permanently restrain the innate tendency the financial sector has towards reckless lending. Since the financial sector makes money by extending debt, it will ultimately succumb to the temptation of funding Ponzi investing, as it has so clearly done in the sub-prime scam – and has also arguably been doing ever since the stock market bubble of the 1980s.

Regulation has proven to be ineffective in constraining this behavior, and indeed the degree of regulatory capture that has occurred in this crisis is truly breathtaking. When institutions that caused the crisis by reckless lending can be deemed 'too big to fail', and were rescued and even encouraged to return to the behavior that caused the crisis in the first place, there is little point in recommending regulations and regulators as a control mechanism for the future.

The only effective constraint is to reduce the desirability of debt to borrowers. This in turn requires finding a means to reduce the attractiveness of debt-financed speculation on asset prices, since that is the main harmful use to which debt is put. I propose two reforms: redefining shares to reduce the attractiveness of speculation on the secondary market, and basing limits to leverage on property not on the income of the borrower, but on the income earning potential of the property.

Jubilee Shares

Shares should be redefined so that, if they are purchased from a company (either in an IPO or a new share issue) they last indefinitely as now, but once they are sold to another individual, they expire after 50 years. These time-limited shares, for which I suggest the name 'Jubilee shares' after the biblical tradition of debt forgiveness, would generate dividends, confer full voting rights, and be able to be onsold; but 50 years after their first sale, they would expire.

The objectives of this proposal are to make the primary share issue market far more important than the secondary, and to make it far less likely that purchases of shares on the secondary market will be made with borrowed money.

The vast majority of turnover on stock markets represents the sale of existing shares between speculators; the creation of new capital plays a comparatively trivial role. With shares redefined in this way, the only way to secure an indefinite stream of dividends would be to participate in an initial share offering. This would hopefully shift the balance of share market activity from the speculative secondary market to the capital-creating primary market.

One of the myths behind which the biggest asset price bubble in history developed was the proposition that share prices were based on a rational estimate of the net present value of future dividend flows. In fact, the valuation process combined leveraged speculation, which itself drove up asset prices, with 'The Greater Fool'.

The fact that all shares currently have a potentially infinite life span is an essential component of the Greater Fool valuation process. If instead shares on the secondary market expired after 50 years, the only reason for purchasing them would be to secure an income stream for that period. Then, valuation would be strictly based on conservatively hypothesized future earnings, and it is highly unlikely that this would be done with borrowed money when the terminal value of such shares was zero.

A Ten-times Rental Income Limit

In the early post-WWII years, lenders were very conservative about loan to valuation ratios (LVRs) for property loans; a typical loan in the 1950s–60s had a LVR of about 70 per cent, so that the borrower's equity in a property began at 30 per cent. In the sub-prime scam, as is well known, LVRs of up to 120 per cent were offered, while even in allegedly well-regulated Australia, LVRs of up to 97 per cent are still offered by major banks, so that the borrower's equity begins at 3 per cent, one tenth the figure that applied in the era of responsible banking.[5]

This drift in LVRs over time was made possible by the fiction that banks assess the debt-servicing capacity of the borrower when offering a loan, something that was not a fiction in the era of responsible lending, but became one as banks succumbed to the temptation to Ponzi financing. Borrowers had a perverted interest in this process occurring, since an increased LVR could allow the more highly geared borrower to trump a more lowly geared one when competing for a given property.

I instead propose reforming lending criteria by limiting the maximum loan that can be secured against a property to ten times the estimated annual rental income of that property. This would reduce the competitive advantage that borrowers get from higher leverage, and replace the current positive feedback loop between leverage and property prices by a negative one: if a property sold for a substantially higher price than ten times its annual rental, this would represent a fall in leverage rather than an increase.

This reform would also encourage the development of a landlord class that actually made money out of property rental, and therefore would have a vested interest in keeping house prices low.

Both these reforms would be subject to the same danger that ultimately defeated the Glass–Steagall Act: their very success in bringing about a period of economic tranquility could lead future regulators to believe that the reforms were hindrances to commerce, leading to their abolition.

However, the process that led to the abolition of Glass–Steagall began with a financial architecture that enabled the banking sector to grow in influence and political power over time, to the stage now where, as noted earlier, the organizations that led the global economy to the brink are themselves deemed 'too big to fail'. One objective of these reforms is to limit the possibilities for the growth of the financial sector beyond the size needed to support its positive contributions to society, by limiting the willingness of the non-bank sector to take on debt. If the non-bank's appetite for debt is limited to productive uses of debt by these reforms, it is possible that the banking sector could never reach the level at which it was able to influence the development of economic policy.

NOTES

1. Now that one can finally speak ill of 'rational expectations', it is clear that it was applied in macroeconomics, not as an empirically or theoretically justified proposition, but with the teleological intent of preserving the belief that money was neutral in the long run, *even though this required assuming that the future could be predicted accurately*. There is no other sensible way to read Lucas's equating of 'rational expectations' with the assumption that future inflation will equal expected inflation: 'If the impossibility of a non-zero value for Expression 6 is taken as an essential feature of the natural rate theory, one is led simply to adding the assumption that Expression 6 is zero as an additional axiom' (Lucas, 1970).
2. 'The granting of credit comes first . . . purchasing power is created to which . . . no new goods correspond. From this it follows, therefore, that in real life total credit must be greater than it could be if there were only fully covered credit' (Schumpeter, 1934: p. 101); 'If income is to grow, the financial markets . . . must generate an aggregate demand that . . . is ever rising. For real aggregate demand to be increasing, . . . it is necessary that current spending plans . . . be greater than current received income . . . It follows that over a period during which economic growth takes place, at least some sectors finance a part of their spending by emitting debt or selling assets' (Minsky, 1982: 6).
3. The government ratio was higher during WWII, but due of course to the extraordinary expenditures occasioned by the war.
4. 'In this system, there is no sense in which the authority has the option to conduct countercyclical policy. To exploit the Phillips Curve, it must somehow trick the public. But by virtue of the assumption that expectations are rational, there is no feedback rule that the authority can employ and expect to be able systematically to fool the public. This means that the authority cannot expect to exploit the Phillips Curve even for one period. Thus, combining the natural rate hypothesis with the assumption that expectations are rational transforms the former from a curiosity with perhaps remote policy implications into an

hypothesis with immediate and drastic implications about the feasibility of pursuing countercyclical policy' (Sargent and Wallace, 1976: 177–8).

5. The Commonwealth Bank offered a 97 per cent LVR as at 20 October, 2010 (see http://www.commbank.com.au/personal/home-loans/loan-to-value-ratio.aspx).

REFERENCES

Bernanke, B.S. (2000), *Essays on the Great Depression*, Princeton, NJ: Princeton University Press.

Bernanke, B.S. (2004), 'What have we learned since October 1979?' panel discussion at conference on Reflections on Monetary Policy 25 years after October 1979, St Louis, MO, Federal Reserve Bank of St Louis.

Bezemer, D.J. (2009), '"No one saw this coming": understanding financial crisis through accounting models', Groningen, The Netherlands, Faculty of Economics, University of Groningen.

Biggs, M., T. Mayer et al. (2010), 'Credit and economic recovery: demystifying phoenix miracles', *SSRN eLibrary*.

Davig, T. and E.M. Leeper (2007), 'Generalizing the Taylor principle', *American Economic Review*, **97**(3), 607–35.

Fullbrook, E. (2010), 'Keen, Roubini and Baker win Revere Award for Economics', *Real World Economics Review Blog*, New York: E. Fullbrook.

Keen, S. (1995), 'Finance and economic breakdown: modeling minsky's "Financial instability hypothesis"', *Journal of Post Keynesian Economics*, **17**(4), 607–35.

Keen, S. (2009a), 'Bailing out the Titanic with a thimble', *Economic Analysis & Policy*, **39**(1), 3–24.

Keen, S. (2009b), 'The Global Financial Crisis, credit crunches and deleveraging', *Journal of Australian Political Economy*, **64**, 18–32.

Keen, S. (2011), 'A monetary Minsky model of the Great Moderation and the Great Recession', *Journal of Economic Behavior & Organization*, forthcoming, available at http://www.sciencedirect.com/science/article/pii/S0167268111000266.

Keynes, J.M. (1936), *The General Theory of Employment, Interest and Money*, London: Macmillan.

Lucas, R.E., Jr (1970), 'Econometric testing of the natural rate hypothesis', in O. Eckstein (ed.), *The Econometrics of Price Determination*, Washington, DC: Board of Governors of the Federal Reserve System and Social Science Research Council, pp. 50–59.

Minsky, H.P. (1982), *Can 'It' Happen Again? Essays on Instability and Finance*, Armonk, NY: M.E. Sharpe.

Sargent, T.J. and N. Wallace (1976), 'Rational expectations and the theory of Economic Policy', *Journal of Monetary Economics*, **2**(2), 169–83.

Schumpeter, J.A. (1934), *The Theory of Economic Development: an Inquiry into Profits, Capital, Credit, Interest and the Business Cycle*, Cambridge, MA: Harvard University Press.

7. Four theses on the global financial crisis

J.E. King*

There are (at least) four lessons to be learned from the global financial crisis. The first lesson is the complete failure of mainstream economic theory to anticipate, explain or provide policies to mitigate the effects of the global financial crisis. The second is the continuing relevance of the nation-state in an era of globalization. Third, there is a whole set of lessons concerning the relationship between private debt and public debt. Finally, the macroeconomic limits to neo-liberalism have become very clear. These four lessons are linked, but it will be convenient to consider them separately. I shall begin with the failure of mainstream theory.

1 THE FAILURE OF MAINSTREAM MACROECONOMIC THEORY

The failure of mainstream economic theory in the face of the global financial crisis has been widely recognized. As one British journalist noted, in one sense the crisis was very good news for economists: 'The recession has apparently led to a surge of school-leavers applying to study economics at university. Applications were up by 15% in January [2009], and similar increases have been recorded for school economics lessons for 16- and 18-year-olds.' But it was not all good news. 'One of the areas prospective economics students might care to study is why most economists failed to foresee the recession, and why those who did made not a blind bit of difference' (Brown, 2009: 14). Similar questions were asked by Queen Elizabeth of the then Prime Minister, Gordon Brown. The answers, in a nutshell, are that mainstream economists were the mental prisoners of formal models that made the global financial crisis unimaginable, and the heterodox economists who rejected these models were ignored, or dismissed as unscientific, by the mainstream.

As I have explained elsewhere (King, 2010), at least six mainstream doctrines have been refuted by the crisis. The first is rational expectations, which, when applied to financial transactions, generates the 'efficient markets hypothesis', from which is deduced the proposition that financial markets invariably produce the 'right price' and therefore require only the lightest of government regulation. This inference involves the elementary logical error of affirming the consequent. The truth of 'If A then B' does not entail the truth of 'If B then A'. Here A is efficiency of financial markets and B is the inability of market participants to outperform the market for any length of time. The fallacy was recognized by some perceptive critics before the onset of the global financial crisis (King, 2009):

> that 'prices are right' and 'there is no free lunch' are *not* equivalent statements. While both are true in an efficient market, 'no free lunch' can also be true in an inefficient market: just because prices are away from fundamental value does not necessarily mean that there are any excess risk-adjusted average returns for the taking. (Barberis and Thaler, 2003: 1057)

Similar conclusions have been drawn by such authorities as the late James Tobin (1987) and the former head of the (British) Financial Services Authority, Adair Turner (2009: 39–42). In the decade or so leading up to the global financial crisis the efficient markets hypothesis did a great deal of harm, both in encouraging foolhardy behaviour on a massive scale by large corporate players in financial markets and in discouraging any serious attempt at regulating their activities. All this would not have surprised the post-Keynesian theorist Hyman Minsky, whose 'financial instability hypothesis' hinges on the emergence of increasingly risky financial innovations as memories of the previous crisis fade (King, 2011).

The second refuted doctrine is the (closely related) principle of 'Ricardian equivalence', which is used to justify deflationary fiscal policy: economic agents are supposed to calculate the precise future implications of debt-financed government expenditures for their own personal tax liabilities and to increase their current and future levels of savings accordingly. This was decisively refuted by the experience of the fiscal stimulus packages introduced in 2008, and in fact David Ricardo himself rejected it (Roberts, 1942). Serious discussion of fiscal policy is now back on the mainstream agenda (Buiter, 2010; Wren-Lewis, 2010). I shall return to this question, and to the contentious issue of 'fiscal sustainability', in the following section.

The third refuted doctrine relates to monetary rather than fiscal policy: only interest rates matter. In mainstream macroeconomic theory, monetary policy operates only through changes in interest rates, which affect saving and (perhaps) business investment. Post-Keynesian economists point to four additional channels, which are loosely related and in all likelihood more important (possibly much more important) than the interest rate channel. These are (i) *credit rationing* in bad times and its opposite (credit abundance?) in good times; (ii) changes in *asset prices*, and in particular *expected* asset prices, and the related phenomena of asset price bubbles and their sudden deflation; (iii) *fear of default*, and (iv) the prospect of *bankruptcy*, both of which are ruled out by the 'no-Ponzi condition' imposed on the Dynamic Stochastic General Equilibrium (DSGE) models used by the mainstream. They introduce a crucial asymmetry in the wealth effects of monetary policy, as has often been noted since Irving Fisher developed his 'debt deflation' theory of financial crisis. All these alternative channels through which monetary policy might operate are discussed by Minsky (2008 [1982]), to whom lip-service is often paid in the wake of the global financial crisis by mainstream macroeconomists who display no understanding of their real implications (e.g. Akerlof and Shiller, 2009).

The fourth refuted doctrine involves the 'New Keynesian' claim that downward flexibility in prices (and wages) is a good thing: price rigidities prevent market clearing, so that excess supplies and demands are the result of a lack of price and wage flexibility. In practice, this seems no longer to be believed, and the rather hesitant mainstream support for fiscal policy in times of cyclical downturn is often justified by the need to prevent the increase in real interest rates that would be caused by a decline in the price level, given the fact that nominal interest rates cannot be negative (Blanchard et al., 2010: 8; cf. Tcherneva, 2009). Keynes himself strongly advocated the virtues of a stable price level. Deflation, Keynes suggested in Chapter 19 of the *General Theory*, had several powerful disadvantages, not least its effect on the state of confidence, on the real rate of interest and on the burden of debt. The objections to a falling price level applied both to the sharp cyclical deflations of 1920–22 and 1929–33 and to the proposal, favoured by many liberal economists, that the price level should decline in the long term *pari passu* with rising labour productivity, money wages remaining constant. 'There are advantages in some degree of flexibility in the wages of particular industries', Keynes argued, 'so as to expedite transfers from those which are relatively declining to those which are relatively expanding. But the money-wage level as a whole should be maintained as stable as possible, at any rate in the short period' (Keynes, 1936: 270). He was correct.

The fifth and most important refuted doctrine is that unemployment is always voluntary, which on Keynes's interpretation is equivalent to the claim that Say's Law holds, so that there is no problem of effective aggregate demand. Glossing Keynes's notoriously convoluted definition in the *General Theory*, someone is involuntarily unemployed if she would be willing to take a job at or slightly below the prevailing real wage but is unable to find one. This was the nub of Keynes's criticism of mainstream theory, and it underpins the 'paradox of thrift', a notion that originated not with Keynes but with the future Nobel laureate, Ragnar Frisch. In a 1932 radio broadcast in Norway (four years before the publication of the *General Theory*), Frisch maintained that it was necessary to encourage consumer spending in order to stimulate output and employment. If instead society tried to save more, the result would be a fall in income and a *reduction* in saving. Frisch's argument was recently recalled, approvingly, by another Nobel prize-winner, Lawrence Klein (2006: 171). It has important implications for government policy, as we shall see below. These five refuted doctrines entail a sixth: their collapse is sufficient also to refute the New Neo-classical Synthesis in macroeconomic theory, which depends upon them (Arestis and Sawyer, 2008; Arestis, 2009).

2 THE CONTINUING RELEVANCE OF THE NATION-STATE

The second lesson of the global financial crisis concerns the continuing importance of the nation-state, as argued by Marxian theorists of imperialism like Ellen Meiskins Wood (2003) and despite the claims to the contrary found in the work of many eminent international relations theorists, from Susan Strange (1994) to Ronen Palan (2006). In an era of informal or 'free market' imperialism, Wood argues, in which formal colonial rule is a thing of the past but United States dominance survives, the other nation-states have a greater role to play than ever before in maintaining the global economic hierarchy. The truth of this proposition has been demonstrated both by the origins of the global financial crisis and by the measures taken to overcome it. On the first question, the following, rather obvious, point needs to be made. Like the Great Depression, the global financial crisis of 2008–9 was 'made in the USA'. This is not to deny that asset price bubbles, fraud, incompetence and systemic failure occurred elsewhere: the Northern Rock disaster in the UK and the nefarious activities of the Icelandic bankers are just two. But the crisis did not originate there, nor did it begin in some nebulous, postmodern, offshore non-location. It had a very specific and precisely defined site: Wall Street. The United States may be in decline as a political and military superpower, losing influence to China all over the global South and apparently unable after ten years to subdue a few thousand rebellious tribesmen in Afghanistan. Its decline as a superpower – since 1991, the only superpower – has been proclaimed by historians as diverse as Paul Kennedy (1987) and Niall Ferguson (2010), but it is still capable of initiating economic havoc and spreading it all over the world, just as it did in 1929–33.

On the second point, the global financial crisis was overcome – if, indeed, it has been overcome – and its effects have certainly been mitigated, through action by national governments: the United States, China, Britain, France, Germany, even tiny Australia. Both monetary and fiscal policy have been employed. Nominal interest rates have been cut, in some cases almost to zero. 'Quantitative easing' has seen the monetization of vast quantities of government debt. 'Troubled assets' (a lovely euphemism for junk bonds and worthless mortgages) have been purchased at face value by central banks and state treasuries. Explicit and implicit guarantees have been provided to private depositors and inter-bank lenders, preventing the panics and the bank failures that intensified the economic collapse in 1930–32. Government expenditure has been greatly increased, both on long-term investment projects and on short-term handouts to stimulate private consumption (Hart, 2009). Budget deficits have increased massively, leading to the controversies about 'fiscal sustainability' that I shall consider in the following section. In this way the 'great recession' has (probably) been prevented from turning into a second Great Depression (it is too soon, in July 2011, to be entirely sure).

In all of this, the international economic institutions were almost totally useless. Indeed, the International Monetary Fund has been worse than useless, irrelevant to the larger national economies but inflicting savage and futile deflation on those small and medium-sized countries (Greece, Hungary, Iceland, Ireland, Latvia, Serbia, Spain) unable to escape its clutches. Contrary to what used to be commonly asserted, globalization has not rendered the nation-state economically irrelevant or impotent. Quite the contrary: when the chips are down, there is still nothing else. Once again, this is often denied by international relations theorists, who continue to exaggerate the importance of the international institutions (see Camilleri and Falk, 2010, Chapter 5, for a recent example from an otherwise excellent book).

3 PRIVATE DEBT AND PUBLIC DEBT

The global financial crisis has seen the greatest conversion of private debt into public debt in human history. This has been acknowledged by perceptive journalists (e.g. Urschitz, 2010) but seems to have escaped the notice of almost all mainstream economists, who ignore the need for stock-flow consistent macroeconomic analysis as advocated by the late Wynne Godley and other heterodox theorists (see Godley and Lavoie, 2007). It has a number of very important implications. First, since the beneficiaries are on the whole much richer than the average citizen, this process of debt conversion will have a profoundly regressive impact on the distribution of wealth and (since capital yields an income) also on the distribution of income. Some poor people will have benefited, notably the former sub-prime mortgagees in the United States, whose debts have evaporated. For the most part, though, the beneficiaries will be rich, most obvious among them the shareholders in financial companies that now (as a result of the Troubled Asset Recovery Plan and other bailouts) hold Treasury Bills instead of Collateralized Debt Obligations, and the overpaid employees of these companies whose inflated bonuses have been restored. It would be good to believe that a team of global forensic accountants was already at work on precise estimates of the magnitude of this redistribution of wealth. Whatever its proportions, it is most definitely an immense scandal.

This leads straight to the second implication: deficit hawks should beware. For the world as a whole, the aggregate 'deterioration' in the public sector's finances is exactly equal to the aggregate 'improvement' in the net worth of the private sector. I use inverted commas to avoid begging the question, since what is 'bad' and what is 'good' in this context is precisely what is at issue. The public finances of the larger nation-states will 'improve' automatically if the recovery continues, but the recovery will be jeopardized by the imposition of Latvian- or Greek-style deflation on the United States or the United Kingdom. A forced 'improvement' in public sector finances will necessarily be accompanied by a 'deterioration' in the financial position of the private sector, and this is absolutely not what the world economy needs right now (see Burger, 2003 for an extended, and prescient, discussion of this question).

That efforts to impose fiscal consolidation will, in any case, be self-defeating is suggested by Victoria Chick and Ann Pettifor in their excellent historical account of British government debt in the twentieth century, which reveals that 'fiscal consolidation increases rather than reduces the level of public debt as a share of GDP and is in general associated with adverse macroeconomic conditions' (Chick and Pettifor, 2010: 1). This was especially true of the 'Geddes axe' that was wielded in the early 1920s. In 1946, they reveal, UK government debt had risen to 252 per cent of GDP (ibid.: 9). And yet the next quarter of a century was a 'golden age' for the British economy. Its problems derived from poor management, low investment, weak productivity growth in manufacturing, an overvalued currency and the resulting balance of payments difficulties; public sector debt was an irrelevancy, which is barely mentioned in the recent *Cambridge Economic History of Modern Britain* (Floud and Johnson, 2004), even in the chapter on fiscal policy. Similar arguments have been made for the United States by Yeva Nersisyan and Randall Wray (2010a,

2010b), who demonstrate the weakness in the mainstream case for fiscal consolidation made by Carmen Reinhart and Kenneth Rogoff (2009).

The precise meaning of 'fiscal sustainability' remains unclear. One recent mainstream graduate text points to the importance of the private sector's willingness to hold government debt:

> If the debt–GDP ratio is expected to rise indefinitely, then concern that government would be unable to meet its debt obligations without having to resort to monetizing the debt – which carries the threat of generating high inflation, or even hyperinflation – would be likely to cause the private sector to be unwilling to hold government debt.

The precise implications of this are, however, ambiguous. A 'necessary condition' for fiscal sustainability is that 'government debt and the debt–GDP ratio are expected to remain finite' (Wickens, 2008: 96). But this is an extremely weak condition, which is consistent with endless budget deficits and a debt–GDP ratio that rises continuously, though at a (very slowly?) declining rate. Whose expectations are relevant here? Will they normally be 'rational' or 'non-rational'? On what criteria? 'The precise choice of an upper limit' on the debt–GDP ratio, Wickens concedes, 'is inevitably somewhat arbitrary' (ibid.: 99), as – presumably – is the former UK Labour government's self-imposed rule that the ratio should remain constant over the whole business cycle (ibid.: 101). The European Union's Stability and Growth Pact sets an (arbitrary) upper limit of 60 per cent, which more than one member country has greatly exceeded. Belgium, in particular, 'did not have a sustainable fiscal policy stance, however measured . . . Nevertheless, despite failing these tests, Belgium has continued to be able to sell its debt' (ibid.: 104).

Wickens's text went to press before the onset of the global financial crisis. Unfortunately, more recent discussions have shed no more light on these issues. Simon Wren-Lewis notes that the 'key limit' on government debt 'is not when a government will probably default, but when the possibility that it will default becomes significant enough for lenders to require a risk premium to offset this chance'. There are no 'robust models' on this question, he concedes, 'in part because this depends on political as much as economic factors' (Wren-Lewis, 2010: 78). Similarly, Willem Buiter cautions that 'we must not be fooled by the contemplation of the very high debt-to-GDP rations found in the USA and the UK immediately after the First and Second World Wars', since 'the political constraints on spending cuts and tax increases are much tighter than they were immediately following the Second World War' (Buiter, 2010: 65). But this begs the question: why should either spending cuts or tax increases be required? Why is the existing debt/GDP ratio, or its short-term trajectory, regarded as unsustainable? Buiter defines fiscal sustainability in Minskyian terms: it is necessary (and sufficient?) that the government avoids Ponzi finance, in which 'existing debt (both interest and principal repayments due) is serviced forever by issuing additional debt so that the debt forever grows at least as fast as the interest rate on the debt' (Buiter, 2010: 56). But this says nothing either about the *ratio* of debt to GDP or about the virtues of 'stabilizing the debt-to-GDP ratio at its current level' (ibid.: 58), a principle that Buiter seems to endorse.

All this reminds me of the old debates among Marxian economists over the falling rate of profit as a potentially fatal contradiction of the capital mode of production (Howard and King, 1992: Chapter 7). Suppose that Marx was right, and the forces leading the rate of profit to decline are stronger than the counteracting tendencies that he himself identified. So what? If the system begins with a high rate of profit (whatever 'high' might mean in this context: 15%? 25%?), and then declines very slowly, at a declining rate, moving towards a very slightly lower asymptote (13%? 23%? a century or two hence?), why should this be seen as a deadly contradiction? There is the same confusion of levels and rates of change, of stocks and flows, that we find in the debate on fiscal sustainability. As Rosa Luxemburg scornfully remarked: 'there is still some time to pass before capitalism collapses because of the falling rate of profit, roughly until the sun burns out' (cited in Howard and King, 1992: 130). Perhaps the same can be said about the growth of government debt.

If the debt/GDP ratio is considered to be a serious problem, for whatever reason, deflationary fiscal policy is not the only way to deal with it. Certainly there are 'political factors' involved. Not least of them are the regressive implications for the distribution of income, since interest payments on government debt go from relatively poor taxpayers to relatively rich bondholders (Nevile, 2009: 33). I think a case can be made for excavating the proposals for a progressive tax on capital, the so-called 'capital levy', which were made by Ricardo in 1815 and by A.C. Pigou a century later, but never implemented. Similar suggestions were again made at the end of the Second World War, once more without success; Gottlieb (1953) provides a useful survey. One British journalist has calculated that a one-off 20 per cent wealth tax levied on the richest 10 per cent of the population would raise enough to pay off the United Kingdom's entire national debt (Philo, 2010). Pigou's plan was both less radical and much more radical than this. A one-off capital levy, with rates rising from 2 per cent at the bottom to 40 per cent or even more at the top would, he estimated, raise a sum equal to one-quarter of private wealth, or roughly £4 billion, which would allow one-half of the internally held domestic debt to be paid off and taxation to be lower, by £240 million per annum, after the war (Pigou,

1918: 155). This was 'not red revolution', he maintained (ibid.: 156), and he himself was a lifelong Liberal. A capital levy would, however, ensure that the burden of reducing the debt would fall on those best able to bear it, the rich, and not on those least able, the poor. In 2011, 'socialist' and Conservative governments alike seem determined to do it the other way round. History suggests that they will not succeed, but they will cause a great deal of unnecessary suffering and injustice along the way.

There is a third, and possibly less obvious, implication of the transformation of private debt into public debt: heterodox economists and media doomsayers should also beware. They should recall both aspects of Minsky's explanation of why 'it' – a global financial crisis of 1930s proportions – did not recur in his lifetime (this is the title of the first American edition of Minsky, 2008 [1982]). The much tighter financial regulation introduced during the New Deal was only half of the story, Minsky suggested. The other half was the transformation of private sector balance sheets as a result of the huge budget deficits that were incurred during the Second World War. This gave the private sector vast quantities of risk-free government securities, greatly increasing the robustness of the US (and British) financial system. As already noted, exactly the same thing has happened in the current global financial crisis. There will, of course, be another global financial crisis, for the reasons that Minsky advanced, some time in the future. But it may not happen any time soon.

4 THE LIMITS TO NEO-LIBERALISM

The final lesson to be drawn from the global financial crisis is that the limits of neo-liberalism have been clearly exposed: it simply does not work in matters of macroeconomics. Howard and King (2008: 1) define neo-liberalism as the doctrine that almost all social problems have a market solution, or a solution in which market relations figure prominently, together with the political practice in which this doctrine has been applied to all manner of social problems, from health and education to military security and the prison system. It might yet be extended to combat global warming, though at the time of writing this appears unlikely. (Incidentally, it is interesting that opposition to emissions trading schemes and carbon taxation comes overwhelmingly from the political right. It is as if the advocates of neo-liberalism lack the courage of their own supposed convictions.) These, however, are all microeconomic applications of the neo-liberal doctrine, albeit, in the case of global warming, potentially a very large one. But the doctrine cannot *in principle* be applied to macroeconomics. Say's Law is false: supply does not create its own demand, and no market-mimicking arrangements can possibly eliminate the problem of effective demand. The truth of this statement was graphically revealed by the global financial crisis and the reaction of nation-states to it. It is in no way affected by the allegedly inexorable march of globalization. In this sense, at least, we still live in the world described by Keynes in the *General Theory*, three-quarters of a century ago.

NOTE

* I have benefited greatly from comments by Mike Howard on earlier drafts of this chapter. He is, however, not responsible for factual errors or expressions of opinion.

REFERENCES

Akerlof, G.A. and R.J. Shiller (2009), *Animal Spirits: How Human Psychology Drives the Economy, and Why it Matters for Global Capitalism*, Princeton, NJ: Princeton University Press.

Arestis, P. (2009), 'New consensus macroeconomics and Keynesian critique', in E. Hein, T. Niechoj and E. Stockhammer (eds), *Macroeconomic Policies on Shaky Foundations: Whither Mainstream Economics?*, Marburg: Metropolis, pp. 165–85.

Arestis, P. and M. Sawyer (2008), 'A critical consideration of the foundations of monetary policy in the new consensus macroeconomic framework', *Cambridge Journal of Economics*, **32**(5), September, 761–79.

Barberis, N. and R. Thaler (2003), 'A survey of behavioral finance', in G.M. Constantindes, M. Harris and R.M. Stulz (eds), *Handbook of the Economics of Finance: Volume 1B: Financial Markets and Asset Pricing*, Amsterdam: Elsevier, pp. 1053–123.

Blanchard, O., G. Dell'Arica and P. Mauro (2010), 'Rethinking macroeconomic policy', Washington, DC: IMF Staff Position Note, SPN/10/03, 12 February.

Brown, D. (2009), 'Why it's not all gloom for economists', *Guardian Weekly*, 17 April, p. 14.

Buiter, W.H. (2010), 'The limits to fiscal stimulus', *Oxford Review of Economic Policy*, **26**(1), Spring, 48–70.

Burger, P. (2003), *Sustainable Fiscal Policy and Economic Stability: Theory and Practice*, Cheltenham, UK and Northampton, MA, USA: Edward Elgar Publishing.

Camilleri, J.A. and J. Falk (2010), *Worlds in Transition: Evolving Governance across a Stressed Planet*, Cheltenham, UK and Northampton, MA, USA: Edward Elgar Publishing.

Chick, V. and A. Pettifor (2010), 'The economic consequences of Mr. Osborne', available at http://www.debtonation.org/2010/06/the-economic-consequences-of-mr-osborne/, accessed 10 June 2010.

Ferguson, N. (2010), 'Decline and fall of the US', *Age* [Melbourne], 29 July, p. 15.

Floud, R. and P. Johnson (eds) (2004), *The Cambridge Economic History of Modern Britain. Volume III: Structural Change and Growth, 1939–2000*, Cambridge: Cambridge University Press.

Godley, W. and M. Lavoie (2007), *Monetary Economics: an Integrated Approach to Credit, Money, Income, Production and Wealth*, Basingstoke: Palgrave Macmillan.

Gottlieb, M. (1953), 'The capital levy and deadweight debt in England, 1815–1840', *Journal of Finance*, **8**(1), March, 34–46.

Hart, N. (2009), 'Discretionary fiscal policy and budget deficits: an "orthodox" critique of current policy debates', *Economic and Labour Relations Review*, **19**(2), July, 39–58.

Howard, M.C. and J.E. King (1992), *A History of Marxian Economics: Volume II, 1929–1990*, Basingstoke: Macmillan and Princeton, NJ: Princeton University Press.

Howard, M.C. and J.E. King (2008), *The Rise of Neoliberalism in Advanced Capitalist Economies: A Materialist Analysis*, Basingstoke: Palgrave Macmillan.

Kennedy, P.M. (1987), *The Rise and Fall of the Great Powers: Economic Change and Military Conflict from 1500 to 2000*, New York: Random House.

Keynes, J.M. (1936), *The General Theory of Employment, Interest and Money*, London: Macmillan.

King, J.E. (2009), 'Economists and the global financial crisis', *Global Change, Peace and Security*, **21**(3), October, 389–96.

King, J.E. (2010), 'Six more refuted doctrines: a comment on Quiggin', *Economic Papers*, **29**(1), March, 34–9.

King, J.E. (2011), 'Hyman Minsky and the financial instability hypothesis', in G.C. Harcourt (ed.), *Handbook of Post Keynesian Economics*, Oxford: Oxford University Press, forthcoming.

Klein, L.R. (2006), 'Paul Samuelson as a "Keynesian" economist', in M. Szenberg, L. Ramrattan and A.A. Gottesman (eds), *Samuelsonian Economics and the Twenty-First Century*, Oxford: Oxford University Press, pp. 165–77.

Minsky, Hyman P. (2008 [1982]), *Can 'It' Happen Again? Essays on Instability and Finance*, New York: McGraw-Hill (first edition Armonk, NY: M.E. Sharpe).

Nersisyan, Y. and L.R. Wray (2010a), 'Does excessive sovereign debt really hurt growth? A critique of *This Time is Different*, by Reinhart and Rogoff', Annandale-on-Hudson, NY: Levy Economics Institute of Bard College, Working Paper No. 603, June.

Nersisyan, Y. and L.R. Wray (2010b), 'Deficit hysteria redux? Why we should stop worrying about US government deficits', Annandale-on-Hudson, NY: Levy Economics Institute of Bard College, Public Policy Brief, 111.

Nevile, J. (2009), 'The current crisis has a silver lining', *Economic and Labour Relations Review*, **19**(2), July, 27–38.

Palan, Ronen (2006), *The Offshore World: Sovereign Markets, Virtual Places and Nomad Millionaires*, Ithaca, NY: Cornell University Press.

Philo, G. (2010). 'It's time to tax the rich', *Guardian Weekly*, 20 August, p. 18.

Pigou, A.C. (1918), 'A special levy to discharge war debt', *Economic Journal*, **28**(110), June, 135–56.

Reinhart, C. and K. Rogoff (2009), *This Time is Different: Eight Centuries of Financial Folly*, Princeton, NJ: Princeton University Press.

Roberts, R.O. (1942), 'Ricardo's theory of public debts', *Economica*, **9**(35), August, 257–66.

Strange, S. (1994), *States and Markets*, 2nd edn, London: Pinter.

Tcherneva, P. (2009), 'Fiscal policy on shaky foundations: Post Keynesian and Chartalist lessons for New Consensus economists', in E. Hein, T. Niechoj and E. Stockhammer (eds), *Macroeconomic Policies on Shaky Foundations: Whither Mainstream Economics?*, Marburg: Metropolis, pp. 209–33.
Tobin, J. (1987), 'On the efficiency of the financial system', in J. Tobin, *Policies for Prosperity: Essays in a Keynesian Mode*, edited by P.M. Jackson, Brighton: Wheatsheaf, pp. 282–96.
Turner, A. (2009), *The Turner Review: A Regulatory Response to the Global Banking Crisis*, London: Financial Services Authority.
Urschitz, J. (2010), 'Das hilflose Zappeln im Schuldennetz' ('Wriggling helplessly in the web of debt'), *Die Presse* (Vienna), leading article, 5 May, available at http://diepresse.co./meinung/kommentare/leitartikel/563097/print.do, accessed 6 May 2010.
Wickens, M. (2008), *Macroeconomic Theory: A Dynamic General Equilibrium Approach*, Princeton, NJ: Princeton University Press.
Wood, E. Meiskins (2003), *Empire of Capital*, London: Verso.
Wren-Lewis, S. (2010), 'Macroeconomic policy in light of the credit crunch: the return of counter-cyclical fiscal policy?', *Oxford Review of Economic Policy*, **26**(1), Spring, 71–86.

8. Monetary policies during the financial crisis: an appraisal

Mervyn K. Lewis

INTRODUCTION

The primary goal of this chapter is to examine the monetary policies pursued in the major developed economies in response to the global financial turmoil. The initial responses revolved around 'conventional' monetary policy which controls the shortest market rate (overnight interbank rate, bill rate or repo rate) with the aim of affecting the general structure of interest rates, economic activity and prices. Authorities in the major countries drove these policy rates to low levels, in some cases effectively zero, much lower than those in the 1930s. When those policies failed to have the desired effects, the monetary authorities turned to so-called 'unconventional' monetary policies in the form of 'quantitative easing', effectively printing money and engaging in massive purchases of government bonds and other securities. In the case of the United States, for example, such a programme took place between January 2009 and March 2010. The Federal Reserve Bank then moved further into uncharted waters by undertaking a second round of quantitative easing and bond-buying between November 2010 and June 2011.

Why have these unprecedented 'unconventional' actions been needed? Obviously the reason is that conventional policies did not work. But why was this the case? How could such low interest rates not stimulate the economy? And, if ultra-low interest rates could not do the job, why would quantitative easing that drives rates even lower be expected to produce a different result? Might, in fact, interest rates be too low?

These are questions considered below, but first a step back is made to evaluate the role of monetary policy beforehand. Quite clearly, monetary policy has been a major component of actions taken by policy-makers to arrest and reverse the economic downturn that followed the global financial crisis, but how important was monetary policy as a cause of the crisis? An examination of this question is the other aim of this chapter. Before doing so, however, the background is set out.

THE BACKGROUND

In the immediate aftermath of the crisis, the focus of those searching for explanations of the causes was almost exclusively on 'micro' factors such as financial regulation (or more particularly, the lack of it). For example, Axel Weber, President of the Deutsche Bundesbank identified three main reasons: lax lending standards, weaknesses in the credit transfer processes, and overly optimistic assessments of structured securities such as mortgage-backed securities and collateralized debt obligations. He found as quite 'strange' the idea that borrowers with little or no capital and a poor credit history could obtain a real estate loan. That observation, in turn, prompted Weber to point to weaknesses in the credit risk transfer process via securitization that seemingly made lenders and investors, if not oblivious to risk, confident that credit risks had been divided up, parcelled out and thus transferred appropriately across the financial markets. Indeed, as Weber noted, it appeared for a while that unstable individual loans could be converted into virtually fail-safe securities through structured financing and trancheing (Weber, 2008). These views were later echoed by Chinese central bank governor Zhou Xiaochuan, who put the blame firmly on Wall Street and factors such as accounting rules, credit rating agencies, securitized lending and lax standards at banks (Batson, 2009). Others have pointed to the role of greed, reckless behaviour (on the part of US homeowners, mortgage brokers, mortgage lenders, Wall Street investment banks, hedge funds and other investors alike), and excessive debt and leverage (Lewis, 2010).

It was only later that attention turned to the root global macroeconomic origins of the crisis – factors which help explain why the sub-prime crisis had such worldwide ramifications (Lewis, 2009). In the words of Pisani-Ferry and Santos (2009: 9), 'there was a collective failure to grasp fully the link between global payments imbalances and the demand for safe (or seemingly safe) financial assets and the manufacturing of those assets'. They continue: 'it was the combination of strong international demand for such assets, largely in connection with the accumulation of current account surpluses in emerging and oil rich economies, and an environment of perverse economic incentives and poor regulation that proved to be explosive'.

Of course, the counterpart to the current account surpluses of China and other countries was the US current account deficit. From a situation of near balance in 1991, the US current account then moved into deficit, which widened dramatically after 2001 to reach $811 billion, or 6.1 per cent of GDP in 2006. At that time, the United States was absorbing nearly 80 per cent of the international savings that crossed borders.

Once the focus shifted from the micro to the macro, attitudes to the fundamental causes of the financial crisis became much more polarized. The US current account deficit has been extensively studied by US economists and commentators. In fact, Iley and Lewis (2007) examine no less than 41 hypotheses and explanatory factors that have been advanced in the extensive literature on the subject. Nevertheless, despite this rich offering, only two explanations have attained major status. These are the 'Bernanke thesis' and 'the Greenspan legacy'.

Ever since Bernanke (2005) advanced the 'global savings glut' hypothesis, policy-makers in the United States have 'insisted that the key macroeconomic problem in the world economy was not its current account but rather China's high propensity to save' (Pisani-Ferry and Santos, 2009: 9). Bernanke's position has engendered considerable interest not only because of its progenitor (then on the Board of Governors of the Federal Reserve System, now its Chairman), but because it runs directly counter to what might seem the most obvious explanation, namely that the US current account deficit is the result of US policies and the economic decisions of US households and corporations. Instead of relating the deficit to excessive borrowing and spending and insufficient savings by US households and the US government, the United States was cast in an accommodating role, rather than an initiating one. Instead of being 'made in the USA', the deficit is perceived chiefly to be the result of decisions made abroad that have produced a glut of savings on world financial markets.

Applied to the context of the global financial crisis, the argument is that when China and other countries switched to market-oriented economies in the 1990s, hundreds of millions of workers were absorbed into the world economy. As GDP growth in the emerging economies soared, consumption could not keep pace with expanding income and savings rose, unleashing a tsunami of capital onto global markets. All of that capital not only pushed down long-term real interest rates to low levels but caused them to become de-linked from the short-term rates that central banks control. On this view, central banks became 'innocent and impotent bystanders in the global macroeconomic shift' (*The Economist*, 2010a: 68). In the case of the United States, flooded with inflows of capital, US savings fell and investment rose as households borrowed and invested in housing, generating the US current account deficit that is the statistical counterpart of the capital account surplus.

There are some who still maintain that the global financial crisis originated in China (including notably Ben Bernanke and Alan Greenspan). Now, however, the Bernanke thesis has gradually given way to the view that the Federal Reserve, in the last four years of Greenspan's chairmanship, kept interest rates too low (and regulation too light).

MONETARY POLICY BEFOREHAND

Current thinking is reflected in the 'illustrated history' in *Bloomberg Businessweek*, 31 October 2010, which starts in 2001 with 'The Fed lowers interest rates to stimulate a weak economy' and continues with 'low mortgage rates encourage homebuying', 'home prices rise encouraging more lending', 'low interest rates hurt investors who seek higher yields', 'Wall Street creates mortgage-backed securities to meet investor demand', 'banks throw money at borrowers', and so on (Coy et al., 2010).

In this alternative story, the US external deficit was made at home, not abroad, as a result of excessive borrowing and spending and too little saving by US households. Those countries (e.g. China) supplying Americans with goods due to the trade deficit were only too happy to lend back the dollars they received so that the spending spree would continue, and thus accommodated insufficient savings in the United States with more savings of their own. From this perspective, the mistake made in the Bernanke thesis was in its failure to mention that central bank policy rates in the wake of the collapse of the dot.com boom in 2001, and September 11, were driven below levels in the Great Depression of the 1930s, which does seem a glaring – and for a central banker all too convenient – omission from any story about the factors behind low US saving and low world interest rates. Greenspan's particular brand of monetary policy saw the Federal funds rate pushed down from 6.5 per cent at the end of 2001 to a (then) record low of 1 per cent in early 2003 and held at that level for over a year, fuelling a real estate boom and massive mortgage equity withdrawal, while the asymmetric 'cushion the busts, ride the booms' philosophy followed by Greenspan encouraged downside risks to be downplayed and risk premiums to be compressed. This 'hothouse' environment acted as an incubator for the mortgage lending expansion.

It is, of course, possible to combine the global 'glut of savings' and the 'Greenspan legacy' stories, as suggested by Iley and Lewis (2007: Chapter 9), in which case a coincidence of two powerful and interacting developments on both sides of the Pacific may have combined to generate large global imbalances, marked in particular by Asian current account surpluses and the US current account deficit. However, if monetary policy is to have something other than a minor supporting role, it is necessary to establish just how 'loose' monetary policy was set in the final years of the Greenspan Fed. Evidence that monetary policy responses were 'overdone' comes from the path of interest rates and monetary growth. For interest rates, three measures are used. The first uses a methodology developed by Frederic Mishkin (1981), but used more recently by Christina and David Romer (2002), in which an *ex ante* real Federal funds rate is estimated.[1] On this measure, the real federal funds rate was set below zero for the first time since the 1970s and then held there for 12 successive quarters. Monetary policy was easily the most expansionary since the mid-1970s. The second measure compares the actual policy rate with the level called for by the Taylor rule (Taylor, 1999). Under the Taylor rule, the policy rate decision is a function of three factors: the inflation gap, the real output gap and the equilibrium real interest rate plus the inflation goal. On this measure, the Federal funds rate was on average 1 percentage point too low in 2001–03 and 1.75 percentage points too low in 2004–05 (Taylor, 2007; Billi, 2009).[2] The third measure compares the actual Federal funds rate with a reference rate calculated to give equilibrium in the banking sector, taking into account industry structure, market and credit conditions (Lim et al., 2010). They conclude that:

> over quite a few years (roughly 2003 to 2006) . . . the actual federal funds rate was seriously misaligned . . . support[ing] the view that the US official rate was kept too low for too long in the early 2000s and that this may have helped create an environment of easy credit prior to the global financial crisis (p. 19).

Low interest rates would normally be accompanied by monetary expansion. In this case, US monetary policy was amplified by the build-up in foreign-exchange reserves and domestic liquidity in countries that tied their currencies to the dollar, notably China and the rest of Asia, since they import American monetary policy under the relatively fixed exchange rate link that they follow. As a result, for a few years after 2001 global liquidity expanded at its fastest pace for three decades. The standard measure of global US dollar liquidity, which adds growth in the US monetary base to increases in US dollar reserves held in custody at the Federal Reserve Bank of New York, peaked at an annual growth rate of almost 21 per cent in August 2004, its most rapid rate of increase since the 1970s (Iley and Lewis, 2007; Lewis, 2009).

If the world is awash with liquidity, it has to go somewhere. Some, no doubt, found its way directly into real estate. Other amounts went into bonds, lowering yields and long-term interest rates, including mortgages, and thus into housing indirectly. In its 2005 Annual Report, the Bank for International Settlements suggested that the fact that the prices of all non-monetary assets (including bonds) rose, could indeed reflect an effort by investors to get rid of excess liquidity.

Greenspan and Bernanke defend Federal Reserve policy against such charges by pointing to the global nature of the house price boom as evidence that US monetary policy was not to blame (*The Economist*, 2010a; Colvin, 2010). However, at a world level, the global savings glut was not the only factor driving down world interest rates. Monetary policy was loosened not only in the United States, but across the three major currency blocs. In 2003, central bank policy rates were set at levels never seen before in what some market practitioners dubbed the '0–1–2 structure', that is, 0 in Japan, 1 per cent in the United States and 2 per cent in the euro area. As we shall see, a broadly similar conjunction of policy interest rates (but at a lower level) was put in place after the crisis.

Also, one does not need to subscribe to the global savings glut hypothesis to draw a direct connection between the US external deficit and the US mortgage market. With the United States in 2005 and 2006 absorbing so much of the international savings, many financial innovations (for example, hedge funds, private equity, structured finance) sought to tap into this flow. A combination of the United States' role as world banker, given its deep and liquid financial markets, allied with the role of the US dollar as international money and the American banking sector's proclivity for financial innovation created a new asset class with 'worldwide appeal' (IMF, 2006). Given the backdrop of historically low long-term interest rates and booming house prices between 2001–05, much of the innovation in structured financing in the United States centred on housing finance. Mortgage debt had been 'commoditized' by the large banks as it was securitized (and frequently resecuritized), bundled into different risk categories and then sold to both domestic and foreign investors.

In summary, the alternative to Bernanke's global savings glut explanation runs in terms of excessively expansionary monetary policy in the United States in the 2001–04 period which drove up US housing prices (notably, at a time when China did not have a large current account surplus). The subsequent asset price inflation undoubtedly made US households feel wealthier and encouraged them to borrow and spend. Median household debt rose by 34 per cent between 2001 and 2004, and nearly half of all US families did not save any portion of their income (Kliesen, 2006). Equity was extracted from housing mainly by the refinancing of home mortgages. At the end of 2005 and early 2006, mortgage equity withdrawal was running at an annual rate of over $800 billion. The fact that foreigners were all too willing to purchase the re-packaged mortgage borrowings and facilitate the housing equity transactions would seem to close the circle.

MONETARY POLICY AFTER THE CRISIS

There was always the question of whether, and to what extent, Bernanke would follow in Greenspan's footsteps. Writing in 2006, Iley and Lewis (2007) posed the issue as follows:

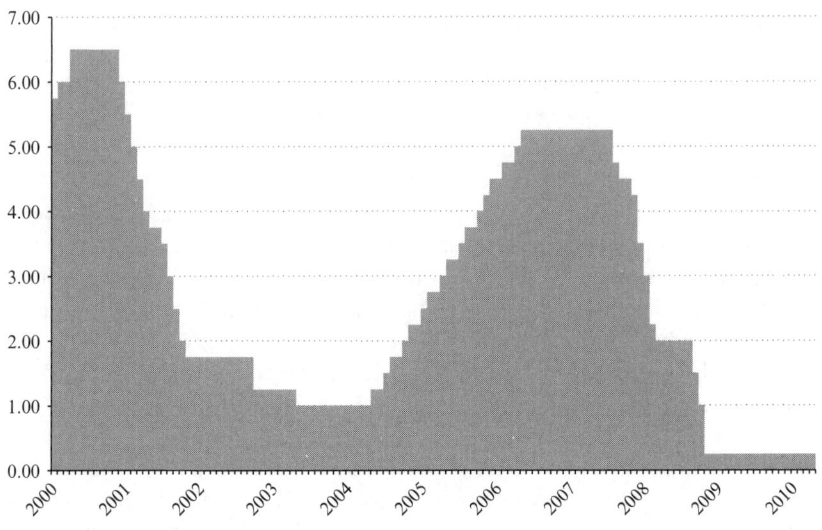

Figure 8.1 Target federal funds rate, 2000–2010

> On our reading of the situation, the basic cause of the widening of the US current account deficit since 2001 has been the exceptionally high asset prices produced by unsustainably low interest rates. National, especially household, saving in the United States has been pushed to record lows and an unprecedently high level of household borrowing has eventuated. . . . the combination of high debt and high asset prices that provides the backdrop to private sector decision-making presents some deflation risks to the US and world economy. Indeed, it was to insure against such deflation that the Fed cut interest rates aggressively in 2001–2003. Ironically, this action helped convert a spent equity boom into one involving house prices. If US households were left to themselves, household borrowing could well 'simmer down', in Greenspan's words, as the housing boom fades, and mortgage equity extraction subsides. The current account deficit might then begin to level out as household spending's share of the economy returns to more normal levels and the household financial deficit recedes. There is always a risk that the adjustment may not proceed in such an orderly way and lead to an asset price shake-out. In this case, it remains to be seen whether the 'Bernanke Fed' will respond to incipient signs of weakness in the housing market with the same alacrity that typically characterised the 'Greenspan Fed', and continue to 'cushion the busts' (pp. 242–3).

It did not take long for the question to be answered. As can be seen in Figure 8.1, the Bernanke Fed has repeated the Greenspan Fed interest rate cycle analysed earlier. Under Greenspan, policy interest rates were lowered by 550 basis points to 1 per cent. Under Bernanke, the Fed funds rate was lowered by 525 basis points to effectively zero (a 0.00–0.25 per cent band) at the end of 2008 (when there were also near zero short-term bond rates). Moreover, policy interest rates have been held at this low level for much longer than the twelve months under Greenspan in 2003–04. At the time of writing (November 2010), there is no sign that policy rates will be lifted soon from the emergency level; indeed, futures markets are not factoring in an increase until towards the end of 2011.

As in the previous interest cycle initiated in 2001, other leading central banks followed the Fed's lead, except that in this case interest rates were pushed lower than the '0–1–2' pattern. In March 2009, the Bank of England cut the bank rate to 0.5 per cent, the lowest level ever in its 300-year history. The European Central Bank opted for a 1 per cent rate, while the Bank of Japan (BoJ) set a target for its key overnight rate of 0.1 per cent. In October 2010, the BoJ lowered the target to a range of between 0.0 and 0.1 per cent, declaring that it would maintain a 'virtual zero interest rate policy' until the deflation threat dissipated and 'medium to long-term price stability is in sight' (Fujikawa and Wessel, 2010).

Despite these dramatic reductions, policy rates even at such low levels were considered insufficient and supplemented by 'quantitative easing', a term used for unconventional ways to continue easing monetary policy by purchasing large quantities of financial instruments from the market (Borio and Disyatat, 2009; Söderström and Westermark, 2009). Central bank actions under this heading included direct lending to the private sector (by the Federal Reserve), purchases of government securities from the non-bank sector (by the Bank of England), and greatly extended open market operations (by the European Central Bank and the Bank of Japan). The first round of quantitative easing (QE1) largely took place in 2009 (in the United States, QE1 saw the Fed purchasing US$1.7 trillion of government and mortgage bonds between January 2009 and March 2010). A second round (QE2) was launched in October 2010 by the BoJ and in November 2010 in the United States (with the Fed to purchase $850–900 billion of medium- to long-term Treasury bonds by the end of June 2011).

In all cases, the idea of quantitative easing was to increase the size of the central bank's balance sheet and inject new cash (base money) into the economy; banks in turn gain additional reserves and the money supply grows (Mathai, 2009). It is perhaps ironic that it has taken the financial crisis for actual monetary policy to align with textbook accounts. In these accounts, the central bank expands the money supply by open market purchases of securities, rather than manipulating policy rates. However, the quantitative easing experiment didn't work as many expected, at least to those brought up on textbook accounts of the money multiplier in which an increase in bank reserves is multiplied into a larger increase in broad money. As can be seen in Table 8.1, money multiplier effects of textbook dimensions failed to materialize and the increase in reserves has been much

Table 8.1 Changes in bank reserves, broad money and bank lending, June 2008–June 2009

	Change in bank reserves held at central bank (%)	Change in broad money (%)	Change in bank lending to private sector (%)
UK	372	2	1
USA	1853	9	4
Eurozone	122	4	2

Sources: Based on Goodhart et al. (2009) and Goodhart (2010).

larger than the expansion of broad money. Reminiscent of the view dating back to 1935 that expansionary monetary policy is 'like pushing on a string',[3] the *Wall Street Journal* (2010) argued that 'the Fed can print more money, but it cannot make people lend, borrow or invest' (p. 27).

Again, as in the 1930s, the culprit was a large increase in banks' holdings of reserves at the central bank, reviving the question posed by Cagan (1965) about the large build-up of reserve ratios of national or member banks in the United States in the 1930s, of whether the reserve holdings were desired or truly excess. In the recent episode, banks at September 2010 had more than US$1 trillion in cash reserves sitting idle in excess reserves at Federal Reserve banks. One view is that 'with little demand for loans and the need to rebuild their balance sheets, banks are hoarding the mountains of cash being shovelled their way by the US Federal Reserve' (Gongloff, 2010). In effect, much of the freshly printed money from QE1 ended up idling away in the banking system. The alternative view (Keister and McAndrews, 2009) is that the reserves are a by-product of the Fed's new lending facilities and asset purchase programmes. A particularly significant change occurred in October 2008, when the Fed began, for the first time, the payment of interest on bank reserves, a change which for all practical purposes can render the money multiplier inoperable. However, no calculations are presented by Keister and McAndrews to account for the $1 trillion reserves, and the explanation they provide is not readily applicable for the parallel experience in the other countries.

Nevertheless, quantitative easing can still proceed even in the absence of the money multiplier effect, as Milton Friedman apparently argued in the case of Japan in 1998.

> The Bank of Japan can buy government bonds on the open market. . . . Most of the proceeds will end up in commercial banks, adding to their reserves and enabling them to expand open-market purchases. But whether they do so or not, the money supply growth would have the same effect as always. After a

> year or so, the economy will expand more rapidly; output will grow, and after another delay, inflation will increase moderately. (Quoted in Wessel, 2010: 27)

That is, the first-round effects of open market operations can still come into play, even if subsequent rounds do not.

This leads us to the question of why QE1 and QE2 were introduced. Quantitative easing seemingly was considered necessary because conventional interest rate policy had not worked, or was regarded as by itself inadequate. With nominal policy rates at, or close to, the zero lower bound (ZLB) constraint, the potential for further cuts had been exhausted. Monetary policy was 'in a corner, short of bullets' (Evans, 2010: 30). Nevertheless, the question that remains to be answered is why conventional policy responses did not work.

Conventional monetary policy in all the major financial markets follows a relatively common template. The central bank controls the shortest money market rate (overnight interbank rate, bill rate) with the aim of altering the interest rates charged to the general public in banking and other financial markets, and eventually economic activity and prices. A number of reasons can be suggested for why such policy may not succeed. First, long-term rates may not decline to the required extent, and engaging in open markets operations at longer maturities under quantitative easing may seek to 'twist' the yield curve in order to stimulate investment and other spending.[4] Second, reflecting the view that the Basle Accord on capital adequacy operates in a pro-cyclical manner (Terry, 2009), banks may be unwilling to lend because of a capital shortage and the need to rebuild capital reserves. Third, recalling Irving Fisher's (1933) 'debt deflation hypothesis' advanced in the wake of the Great Depression, a process of de-leveraging in the private sector may have left many creditors unwilling to borrow. In effect, the low interest rates fail to offset the depressing effect of the liquidation of bad debts.

CAN INTEREST RATES BE TOO LOW?

Conventional wisdom is that interest rates should be raised during an upswing in the economy and lowered during a downswing. But how low should rates go? There are, consequently, some other points that need to be taken into account in the assessment of monetary policy responses, and these revolve around the question: can interest rates be lowered too far?

One issue is that if interest rates are lowered to zero, banks can borrow at very low rates, invest in government bonds and other safe long-term securities, and still make handsome profits. In fact, the ultra-low rates are seen as 'a semi-deliberate subsidy to help nurse banks back to health' (*The Economist*, 2010b: 70). A leading critic of this policy is Thomas Hoenig, President of the Federal Reserve Bank of Kansas City, and a notable dissenter on Federal Open Market Committee decisions. He opposes super-low interest rates because:

> Wall Street banks and large corporations are currently able to borrow for almost nothing and either hoard cash, make acquisitions, or invest in long-term Treasuries for a guaranteed profit. Retirees and other bank depositors effectively subsidize this borrowing and earn almost nothing on their savings. It's a distortion, and it favours the large institutions over smaller ones and Wall Street over the saver. I just don't like it. It's not fair. (Reported in Barrett and Lanman, 2010: 78)

According to calculations made for *Bloomberg Business Week* by research firm SNL Financial, in the two years after the Federal Reserve started cutting interest rates in September 2007, US banks booked an extra $50 billion of interest income (Henry, 2010). In achieving this result, the banks have been aided by the fact, noted above, that longer-term rates have remained relatively high, while the strong preference for Federally insured accounts has allowed banks to lower rates on savings accounts. In these circumstances, why would banks want to engage in potentially risky lending? Further, if depositors simply keep funds in short-term cash deposits, banks' liabilities become increasingly short-term and their reluctance to lend intensifies because of medium-term funding gaps in their liabilities structure.

Following on from Hoenig's observations, another issue with the ultra-low interest rate policy is that it has been 'hell on savers' (Henry, 2010: 63). Conventional interest policy, at least in terms of the UK 'credit counterparts' approach (Lewis and Mizen, 2000: Chapter 13), focuses on the asset side of banks' balance sheets, and is designed to encourage increased lending by lowering borrowing costs. Because so many in Anglo-Saxon countries borrow against their own home and use credit, there is a predisposition to consider interest rates from the viewpoint of people with a mortgage. Yet, there is another side of the coin. The level of interest rates also has a big influence on the income received from saving, as indicated by the aphorism quoted by Walter Bagehot 'John Bull can stand many things but he cannot stand two per cent', expressing savers' distaste for very low interest rates (Buttonwood, 2010) – and 2 per cent was indeed as low as Bank of England interest rates went in its first three centuries of operation. For many people in retirement with a portfolio containing 'cash' (i.e. money market investments) and securities (i.e. bonds, mortgages) higher interest rates are a blessing and lower rates force a curtailment of expenditure.

For those saving toward retirement, for example through superannuation schemes, low interest rates mean that more capital will need to be built up in order to buy an income in retirement through investments or through an annuity. There is the need to 'save now rather than starve later' (ibid.: 76), and this saving must be done by reducing current spending. Interest rate reductions hurt savers' incomes at the same time as they make borrowers better off. Savers are further punished in real terms should inflation later rise. In an environment in which borrowers may be reluctant to take on more debt, might interest rates that are 'too' low do more harm than good?

Indeed, such a scenario has been argued in the case of Japan following the collapse of the 'bubble economy' in 1990. The Bank of Japan's target overnight call rate that peaked at 6 per cent per annum in 1990 had collapsed to zero by 1998. Except for a brief period in 2000, the target rate remained at zero until mid-2006 (only to fall again in this case to 0.0 – 0.1 per cent per annum in the wake of the global financial crisis). Consequently Japanese interest rates were held effectively at zero for nearly a decade, yet failed to revive the economy. The standard explanation (e.g. Ernst & Young, 2010) is that banks, beset by non-performing loans and losses on other assets, and needing to rebuild capital, refused to lend, and the customary transmission process of monetary policy was broken. At the same time, in order to resolve their balance sheet problems, non-financial corporate sector borrowers devoted their energies to de-leveraging and paying down debt, and were unwilling to borrow at any price (Koo, 2009: 5). Nevertheless, the low interest rates supported corporate restructuring and helped banks to write down bad loans, nursing corporate Japan back to health, but at the expense of the household sector whose interest income was virtually wiped out (Nakamae, 2007; 2010). Household interest income fell from 39 trillion yen in 1991 to less than 5 trillion yen following the interest rate cuts (even though interest-bearing deposits of Japanese households increased from 600 to 800 billion yen). Despite a fall in the household savings ratio from 15 per cent in 1991 to 2.5 per cent in 2006, Japanese consumption remained stagnant for more than a decade. On this basis, Nakamae argued that an increase (more correctly, a normalization) of Japanese interest rates from zero would revive households' interest income and expand consumption. It might also have seen a resurgence of small companies, which are reliant on domestic (rather than export) demand and account for three-quarters of employment in the economy. In effect, interest rates were too low for the economy's good.[5]

Finally, a third issue with low rates comes from the potential distortions to the allocation of capital and risk-taking, of which the Bank for International Settlements warns in its latest annual report (BIS, 2010). The BIS notes:

> . . . keeping interest rates very low comes at a cost – a cost that is growing with time. Experience teaches us that prolonged periods of unusually low rates cloud assessments of financial risks, induce a search for yield. . . . Furthermore, the resulting yield differentials encourage unsustainable capital flows to countries with high interest rates. . . . Inflows are important contributors to growth, especially in emerging market economies. In the current situation, however, they may lead to further asset price increases and have an inflationary impact on the macro-economy (pp. 45–6).

According to one commentator, Benjamin Franklin's original aphorism should be updated to 'in this world there is nothing certain, except death and taxes and asset bubbles' (Oliver, 2010). Greenspan's ultra-low interest rate policy in 2001–04 preceded, and arguably fuelled, the US housing bubble of 2005–6. Will the Bernanke Fed generate another asset boom and bust? It would seem that, in seeking to lower interest rates below those resulting from the policy rate reductions, QE2 is deliberately designed not only to encourage homeowners, consumers and businesses to borrow, spend and invest but to 'also drive investors into stocks, corporate bonds and other riskier investments offering higher returns' (Hilsenbath, 2010: 22). To argue, as many do, that this policy is unlikely to spark an asset boom in the United States, at least under present circumstances, ignores the potential global consequences that could follow. To the extent that countries maintain fixed currency pegs to the US (such as Hong Kong) or resist upward pressure in their currencies by buying US dollars (for example China) or keep their interest rates artificially low, they will be importing easy US monetary policy and adding to the increase in global liquidity (as happened under Greenspan). That liquidity could in turn fuel the next boom. Will it be in gold, Asian property, Asian equities, commodity and food prices, resources stocks or renewables? Or, will it be possible to stop things from getting out of control? Only time will tell.

NOTES

1. The estimation proceeds as follows. First, an *ex post* real Federal funds rate is calculated, subtracting the GDP deflator as the inflation measure from the effective Federal funds rate. The *ex ante* real rate is then estimated by regressing the *ex post* rate on a constant time trend and four lags of the nominal Federal funds rate, the deviation of GDP from trend and inflation. The fitted values of this equation are estimates of the *ex ante* real Federal funds rate.
2. Billi also compares the policy setting with that called for by the optimal Taylor rule based on a macroeconomic model of the economy that comprises a Taylor rule, Phillips curve, a household spending relationship, and a loss function. It is found that the Federal funds rate was on average 1.25 percentage points too low in 2001–03 and 1.5 percentage points too low in 2004–05 (Billi, 2009).

3. Although the expression is widely attributed to Keynes, it would appear to have first surfaced in Congressional Hearings on 18 March 1935. According to Roger G. Sandilands and John Harold Wood, the phrase was introduced by Congressman T. Alan Goldsborough in 1935, supporting Federal Reserve chairman Marriner Eccles in Congressional hearings on the Banking Act of 1935:

   '**Governor Eccles**: Under present circumstances, there is very little, if any, that can be done.
   Congressman Goldsborough: You mean you cannot push on a string.
   Governor Eccles: That is a very good way to put it, one cannot push on a string. We are in the depths of a depression and . . . beyond creating an easy money situation through reduction of discount rates, there is very little, if anything, that the reserve organization can do to bring about recovery.'

   See http://www.barrypopik.com/index.php/new_york_city/entry/you_cant_push_a_string/, accessed 11 December 2010.
4. Again there are parallels between recent policy and monetary events in earlier times. In 1961, under 'Operation Twist', the Fed sought to lower long-term rates relative to short-term rates in order to stimulate the economy. For an assessment see Ross (1966).
5. Nakamae suggested other benefits would flow from raising or normalizing interest rates. It would stem the leakage overseas of Japanese savings in search of higher returns, and thus strengthen the yen, lower the import costs of small businesses, and reduce the vulnerability (revealed clearly in 2009) of the Japanese economy to overseas demand for its exportables. The author is grateful to Andrew Smithers for supplying the references to Tadashi Nakamae's views.

REFERENCES

Barrett, P.M. and S. Lanman (2010), 'Thomas Hoenig is Fed Up', *Bloomberg Businessweek*, 27 September–3 October, pp. 74–8.

Batson, Andrew (2009), 'Experts deny Asian "savings glut" caused the global crisis', *The Australian*, 6 July, p. 22.

Bernanke, B.S. (2005), 'The global savings glut and the US current account deficit', Sandridge Lecture, Virginia Association of Economists, Richmond, Virginia, 14 April.

Billi, R.M. (2009), 'Was monetary policy optimal during past deflation scares?', *Economic Review*, Federal Reserve Bank of Kansas City, pp. 67–98.

BIS (2010), 'Low interest rates: do the risks outweigh the rewards?', BIS 80th Annual Report, Basel, Switzerland: Bank for International Settlements, pp. 36–46.

Borio, C. and P. Disyatat (2009), 'Unconventional monetary policies: an appraisal', BIS Working Papers No. 292, Basel, Switzerland: Bank for International Settlements.

Buttonwood (2010), 'Another paradox of thrift', *The Economist*, 18–24 September, p. 76.

Cagan, Phillip (1965), *Determinants and Effects of Changes in the Stock of Money, 1875–1960*, New York and London: National Bureau of Economic Research, Columbia University Press.

Colvin, Geoff (2010), 'Alan Greenspan fights back', *Fortune*, 1 March, pp. 56–60.

Coy, P., P.M. Barrett and C. Terhuyne (2010), 'Shredding the dream', *Bloomberg Businessweek*, 25–31 October, pp. 76–86.

The Economist (2010a), 'It wasn't us', *The Economist*, 20 March, p. 68.

The Economist (2010b), 'Easy-money riders', *The Economist*, 17 July, p. 70.

Ernst & Young (2010), 'What lies ahead? The Japan precedent', London: Ernst & Young.

Evans, K. (2010), 'In a corner, short of bullets', *Wall Street Journal*, 28–9 August, p. 30.

Fisher, Irving (1933), 'The debt-deflation theory of great depressions', *Econometrica*, **1**, 337–57.

Fujikawa, M. and D. Wessel (2010), 'The scramble is on to reflate stalled economies and restrain currencies', *The Australian*, 7 October, p. 25.

Gongloff, Mark (2010), 'Libor may no longer be the leading credit-stress indicator', *The Australian*, 6 September, p. 25.

Goodhart, C.A.E. (2010), 'Money, credit and bank behaviour: need for a new approach', Giblin Workshop, University of Tasmania, 15 February.

Goodhart, C., M. Baker and C. Sleeman (2009), 'QE: necessary, successful and ready to wind down', *UK Economics*, Morgan Stanley Research Europe, 23 November.

Henry, David (2010), 'Lousy CD rates? Guess who wins', *Bloomberg Businessweek*, 15 February, p. 63.

Hilsenbath, J. (2010), 'Fed's $US600bn to fire up the economy', *Wall Street Journal*, 5 November, p. 22.

Iley, R.A. and M.K. Lewis (2007), *Untangling the U.S. Deficit. Evaluating Causes, Cures and Global Imbalances*, Cheltenham, UK and Northampton, MA, USA: Edward Elgar Publishing.

International Monetary Fund (2006), 'United States: selected issues. Chapter 1: The attractiveness of US financial markets: the example of mortgage securitization', Washington: International Monetary Fund, pp. 4–13.

Keister, T. and J.J. McAndrews (2009), 'Why are banks holding so many excess reserves?', *Current issues in Economics and Finance*, Federal Reserve Bank of New York, **15**(8), 1–11.

Kliesen, K.L. (2006), 'Families digging deeper into debt', *The Regional Economist*, Federal Reserve Bank of Saint Louis, July, pp. 12–13.

Koo, R.C. (2009), 'The age of balance sheet recessions: what post-2008 US, Europe and China can learn from Japan 1990–2005', available at http://www.imf.org/external/am/ 2009/pdf/APDKoo.pdf, accessed 5 June 2010.

Lewis, M.K. (2009), 'The origins of the sub-prime crisis: inappropriate policies, regulations, or both?', *Accounting Forum*, **33**(2), 114–26.

Lewis, M.K. (2010), 'An Islamic economic perspective on the global financial crisis', in Steve Kates (ed.), *Macroeconomic Theory and its Failings: Alternative Perspectives on the Global Financial Crisis*, Cheltenham, UK and Northampton, MA, USA: Edward Elgar Publishing.

Lewis, M.K. and P.D. Mizen (2000), *Monetary Economics*, Oxford: Oxford University Press.

Lim, G.C., S. Tsiaplias and C.L. Chua (2010), 'Bank and official interest rates: how do they interact over time?', Melbourne Institute Working Paper No. 4/10, Melbourne Institute of Applied Economic and Social Research.

Mathai, Koshy (2009), 'What is monetary policy?', *Finance and Development*, **46**(3), 46–7.

Mishkin, F (1981), 'The real interest rate: an empirical investigation', *Carnegie-Rochester Conference Series on Public Policy*, **15**, 151–200.

Nakamae, Tadashi (2007), 'Weak yen conundrum', *The International Economy*, Winter, pp. 42–5.

Nakamae, Tadashi (2010), 'How Japan could lead return to durable growth', *Financial Times*, available at http://www.ft.com/cms/s/a5295546-3c0a-11df-9412-00144feabdc0,dwp_uuid=518cc03a-2285-11dd-93a9-000077b07658, accessed 28 May 2010.

Oliver, Shane (2010), 'Waiting for the next big bubble', *The Australian*, 9 October, p. 8.

Pisani-Ferry, J. and I. Santos (2009), 'Reshaping the global economy', *Finance & Development*, **46**(1), 8–12.

Romer, C. and D. Romer (2002), 'The evolution of economic understanding and postwar stabilisation policy. Rethinking stabilisation policy', Federal Reserve Bank of Kansas City, available at http://www.kansascityfed.org/publicat/Sympos/2002/pdf/S02 RomerandRomer.pdf, accessed 23 May 2010.

Ross, M.H. (1966), '"Operation Twist": a mistaken policy?', *Journal of Political Economy*, **74**(2), 195–9.

Söderström, U. and A. Westermark (2009), 'Monetary policy when the interest rate is zero', *Sveriges Riksbank Economic Review*, **2**, 5–30.

Taylor, John (ed.) (1999), *Monetary Policy Rules*, Chicago, IL: University of Chicago Press.

Taylor, John (2007), 'Housing and monetary policy', Federal Reserve Bank of Kansas City, *Jackson Hole Economic Symposium*, pp. 463–76.

Terry, Chris (2009), 'The new Basel Capital Accord: a major advance at a turbulent time', *Agenda*, **16**(1), 25–43.

Wall Street Journal (2010), 'Helicopter Ben at the ready', *Review & Outlook*, *Wall Street Journal*, 12 August, p. 27.

Weber, A.A. (2008), 'Financial market stability', *Review*, **78**, Financial Markets Group Research Centre, pp. 1–2.

Wessel, David (2010), 'Friedman would accept pumping money to stimulate the economy', *Wall Street Journal*, 29 October, p. 27.

9. After the crash of 2008: financial reform in an age of plutocracy

Robert E. Prasch*

> At the heart of every [financial] crisis is a political problem – powerful people, and the firms they control, have gotten out of hand. Unless this is dealt with as part of the stabilization program, all the government has done is provide an unconditional bailout.
>
> Simon Johnson, Economist, MIT & former Chief Economist, IMF, in testimony submitted to the US Congress, 19 November 2009

> In Washington, the view is that the banks are to be regulated, and my view is that Washington and the regulators are there to serve the banks.
>
> Spencer Bachus (R – AL), Chair-designate, Financial Services Committee, US House of Representatives, 13 December 2010

I THE POLITICS OF THE 'DAY AFTER': WHO WILL SHOULDER THE LOSSES?

Several studies have considered how the current financial catastrophe came about, along with the ideas and decisions that facilitated it (Cassidy, 2009; Johnson and Kwak, 2010; McLean and Nocera, 2010; Muolo and Padilla, 2008; Prasch, 2010). Less frequently contemplated has been the question as to who will take the substantial losses from the tremendous quantity of poor quality financial assets associated with the housing bubble. Small losses, rightly or wrongly, are generally treated as a 'personal problem'. But when losses become this large, who is to take them is inevitably transformed into a pressing political question.

As things stand, three broad classes of persons have emerged as leading candidates to absorb these losses. They are: (1) the shareholders and bonus earners at the major banks, that is to say the firms that actually put together these securities and sold them into the markets; (2) the creditors and other counterparties of these same banks, including those who guaranteed this debt with insurance contracts known as 'credit-default swaps'; and (3) taxpayers. The latter are vulnerable either directly through the Department of the Treasury, or indirectly through the lending facilities of the Federal Reserve System, Federal Home Loan Bank System, and the Federal Deposit Insurance Corporation.

Of course, from the beginning it was understood that homeowners, along with the real estate and construction industries, would lose. At the time of writing 12 million families have already lost their homes along with the savings that they believed that asset represented. With homeowner wealth diminished and the real estate and construction industries in such trouble, it is no surprise that the unemployment rate achieved postwar highs. Today it seems almost to be stuck in place.

Incumbent politicians, bank spokespersons, and too many economists like to present themselves, along with their analysis, as being above the 'din' of everyday politics. The long-standing and widely-approved political rhetoric of times such as these is that all of us must 'share sacrifices'. But in the real world, few things are as political as the allocation of large unexpected losses. This truth was revealed to the victims of the Great Mississippi Flood of 1927 and to the steerage passengers on the rapidly sinking *Titanic*. In each instance they learned that the 'sacrifice' about to be borne would be anything but proportionately 'shared'. As a rule, tacit power becomes explicit during a disaster. So it is today.

The group that first grasped the enormity of the current catastrophe was the senior management of America's largest financial firms (although we now know that several of them were either oblivious or in denial). They, almost alone, had 'real time' access to critical information concerning the size, quality and performance of the debts on the books of their institutions. This prior knowledge gave them the opportunity to move quickly to protect themselves.

Some bought themselves and their firms some time by engaging in 'creative accounting' to hide problems from the markets and possibly regulators (Richard Fuld of Lehman Brothers with the assistance of Ernst & Young). Some sold large blocks of stock in their own institutions (Angelo Mozilo of Countrywide Financial) even as others (Stan O'Neill of Merrill Lynch) reached for lavish 'golden parachutes' as their firms imploded. Some did all three. None of this was exceptional and even less of it was ethical. Some of it may have been illegal. Little of it was surprising.

Having ready access to ideologically friendly regulatory institutions presented senior bankers with a second advantage in the scramble to minimize their own, and their firms', portion of the 'shared sacrifice'. Yet, despite the substantial backroom deals made between the authorities and the major banks, and the famously generous terms provided, the listed price of bank shares declined dramatically. Many financial institutions went into receivership, but these were mostly small- and medium-sized banks and a few larger firms that once competed directly with Goldman Sachs.

Bank creditors and counterparties, to the extent that they were owed money by the largest American banks, did substantially better. The reason, of course, was that from the beginning of the crisis (which I date to the first large central bank interventions on 9–10 August 2007), the government's agenda was to prevent the major banks from having to engage in a 'fire sale' of 'troubled' assets to shore up their capital. This, as we will see, was accomplished by concocting innumerable ways to allow them to minimize the loan write-downs that would have to be formally acknowledged. While it may not have been the primary intention, this program worked to the distinct advantage of the creditors and counter-parties of these large institutions. Again, such extraordinary measures were not generally granted to small- or medium-sized banks, of which more than 350 have been put in receivership by the Federal Deposit Insurance Corporation (FDIC) since 2007.

The third group eligible to accept large losses is, of course, taxpayers. This likelihood was considerably enhanced to the extent that their elected representatives were not inclined – for a variety of political, financial and personal reasons, including simple embarrassment – to admit to the depth or breadth of the problem. Lacking firm representation during the crisis, a consequence was that taxpayers were de facto selected to be the group to absorb the lion's share of these losses. There are several reasons for this failure of representation despite the nation's ostensibly democratic political institutions.

The first is that this disaster has a strong bipartisan parentage, one going back at least 35 years (Galbraith, 2008). Any blame would quickly rebound upon the leadership of one's own party, so discussions of the origin of the problem have been marginalized. This also explains the large, and largely disingenuous, chorus of voices taking the 'high road' and saying that 'now is not the time to find blame', while simultaneously asserting that 'no one could have seen it coming'. Second, the senior leadership of both parties remains deeply committed to an ideology that insists that financial markets are self-regulating. Even for those who do not believe it, the dominant strategy is to pretend to, so as to avoid being asked why you did not sound the alarm or act earlier to protect the public. The third is what we might call the 'Sutton Rule'. Asked why he robbed banks, Willie Sutton famously answered, 'because that's where the money is'. Under American campaign laws and practices, substantial sums of money are required for elections, and bankers have access to such sums. Fourth, many politicians and their more astute and ethically flexible advisors enjoy ready access to the 'revolving door' between high political office and Wall Street. These 'opportunities' provide public officials with highly lucrative and not overly burdensome sinecures between periods of 'public service' (Phil Gramm, Rahm Emanuel, Lawrence Summers, Jeb Bush, Tony Blair and the late Richard Holbrook are only a few prominent examples of the many who have enriched themselves in this manner). The hope for such sinecures is also an effective disciplining device for the even larger number of politicians, regulators, and legislative assistants who aspire to such jobs. Fifth, and perhaps of most importance, taxpayers are a large group of people with multiple and various motivations, political interests and ideological commitments. They also have pressing concerns and pleasant distractions such as raising a family, doing household chores, or going to work. By contrast, senior bank managers are a small number of persons sharing a powerful commitment to the maximization of their own wealth. They also have access to virtually boundless social, legal, political, financial and public relations resources with which to shape and sway popular opinion – and they have deployed these liberally (McCarty et al., 2010; Johnson and Kwak, 2010).

Despite these multiple advantages, this crash was so large, the misery created so widespread, and the bankers' actions that facilitated it so transparently venal, that it looked as if the interests of taxpayers and citizens might get some traction. Alas, it did not turn out that way.

II RESUSCITATE OR RESTRUCTURE? THE PROBLEM OF 'VISION' IN THE RESPONSE TO THE FINANCIAL CRISIS

Why was it, despite the clearly wrecked balance sheets of the nation's largest banks, that the authorities did not comply with the Federal Deposit Insurance Corporation Improvement Act of 1991? Drawing upon the major lesson of the Savings and Loan (S&L) crisis of the 1980s, this law mandates that the authorities take Prompt Corrective Action (PCA) when a bank is in trouble. The reason for this law was that after the dismal S&L episode the consensus lesson was that a policy of regulatory forbearance (that is keeping insolvent institutions open) increased the levels of fraud, economic dislocation, and eventual clean-up costs. Why, then, were the nation's largest failed banks not put into receivership? After all, it was the law (Black, 2010b).

A key obstacle was that the vision of the self-regulating market, and especially the self-regulating financial market, *remains* at the core of American regulatory practices (Cassidy, 2009: Chapters 1–8; Johnson,

2009; Kregel, 2007; Prasch, 2011a). This would appear to be counter-intuitive. After all, by the time of the 2008 presidential election, several of the leading lights of this catastrophically failed doctrine, including some of its most prominent champions, had acknowledged that what they once so ardently believed had been demonstrated to be disastrously false. Even Alan Greenspan admitted to the US House of Representatives that, 'Those of us who have looked to the self-interest of lending institutions to protect shareholders' equity, myself included, are in a state of shocked disbelief' (Alan Greenspan, as cited in Andrews, 2008).

Given this state of affairs, it was and remains fascinating to witness the degree to which this fully discredited 'vision' remains the central principle behind the response to the crisis. Yet the decisions, actions and statements made by the Fed, the Bush and Obama Administrations, the Congress, the Department of Justice, and other regulatory and oversight agencies each and severally affirm this observation. It was and is repeatedly and endlessly asserted that the financial crisis was exclusively the result of an unpredicted and unpredictable 'panic' that spontaneously and inexplicably overwhelmed the nation's major financial institutions. While structural problems are mentioned periodically, they are clearly downplayed in all official pronouncements.

Let us pause to contemplate the implications of this perspective. It maintains that the nation's largest and most prominent financial institutions were for the most part ably and responsibly managed by persons of high intelligence and impeccable integrity. If mistakes were made, and it is allowed that some were, they are exclusively attributed to errors made in the honest but perhaps overly zealous pursuit of 'shareholder value' that, it is asserted, came from providing essential and desirable services to Wall Street and the 'real economy' more generally. Stated simply, the view of administration officials, senior bankers, and those paid to do their thinking was, and remains, that the crisis of 2007–09 was a classic liquidity event induced by an irrational, unfounded, but self-reinforcing crisis of confidence. Consistent with this view, bankers have repeatedly informed anyone who will listen that they too are innocent victims.

III RESPONDING TO THE CRISIS

Given these premises, the 'solution' followed directly. The immediate task was to protect essential banking functions and in particular the payments system. To that end, it was necessary for the authorities to quickly and unreservedly provide substantial 'liquidity' to the system.[1] In late 2008, as matters unexpectedly and inexplicably worsened, these initial moves were reluctantly bolstered by the extension of wide-ranging federal guarantees to the money and commercial paper markets, the takeover of several prominent institutions such as Fannie Mae, Freddie Mac, and AIG, and extensive short-term loans granted directly to the banks (technically Repo contracts) collateralized by a portion of the enormous quantities of mortgage-backed assets remaining on the books of the major banks.[2] It is sometimes grudgingly acknowledged that these moves had less than fortunate distributional consequences, with a distinct tendency to reward poor prior performance, but it has been as frequently asserted that this was the best anyone could do in such an uncertain, volatile and rapidly changing financial situation. Chaos had to be averted, and that was achieved (Blinder and Zandi, 2010).

These Fed/Treasury/Home Loan Bank Board/FDIC directed loans, guarantees and bailouts were conducted secretly so as to preserve the 'good name and reputation' of the bankers and firms that had failed so catastrophically. The reason given for this secrecy, an argument made in several judicial proceedings in the course of resisting a Freedom of Information Act suit from Bloomberg News, was that it was necessary to facilitate the restoration of 'confidence' in major financial firms.

This argument was, on its face, highly implausible. Investors, especially those with substantial sums to protect, knew that a lot of firms were insolvent and for that reason dependent upon the Fed's largesse for their survival. They could also deduce a reasonable estimate of the aggregate size of the bailout from the Fed's publically available balance sheet. It was immediately clear that the total quantity of support was very substantial.

Yet the Fed insisted that not knowing the specifics of the firms bailed out, the exact sums granted to each, or the interest rates charged, would shore up investors' confidence in the solidity of the system. The collapse in the market's valuation of the major financial firms after the bailouts provided a clear resolution to this 'debate'. Most people, especially those who had or were responsible for large sums of money, had a fairly good idea of which banks were broke, and shied away en masse.

A substantially more plausible explanation for the insistence on secrecy was that the information was being withheld to protect the Fed, and the beneficiaries of its largesse, from well-deserved public outrage and consequent political retribution (Ferguson and Johnson, 2009a; 2009b). It is equally likely that the authorities did not want the public to know the exact size and terms of these loans so that the Fed, the Treasury, and the White House could continue to represent their program as a lender-of-last-resort operation rather than a straightforward subsidy of deeply insolvent and undeserving firms.[3]

Fed Chair Ben Bernanke did demonstrate a degree of political adroitness just prior to the November 2008 elections. Claiming that he had neither the resources nor authorization to provide additional bailouts, he and Treasury Secretary Hank Paulson (the former Co-Chair of Goldman Sachs) decided that the Congress and the Executive branch should 'buy into' its bailout agenda. This had the dual effect of instantiating that the bank bailouts were a bipartisan effort while providing the Fed with political cover, which made sense in light of a pending election (Ferguson and Johnson, 2009a; 2009b). Not fully anticipated was the passion with which the public, who for the first time were being allowed some voice in what was taking place, would threaten or cajole their Congressional Representatives before the first and second roll-call votes that ended with the authorization of $700 billion for the (in)famous Troubled Asset Relief Program (TARP).

Let us recall, once again, that the presumption underlying TARP was that the core problem was bank illiquidity, not insolvency. Regrettably, the public did not accept this – by Fall 2008 – transparently false and dishonest explanation. They, correctly, understood that the banks were insolvent and further identified TARP as a crony-driven bailout. And indeed when the public balked, the bill failed initially in the House of Representatives, and the Dow Jones Index duly fell 777.68 points (6.98 per cent) on 29 September 2008.

From an elite perspective, the public's correct assessment of the situation posed something of an inconvenience, although not one so substantial as to derail the agenda. Seeing the wealth of their friends and themselves diminishing rapidly, elites did express a heartfelt anger that was as unanimous as it was deafening. To the 'great and the good' it was offensive that the 'great unwashed' would have the temerity to respond so vigorously and negatively to what their betters had deemed to be the best use of hundreds of billions of taxpayer dollars. Happily for the likes of Thomas Friedman and other savants of the conventional wisdom, order was soon restored, and the bill authorizing TARP passed on the second vote. It was insisted, however, that the House of Representatives was solely responsible for the Dow Jones Index's decline on 29 September. What wasn't explained was why the Dow continued to fall after TARP had passed; it experienced declines of 5 per cent or more on 7, 9, 15 and 22 October, 5 November and 1 December of 2008. Could it be that the existence or non-existence of TARP made little difference?

IV THE TARP AND 'STRESS TESTS' IN THEORY AND PRACTICE

Originally, TARP funds were to be used by the Treasury to directly purchase bundles of 'troubled' (translation: catastrophically failed) asset-backed securities such as Mortgage-Backed Securities (MBS), Collateralized Debt Obligations (CDO), and even Collateralized Debt Obligations Squared (CDO^2) directly from the banks (Nobel Laureate Joseph Stiglitz drew the ire of 'respectable' opinion when he so wonderfully labeled this program 'Cash for Trash'). The idea, if we can call it that, was that once the banks were freed of these 'momentarily' illiquid assets, they would willingly lend new funds, the economy would have a robust recovery, investors' 'panic' would ease, and the Treasury would be able to resell these now-recovered and nicely-performing assets back into the markets, almost certainly for a profit.

Only later did the Treasury realize that they were caught on the horns of a dilemma. If they bought the 'troubled' securities at full price the public would immediately perceive that the program was simply a bailout (Ferguson and Johnson, 2009a, 2009b; Johnson and Kwak, 2010: Chapter 6). Alternatively, if they bought these assets at prices that even remotely reflected their actual worth, they would have to be steeply discounted from the level at which they were listed on the 'asset' sides of the banks' accounting statements. Under the mark-to-market accounting rules then in effect, the banks would be forced to recognize these prices when evaluating their remaining inventory of identical or similar assets. This sudden write-down in asset values would immediately reveal the gaping holes in bank balance sheets and probably force many prominent institutions into receivership.

This, rather than public outrage, was the reason that the original plan had to be shelved. To proceed safely, changes had to be made in the rules of the Financial Accounting Standards Board (FASB), specifically FASB 157-e, thereby allowing banks to revert to risk-adjusted discounted cash-flow methods of valuing these assets. With the admirable behind-the-scenes cooperation of the newly inaugurated Obama Administration, the US Chamber of Commerce, bank lobbyists, the OCC, the SEC, and a vocal bipartisan majority of the House Financial Services Committee, the FASB was pushed aggressively to approve this change in the accounting rules. Pressed by Congress to act within the extraordinarily short period of three weeks, these changes were announced by the FASB on 2 April 2009. Then, and later, the authorities ignored the warnings and misgivings publically expressed by two of the most important professional organizations of accountants – the American Institute of Certified Professional Accountants (AICPA) and the Center for Audit Quality (CAQ).

With all reservations safely set aside, the rule was changed and illiquid mortgage-backed assets could now be assigned substantially higher valuations on bank balance sheets. The nation's major banks were suddenly

– magically – more profitable. While little was disclosed, then or now, it was widely thought that the greatest beneficiaries of this accounting sleight of hand were Citibank, Bank of America and Wells Fargo, as they were holding the largest quantities of these failed assets. The estimated enhancement in value was approximately 20 per cent.

With the rules of accounting now favorably modified, and the balance sheets of the largest banks newly refurbished, it was now safe to bring closure to the Obama Administration's first major financial rescue initiative – the 'stress tests' that were being applied with much fanfare to the 19 largest financial institutions. On 7 May, it was triumphantly claimed that only 10 of these 19 banks required additional capital and that the amount of supplementary funds required was a paltry $75 billion (Black, 2010c). Evidently, we were to believe that with all the horrendous losses in real estate lending, including the assets constructed out of these loans, the banks were close to being fully capitalized. And I have a bridge in Brooklyn for sale . . .

Although it was not immediately apparent, these 'results' affirmed what most thinking adults already understood – the 'stress tests' were merely political theater, albeit distinctly not in the tradition of Bertolt Brecht. Since the details of the tests and their standards were neither revealed to the public nor made available in any other way, the 'results' were only as good as the word of the administration.

Despite the striking continuity of economic ideas and personnel between the Bush and Obama advisors, accepting this word was nevertheless a good idea. The reason was not that the stress test results should have been interpreted as a proof that these big banks were fine, as clearly they were not. Rather, the importance of these tests was that the very act of proclaiming these 19 banks safe effectively pledged the new administration to supporting them. Politically, there was no way that these banks could be pronounced insolvent months or even a year or two after having allegedly been put through a rigorous and painstaking review. This certainly made them a safe haven for investors' money. Simultaneously, and I might add brilliantly, this performance dodged the political cost associated with a public acknowledgement that enshrining these 19 firms as 'Too Big To Fail' (TBTF) was to be the official position of the recently-inaugurated agents of 'hope and change' – the new Democratic administration and its substantial Congressional majorities. The stress tests, then, effectively eliminated any lingering doubt on the part of the world's financiers that the Bernanke–Geithner–Paulson policy of TBTF would be abandoned or modified by the incoming team of Bernanke–Geithner–Summers. Indeed, in something of an ironic twist, it has been the 'Tea Party' movement and its allies within the Republican right, not the Democrats, that has garnered popularity and political success by articulating a principled opposition to the policy of TBTF.[4]

Periodic utterances to the contrary, with this move President Obama committed the United States to socializing the losses of the nation's largest banks without asking for anything in return. No influence over management, no restraint on bank practices, no reduction in leverage or risk-taking, no say over unseemly bonuses, not even a commitment to a constructive position on reregulation. Nothing. Having asked for nothing, it was both remarkable and amusing to find that the administration was surprised – and disappointed – to discover that they got nothing in return. Yet they were. After the bailouts of the last months of the Bush Administration, and the 'stress tests'/guarantees of the first months of the Obama Administration, the managements of these failed institutions knew that – at least for themselves – the crisis had passed. They immediately made plans to grant themselves large bonuses to reward their own 'performance', and mobilized their lobbyists to resist reregulation on any terms but those they dictated.

As recounted, these sordid episodes of changed accounting standards and Potemkin stress tests were presented as 'proof' that the banks were now solvent and that the economy was well on its way to recovery. While neither statement was true, the banks were now in a position to begin rebuilding their balance sheets. This was readily accomplished through an indirect subsidy from the Fed. Banks were allowed to engage in a 'carry trade' that essentially involved (secretly) borrowing large sums from the Fed, and using these funds to take large positions in US Treasury bonds or other relatively risk-free assets, while booking the differential as profit. Being TBTF also gave these banks a substantial advantage in the regular money markets as, unlike their less fortunate competitors, they could borrow at the risk-free rate (Baker and McArthur, 2009). As mentioned, being immune to shame, bank managements then embarrassed their White House benefactors by awarding themselves with outsized bonuses as a presumptive payment for their superior 'risk-taking' and 'risk-management' skills!

The Fed, for its part, sacrificed a fair return on these funds. Since the Fed normally turns over its substantial operating profits to the Treasury, the implication was that for the duration of this operation, this sum would be substantially smaller than what otherwise might be expected. In this manner, through reduced transfers to the Treasury, Americans have indirectly subsidized these large failed financial institutions (Black, 2010c).

V CONCLUSION: THE DODD–FRANK WALL STREET REFORM AND CONSUMER PROTECTION ACT

Unsurprisingly, in light of what had come before, the flawed ideological premises and the 'invisible hand' of bankers' political influence were each highly influential throughout the process that ended with the much-heralded Frank–Dodd Wall Street Reform and Consumer Protection Act of 2010 (Popper, 2010; McCarty et al., 2010). Aside from bankers, their lobbyists, and the politicians directly engaged, most observers understood that what transpired was a woefully inadequate response (Black 2010d; Taibbi, 2010).

The Obama Administration and its Congressional allies have been insisting to one and all that the Frank–Dodd Wall Street Reform and Consumer Protection Act of 2010 was the 'most substantial reregulation of the financial system since the Great Depression'. This claim fails to mention that Dodd–Frank simply did not address the most important issues, including Too Big To Fail banks (Black, 2010a; Buiter, 2009; Cho, 2009; Flannery, 2010), the overleveraging of highly interconnected financial institutions, the perverse incentives built into executive pay (Bebchuk, 2010; Crotty, 2008), the conflicted credit-ratings agencies (Partnoy, 2006), the inadequate funding and capture of the regulatory agencies (Johnson and Kwak, 2010), and the identification and prosecution of financial fraud.

Also ignored by these triumphant claims was how much of the actual rule-making over issues such as the regulation and supervision of derivative exchanges, proprietary trading by banks holding insured deposits, capital requirements, and so on, have been delegated to the staff of various regulatory agencies to be worked out at a later date (Morgenson, 2010a; 2010b; Levine, 2010; Story, 2010). As all of the adults know, in a world where the political influence of failed banks and bankers has not – and will not – be checked, this postponement essentially grants the banks and their lobbyists 'a second bite at the apple'. The administration knows this, the banks know this, the bank lobbyists know this, and financial journalists should know this. Yet nothing is being done. Joe Nocera of *The New York Times* nicely summarizes the contrast with the 1930s:

> Indeed, watching Congress struggle just to pass even these timid reforms gives one a greater appreciation for what Congress accomplished during the Great Depression . . . No doubt the bank lobby of that era complained that their business would be ruined. But Congress went ahead and did it anyway. (Nocera, 2010)

For the most part, the banks suborned the rescue and reregulation process in plain sight. While some elements of what occurred were hidden, reasonably astute persons could largely infer what was actually going on. Yet it happened anyway. Power exerted itself just as it became time for 'shared sacrifices'. Financial burdens were doled out in almost exactly the reverse order of responsibility for what had occurred, and the process received bipartisan political blessings along the way. This, in a word, is what plutocracy is all about.

NOTES

* The author would like to thank James K. Galbraith, William K. Black, Jim Crotty and Falguni Sheth for multiple conversations over the past several years that have helped me better understand the causes and consequences of the Crash of 2008, including the multiple regulatory and political failures. They are, of course, not responsible for the errors or perspectives in this chapter.

1. Lender-of-last-resort operations were codified as principles by Walter Bagehot (1873) and are nicely summarized in Martin Mayer (2001, Ch. 5). They are that central banks should (1) lend freely; (2) on good securities; at (3) a high rate of interest. These principles have been meticulously followed in the case of sovereign nations such as Iceland and Ireland. The Fed, as was suspected all along – although the evidence has only recently come to light – grossly violated the last two of these conditions. That is to say that they loaned freely on poor securities at laughably low rates of interest. Stated simply, they provided a massive and hidden subsidy to fantastically insolvent financial institutions, including a number of foreign banks.
2. Among many others, I was surprised to learn that the major banks were holding large quantities of asset-backed securities on their books when the crisis hit. Several explanations have been advanced. It seems to be a combination of (1) unsold inventory that piled up as the crisis unfolded; (2) securities taken back on the books of the banks as a consequence of the banks having issued lines of credit or 'liquidity puts' to the 'off balance sheet' Structured Investment Vehicles (SIVs) that they created to hold these loans; and (3) banks were holding some tranches of CDOs because they had actually believed their own hype, thought that they were underpriced, and for that reason would be an excellent investment. Another possibility is that the short-term interests of managements were so dominant that they simply could not bring themselves to be concerned with the future of the institutions they managed. Some highly informed persons have taken this extreme attitude to be evidence of malfeasance, if not outright fraud.
3. Thanks to the Federal Reserve Sunshine Act guided through the Senate by Bernard Sanders (I-VT) and in the House by Congressman Ron Paul (R-TX), the Fed was finally (1 December 2010) forced to disclose the details of the loans they made between 2007–09. While there are few surprises vis-à-vis the identities of the firms and the size of the loans, the terms of these loans turned out to be even more generous than the most cynical of us had imagined. And I can be cynical.
4. In one of the most dishonest moments of this entire episode – and there have been so many – on 16 December 2010, Secretary of the Treasury Timothy Geithner reported to the US Senate that the TARP program 'brought stability to the financial system and the economy at a fraction of the expected costs'. The estimate he offered was $25 billion. His carefully prepared statement suggested that the government would, if anything, come out ahead on the sweetheart deals and massive subsidies granted to the financial sector by the Fed and other government institutions. It was disappointing, but not surprising, that this statement was accepted by the media and the District's 'chattering classes' as proof that in the end the financial sector was not bailed out (Black, 2010d).

BIBLIOGRAPHY

Andrews, Edmund (2008), 'Greenspan concedes error on regulation', *The New York Times*, 24 October, B1.

Bagehot, Walter (1873), *Lombard Street: A Description of the Money Market*, Henry S. King & Co.

Baker, Dean and Travis McArthur (2009), 'The value of the "too big to fail" big bank subsidy', Center for Economic and Policy Research, Issue Brief (September).

Bebchuk, Lucian A. (2010), 'Regulating bankers' pay', *Georgetown Law Journal*, **98**, 247–87.

Black, William K. (2010a), 'Too big to regulate: systematically dangerous institutions – the US, Iceland, and Ireland', *Benzinga.com*, 6 December.

Black, William K. (2010b), 'If Obama thinks that response to the S&L debacle failed, why is he adopting it?', *The Huffington Post*, 1 November.

Black, William K. (2010c), 'No Mr President, Larry Summers did not resolve the financial crisis for a pittance, he just papered over the problem', *The Huffington Post*, 28 October.

Black, William K. (2010d), 'Why the Financial Reform Bill won't prevent another crisis', *CNNMoney.com*, 26.July.

Blinder, Alan and Mark Zandi (2010), 'How the great recession was brought to an end', available at http://www.economy.com/mark-zandi/documents/End-of-Great-Recession.pdf.

Bubchuk, Lucian A. (2010), 'How to fix bankers' pay', *Daedalus*, **139**(4) (Fall).

Buiter, Willem H. (2009), 'Too big to fail is too big', *FT.Com/Maverecon*, 24 June.

Cassidy, John (2009), *How Markets Fail: The Logic of Economic Calamities*, New York: Farrar, Straus and Giroux.

Cho, David (2009), 'Banks "too big to fail" have grown even bigger: behemoths born of the bailout reduce consumer choice, tempt corporate moral hazard', *Washington Post*, 28 August.

Crotty, James (2008), 'Structural causes of the Global Financial Crisis: a critical assessment of the "New Financial Architecture"', Working Paper No. 180, Political Economy Research Institute, Amherst, MA: University of Massachusetts.

Ferguson, Thomas and Robert Johnson (2009a), 'Too big to bail: the "Paulson Put" presidential politics, and the global financial meltdown: Part I: from shadow financial system to shadow bailout', *International Journal of Political Economy*, **38**(1) (Spring), 3–34.

Ferguson, Thomas and Robert Johnson (2009b), 'Too big to bail: the "Paulson Put" presidential politics, and the global financial meltdown: Part II: fatal reversal – single payer and back', *International Journal of Political Economy*, **38**(2) (Summer), 5–45.

Flannery, Mark J. (2010), 'What to do about TBTF?', presented at the Federal Reserve Bank of Atlanta Financial Markets Conference, 'Up from the ashes: the financial system after the crisis', 12 May.

Galbraith, James K. (2008), *The Predator State: How Conservatives Abandoned the Free Market and Why Liberals Should Too*, New York: Free Press.

Helleiner, Eric (1994), *States and the Reemergence of Global Finance: From Bretton Woods to the 1990s*, Ithaca, NY: Cornell University Press.

Johnson, Simon (2009), 'Written testimony submitted to the Congressional Oversight Panel', 19 November.
Johnson, Simon (2010), 'Implications of the "Volker rules" for financial stability', testimony submitted to the Senate Banking Committee, 4 February.
Johnson, Simon and James Kwak (2010), *13 Bankers: The Wall Street Takeover and the Next Financial Meltdown*, New York: Pantheon.
Kotlikoff, Laurence J. (2010), 'Mervyn King has it right – our financial system is the worst', *The Huffington Post*, 9 November.
Kregel, Jan (2007), 'The natural instability of financial markets', Working Paper No. 523, Annandale-on-Hudson, New York: The Levy Economics Institute of Bard College.
Lazonick, William and Mary O'Sullivan (2000), 'Maximizing shareholder value: a new ideology for corporate governance', *Economy and Society*, **29**(1), 13–35.
Levine, Ross (2010), 'An autopsy of the US financial system', Working Paper No. 15956, National Bureau of Economic Research.
Lewis, Michael (2010), 'The mystery of disappearing proprietary traders', *Bloomberg.com*, 29 September.
Mattingly, Phil and Robert Schmidt (2010), 'How senate's "stupid" derivatives rule emerged, survives', *Bloomberg.com*, 6 May.
Mayer, Martin (2001), *The Fed: The Inside Story of How the World's Most Powerful Financial Institution Drives the Markets*, New York: The Free Press.
McCarty, Nolan, Keith Poole, Thomas Romer and Howard Rosenthal (2010), 'Political fortunes: on finance and its regulation', *Daedalus*, **139**(4) (Fall), 1–13.
McLean, Bethany and Joe Nocera (2010), *All the Devils are Here: The Hidden History of the Financial Crisis*, New York: Penguin.
Minsky, Hyman P. (1982), *Can 'It' Happen Again?*, Armonk, NY: M.E. Sharpe.
Morgenson, Gretchen (2010a), 'It's not over until it's in the rules', *The New York Times*, 29 August, p. BU1.
Morgenson, Gretchen (2010b), 'Strong enough for tough stains?', *The New York Times*, 26 June, p. BU1.
Muolo, Paul and Mathew Padilla (2008), *Chain of Blame: How Wall Street Caused the Mortgage and Credit Crisis*, Hoboken, NJ: John Wiley & Sons.
Nocera, Joe (2010), 'A dubious way to prevent financial crisis', *The New York Times*, 5 June, p. B1.
Partnoy, Frank (1999), 'The Siskel and Ebert of financial markets: two thumbs down for the credit rating agencies', *Washington University Law Quarterly*, **77**(3), 619–712.
Partnoy, Frank (2006), 'How and why credit rating agencies are not like other gatekeepers', in Yasuyuki Fuchita and Robert E. Litan (eds), *Financial Gatekeepers: Can They Protect Investors?*, Washington, DC: Brookings Institution Press.
Popper, Nathaniel (2010), 'Financial Reform Law offers look at lobbyist efforts to shape it', *Los Angeles Times*, 15 November.
Prasch, Robert E. (2004), '"Shifting risk": the divorce of risk from reward in American capitalism', *Journal of Economic Issues*, **38**(2): 405–12.
Prasch, Robert E. (2007), 'The economics of fraud', manuscript, Middlebury College Department of Economics.
Prasch, Robert E. (2010), 'Bankers gone wild: the crash of 2008', Chapter 11 in Steve Kates (ed.), *Macroeconomic Theory and its Failings: Alternative Perspectives on the Global Financial Crisis*, Cheltenham, UK and Northampton, MA, USA: Edward Elgar Publishing.

Prasch, Robert E. (2011a), 'The instability of financial markets: a critique of efficient markets theory', Chapter 5 in Joelle J. Leclaire, Tae-Hee Jo and Jane E. Knodell (eds), *Heterodox Analysis of Financial Crisis and Reform: History, Politics and Economics*, Cheltenham, UK and Northampton, MA, USA: Edward Elgar Publishing.

Prasch, Robert E. (2011b), 'The financial crash of 2008: an illustrative instance of the separation of risk from reward in American capitalism', Chapter 3 in Martha Starr (ed.), *Consequences of Economic Downturn: Beyond the Usual Economics*, New York: Palgrave Macmillan.

Ratnovski, Lev and Rocco Huang (2009), 'Why are Canadian banks more resilient?', IMF Working Paper No. 09-152.

Russell, Ellen (2010), 'The case for constructive ambiguity in a regulated system: Canadian banks and the "too big to fail" problem', Working Paper No. 223, May, Political Economy Research Institute.

Shiller, Robert (2005), *Irrational Exuberance*, Princeton, NJ: Princeton University Press.

Stern, Gary H. and Ron J. Feldman (2004), *Too Big To Fail: The Hazards of Bank Bailouts*, Washington, DC: Brookings Institution Press.

Stern, Gary H. and Ron Feldman (2009), 'Addressing TBTF by shrinking financial institutions: an initial assessment', Federal Reserve Bank of Minneapolis (June).

Story, Louise (2010), 'A secretive banking elite rules trading in derivatives', *The New York Times*, 1 December, p. A1.

Taibbi, Matt (2010), 'Wall Street's big win: finance reform won't stop the high-risk gambling that wrecked the economy – and Republicans aren't the only ones to blame', *Rolling Stone*, no. 1111, 4 August.

Wiseman, Paul and Pallavi Gogoi (2009), 'FDIC chief: small banks can't compete with bailed-out giants', *USA Today*, 20 October.

10. The new institutional economics and the global financial crisis

Martin Ricketts

INTRODUCTION

The narrative of the global financial crisis is now very familiar. An asset price bubble, particularly associated with residential property, exposed financial organizations to risks that they did not recognize sufficiently. Like generals flushed with past successes, the chief executives of many of these organizations advanced confidently into terrain that more detached, cautious and historically aware observers might reasonably have warned contained dangerous features potentially lethal, not only to their own troops, but also, as a result of consequences felt elsewhere, fatal to an entire campaign. Economic organizations are interdependent just as individual people are interdependent. No economic organization 'is an island entire of itself' – in spite of historical attempts to construct one. Even large nation-states or empires are rarely self-sufficient, while, at the other end of the scale, even religious communities and small social communes depend to some degree on outsiders. Interdependence is the norm, and as the bell tolled for Northern Rock in September 2007 in the UK, when depositors queued to withdraw their funds; or for Lehman Brothers in September 2008 in the USA, when clients fled and Chapter 11 bankruptcy ensued; senior people in the banking industry (at least for a brief period) did not need John Donne to tell them for whom it tolled.

If all organizations are interdependent it must nevertheless be admitted that the systemic consequences of failure vary massively. The fate of small religious communes will not disturb many other people as the effects gradually ripple out from the centre of any disturbance and fade away. Even fairly large-scale enterprises (in terms of employment or capital invested) can fail without causing emergency conferences to be called across the world. Financial services are apparently special in terms of the collateral damage that may accompany bankruptcy. Instead of a shock gradually abating as the force dissipates with distance, a financial crisis can set off a dynamic chain of events that gains in intensity and sucks in victims at an increasing distance from the epicentre.

The reasons for this characteristic are well known. Ultimately the stability of financial institutions depends upon confidence. Everyone understands that each financial organization is incapable of repaying all its creditors out of reserves at very short notice. No individual will care about this very much, providing that each believes that the others are confident in the ability of the bank to repay and that they will therefore only be calling on the bank in response to private circumstances and requirements. Providing the banks' financial reserves are sufficient to handle the likely net demands of creditors at any point in time, all will be well. If some 'unlikely' events take place and confidence is disturbed, however, the danger of a spiral of bankruptcies is very great as large numbers of people are impelled to act in ways that are individually rational but collectively destructive – withdrawing deposits and failing to renew loans – the greatly to be feared 'run on the bank'. It is precisely to meet this type of contingency and thus bolster confidence that funds will always be available, that the classic 'lender-of-last-resort' function of central banks evolved during the nineteenth century.

The other fundamental reason for the destructive power of financial crises is simply that 'financial services' are an input into virtually every transaction that takes place in a modern economy. Economic activity is about exchange, and money facilitates exchange by reducing the cost of transacting. The present extent of division of labour would be unsustainable without the financial services that support it. As Carl Menger (1871) pointed out in his *Principles of Economics*, the services of a simple medium of exchange can evolve spontaneously from the mutual interaction of self-interested traders, and probably did so long before the intervention of the state. It is possible to argue that more sophisticated financial services involving the bringing together of borrowers and lenders in support of a more geographically extended trade network and more capital-intensive production processes will also gradually emerge from the demands of the transactors themselves. But the modern financial services industry is a creature of the state. When once highly leveraged financial institutions have come into existence, especially when operating in a system of fiat money unconvertible into precious metals or commodities of any description, the confidence required to sustain them is a kind of 'public good' that invites state support at times of crisis – and this has been duly provided. The extent and form of this support are contentious areas but even those espousing broadly 'free market' principles usually (though not universally) confer on the state important responsibilities for maintaining the currency and controlling credit on essentially 'public interest' grounds.

These points are commonplace and elementary but their implications are very often neglected or overlooked. As politicians struggle to convince the public that 'we're all in this together' in the face of mounting public debt and a fiscal crisis that has inevitably succeeded the credit and banking crisis, it is important to be aware that we always were 'in it together'. Finance is not just another business. It is the business of facilitating business. Exchange can be studied without reference to money, or markets in credit instruments defined in terms of money. Business could, in principle, go on without them. Work effort could be offered in exchange for specified goods; consumption could be forgone now and resources provided for productive investment in exchange for goods and services in the future; even insurance might conceptually be arranged by mutual agreement on the distribution of claims to real output contingent upon actual events. Indeed, this is what we teach students is 'really' going on in labour, capital and contingent claims markets; and microeconomics textbooks emphasize that ratios of money prices simply represent the 'real' terms upon which trade is taking place. But if the potential gains to trade can be studied without reference to money, their actual realization is heavily dependent on monetary institutions. Ultimately, financial services are socially valuable because they reduce the transactions costs that would otherwise inhibit every type of exchange and thereby enable increasing levels of specialization and exchange. Historically the productive forces released by the development of increasingly sophisticated types of financial intermediation have undoubtedly been very great, but as dependency on a more and more extended pattern of trade has evolved, so too has the potential cost of financial disruption.

GOVERNANCE IN FINANCIAL MARKETS

As central banks extended emergency liquidity to financial institutions unable to find it from other sources, and as governments committed taxpayers to re-capitalize those banks stranded with high levels of 'troubled assets' – indeed almost anything to prevent mass panic – the global financial crisis could naturally be viewed as a failure of markets. From the perspective of the new institutional economics, however, it is more helpful to characterize the crisis as a failure of 'governance'. The process of financial intermediation must involve the participants in overcoming, or at least mitigating transactional hazards. Ronald Coase's (1937) observation that 'there is a cost of using the price mechanism' – by which he meant transacting 'outside the firm' using relatively impersonal, short-term, arm's length contracts – can stand as the founding insight of modern institutional economics. Transacting is costly, and the process of economizing on these costs leads to the institutional and organizational structures that inhabit the economic landscape at any point in time. Financial transactions are notoriously hazardous and the provision of governance structures to facilitate them by inculcating confidence and trust is the underlying social role of banking and other financial services and the ultimate source of the rents that are generated there.

From the point of view of the new institutional economics, therefore, the origins of the global financial crisis can be found in rent-seeking and the failure of governance arrangements designed to suppress it. The use of reputational capital to facilitate trade in financial instruments is socially productive when that trust is well founded. Mutual gains to transactors accompany these activities and rent is created and augmented. Facilitating trade by implicitly misleading transactors concerning the hazards that confront them in pursuit of short-term advantage is to dissipate evolved reputational capital – capital that might be specific to particular organizations or that might more generally be associated with extended groupings of market makers. Raiding this evolved reputational capital (either within or across organizations) is akin to depleting 'the commons' in the natural world and suggests that institutional arrangements for protecting this crucial resource were not sufficiently strong. In these circumstances the gains to some transactors are achieved by imposing losses on others, and social surplus is destroyed in the process.

It is sometimes asserted that the global financial crisis was caused by the greed of the bankers. The problem with such a statement is that it implies no particular reform process other than a kind of moral reformation. Economics (including the new institutional economics) takes it for granted that people are greedy (or at least predominantly self-regarding). This does not mean that people are incapable of rising above the pursuit of worldly riches or their own self-interest, but it does imply that 'the economic institutions of capitalism', whether markets or hierarchies, are best structured when they work with the grain of human nature and do not expect too much from unalloyed virtue un-buttressed by social and institutional supports.

EXAMPLES OF INSTITUTIONAL FAILURE

Sub-prime Mortgages

The lack of attention to matters of governance is clearly revealed in the market that is most associated with the genesis of the global financial crisis

– the provision of mortgage finance to 'sub-prime' borrowers. There is nothing wrong with facilitating the purchase of houses by poorer people. What is wrong is to assume that it can be done by actually reducing the 'governance services' associated with such transactions and substituting the greater use of arm's length trading. Historically the institutions that evolved to provide housing loans to the aspiring working and middle classes were mutual societies.[1] In a less gullible age few would have been under any illusions about the dangers of borrowing short and lending long, and all would have been keen to restrict membership and loans to reliable borrowers. This required the institutions to be local and the members to be known to one another. Private or 'hidden information' is exactly what was not wanted because it leads directly to the phenomenon of adverse selection – the inability to assess with sufficient reliability a good borrower from a bad one. Unknown or distant borrowers are also beyond the sway of peer pressure and local monitoring and thus more likely to give rise to the problem of 'moral hazard' – a reduced incentive to undergo personal hardship in order to avoid default. The success of 'microfinance' organizations in facilitating small-scale development in many developing countries indicates that extending credit to poor people is perfectly good business if attention is paid to matters of governance.[2]

These observations should not be interpreted as an assertion that under modern conditions mortgage lending is always most efficiently conducted using mutual, small and local organizations. Larger organizations with greater geographical reach and access to resources outside a restricted circle clearly have advantages in terms of risk spreading and risk pooling. The early history of financial institutions is littered with case studies of the trade-off between the advantages of local and smaller companies or societies better able to police their contracts or membership, and the advantages of larger, better capitalized companies able to hedge risks but less well informed about local circumstances and with managers less well controlled by those with rights of 'ownership'. Organizational and technological innovations continually modify the available trade-offs and seem generally to have favoured the building of larger institutions. The point is that in every historical period the trade-off has existed, and it has always been a matter of the finest commercial (in its broadest sense) judgement where the 'best' solution lies in any given set of circumstances.

It is hard to believe that much commercial or business judgement was brought to bear on the huge institutional changes that preceded the crisis in sub-prime mortgages. This was not simply a matter of banks adopting mutual, private or joint-stock ownership (though a significant trend away from mutuals and partnerships towards the public limited company has been a characteristic of the last thirty years). Neither was it simply a matter of size or geographical reach (though banks were increasingly large and international in scope). The crucial innovation that eventually precipitated a crisis of confidence was the creation of complex tradable financial instruments from the underlying mortgages created in the residential property sector by dividing them up and constructing packages from the 'diced' components. Instead of mortgages being held as assets on the balance sheet of an institution they could be sold to other investors as complex debt obligations with varying contrived risk return characteristics and with the underlying property notionally acting as security.

The potential theoretical advantages of this financial innovation should not be overlooked. Markets in state contingent claims enable risk to be spread widely (thus reducing the social cost of risk) and they permit economic agents to choose between the risk and return opportunities available (thus ensuring that portfolios reflect the risk preferences of the economic agents participating in the market). An innovation that permits people to achieve greater security at lower expected cost through the availability of a new financial instrument is in principle socially beneficial. The mistake, however, was to see the development of these markets and novel financial instruments in a purely technical and statistical light and to overlook their associated governance requirements. If mortgages are not held by a bank until fully redeemed but traded on markets in 'securitized' form, the incentive to ensure the quality of the underlying asset is much less 'direct'. Of course a reputation for good appraisal of borrowers and accurate assessment of relative risk classes of asset might be important to a bank's ability to trade complex derivatives of its mortgages, just as a good reputation is important to a trader in second-hand cars. Nevertheless, in a situation where the buyer of a collateralized debt obligation has no *ex ante* way (short of assaying each security) of independent verification, and thus where there is little alternative (short of loading the market with prohibitive levels of transactions costs) to trusting the market makers and ratings agencies, there is substantial danger that quality standards will be gradually eroded in the interests of short-term profitability and at the expense of long-term reputation.

With the benefit of hindsight it now seems clear that financial institutions were insufficiently alert to these dangers. It seemed to have been taken for granted that the extensive trading of mortgage-backed debt instruments would not have significant behavioural consequences and that the probability distributions underlying the traded assets could be reliably assessed and were (like earthquake probabilities or the weather) effectively beyond human influence. In other words the governance requirements in these markets were greatly underestimated.

Bankers' Bonuses

The same apparent disregard of potential contractual danger is revealed by the dispute over pay and bonuses in the banking sector. Indeed bankers' bonuses have become in Europe and the USA the subject of heated political interest and (mostly) condemnation. Many people in the banking sector, it transpired, were not merely well rewarded for their efforts but had contracts linking a large proportion of their pay to the financial returns earned in the trading or other activities that they undertook. The banking and financial services sector was a heavy user of 'incentive contracts'. Again it is necessary to start by emphasizing that in certain circumstances there is every reason to use incentive contracts rather than contracts that simply pay for time on the job. The important organizational and business question is whether the circumstances in the banking sector were correctly assessed as being suitable for these contractual arrangements.

Linking a person's reward to the results of his or her effort is not, on the face of it, a bad idea. Indeed where effort is very costly to observe, and monitoring is therefore of limited use, a simple contract specifying a payment in exchange for the successful completion of a given objective (assumed verifiable at low cost) would be the obvious response. The situation becomes more complicated if the relationship between a person's effort and the outcome is influenced by factors outside his or her control. There is, in other words, uncertainty about the outcome, even though greater effort and skill will always (other things constant) improve the result. To pay a person a fixed wage under these conditions is hazardous because shirking is hard to detect. A poor outcome can always be explained by (unobservable) adverse circumstances. To pay a person a share of the result will obviously partially overcome this problem, but at the cost of making him or her bear part of the risk. The natural result of this line of reasoning is that incentive contracts are likely to be used where monitoring is costly, desired results are definable and observable at low cost, the environment is risky, and contractors are not too risk averse.

The traditional 'franchise contract' can be interpreted in precisely this way.[3] The franchisee pays a fee to the franchisor for permission to trade under a particular brand name and then has very high-powered incentives to be successful because a high proportion of any profit on the franchisee's operations is retained. A risk-neutral franchisee should keep all the profit because then he or she would shoulder all the risk and equate the marginal cost of effort to the marginal expected return. If there are risk-neutral people around, they are obviously the efficient risk-bearers. Risk aversion is perhaps more likely, and in these conditions the employer and employee or franchisor and franchisee would be expected to share the risk between them. The optimal contract will equate marginal gains to greater effort with marginal losses from greater risk-bearing costs as the bonus element (or profit share) increases.

Looked at from the perspective of the simple theory of principal and agent, therefore, it is possible to see bonus arrangements as a method of aligning the interests of a bank's employees with those of its owners. The problem is that this theory concentrates on a single contractual hazard – effort incentives in the face of high monitoring costs. It is far from clear that this is the only (or even the main) contractual problem or that the assumptions behind the conventional analysis apply to the banking sector.

In most agency relationships there are diverse contractual hazards running in both directions. A franchisor, for example, might avoid the danger of shirking on the part of the franchisee by simply charging the latter a franchise fee for the use of a brand name or other specialized capital. It is usually important, however, for franchisees to maintain the quality of the service provided, and action by some franchisees to reduce costs and 'free ride' on the brand name could have disastrous consequences for the reputation of a franchise chain. Thus, the franchisor as owner and guardian of this jointly used asset usually has responsibility for group marketing, the determination of methods and standards of service, staff training, and the monitoring and enforcement of these standards. We therefore expect to see the franchisor receiving a royalty as well as a lump sum for what are effectively regulatory or 'governance services'. We also expect to observe much lower-powered incentives to franchisees (a smaller profit share) in circumstances where the temptation to 'chisel' on quality is high and costly to detect and where the external costs (that is external to the individual franchisee and internal to the group as a whole) are large.

These observations about the economic theory of principal and agent allow us to see the bankers' bonus controversy in the somewhat broader context of contractual hazards. In the case of banking services, for example, no one would expect jobs to be auctioned off to the highest bidders with the winners permitted to keep all the returns achieved over a specified time interval – even though this system would undoubtedly provide extremely high-powered incentives. The actual bonus arrangements subject to such public criticism after the global financial crisis do not approach this extreme case, but the charge levelled at the banks is that they collectively underestimated the dangers associated with the bonus system. In particular it encourages excessive risk-taking and short time horizons. Unless the bonus system is very well designed and calibrated, individual rewards can encourage behaviour that undermines the organization as a whole. Cases have occurred of 'rogue traders' bringing down famous names in banking,[4] but perhaps it is not these individual catastrophes, fascinating though they often are as human tragedies, but the gradual and cumulative erosion of natural scepticism and restraint across an entire industry that is ultimately more dangerous. The latter threatens an entire financial system. The former can act as a warning and example.

Post-crisis Reforms

After the immediate provision of special liquidity schemes by central banks and of programmes of government support for 'troubled assets' or the reinforcement of banks' balance sheets with public money, the question of longer-term reform has come to the fore. Much of the public discussion has concentrated on the imposition of more intrusive regulatory supervision and derives, as suggested in the introduction, from the conviction that the crisis was a manifestation of market failure. Proposed changes include increases in capital and other reserve ratios across the banking sector; the introduction of transaction taxes to suppress speculative trading activity; the introduction of levies on profits made in the banking sector; direct intervention to regulate incentive packages within financial services; and the separation of retail from investment banking as was the case under the Glass–Steagall legislation (1932) in the United States passed in the aftermath of the 1929 crash.

From an institutional point of view these proposals flow from a perceived need to strengthen the regulation of financial markets in response to the crisis but they do not directly address the primary question of why governance arrangements proved to be inadequate. Perhaps reserve ratios might have been somewhat on the low side for prudence. Perhaps the trading of increasingly complex financial instruments has, over recent years, been pressed too far and given rise to hazards that have been overlooked. Perhaps incentive packages have not done much to nurture caution. Perhaps the integration of investment with retail banking gives rise to systemic dangers that should have been taken more seriously. But the underlying question is why a very disruptive financial crisis developed before these problems were noticed. The answer implied by the reform proposals mentioned above is that the markets were not sufficiently well supervised by the regulatory authorities. Left unsupervised there was a race to the bottom. The dire consequences of adverse selection according to this view are associated with lack of regulation.

There is, however, an alternative view. The information problems that give rise to adverse selection can be addressed through various institutional mechanisms – especially the evolution of trust and private governance arrangements to protect it. Government regulation is capable of undermining this process. The old observation that 'bad money drives out good' derives not from a world in which people freely choose what money to trust, but a world in which a regulator insists on the equivalence of coins known by market transactors to be of different quality. The idea therefore that the crisis was the result of insufficient regulation is not as clear cut as sometimes assumed. Regulatory agencies with extensive statutory powers existed during the run-up to the crisis and had been set up precisely to oversee the activities of participants in financial markets. This public oversight to some extent substitutes for private oversight. If market participants are re-assured by the existence of regulatory agencies, they will cut back on their own investments in monitoring quality and take less interest in the private governance arrangements put in place by individual institutions. The provision of governance services has been moved on the grounds of public benefit from the private to the public sector, a move that creates hazards because it undermines the incentive on the part of an individual financial institution to bear significant costs in order to create a reputation for greater safety.

A reform agenda that draws on the new institutional economics would therefore seek to use the competitive process to support strong governance in financial institutions and to reduce the danger of contagion in the event of failure. The objective would not be to produce uniformly 'safe' institutions but would permit the emergence of a range of competing institutions characterized by varying responses to the hazards that they face. Rather than intervening in particular areas by closing down particular incentive packages, mandating specified reserve requirements for different types of business, insisting on the separation of retail from investment banking and so forth, the aim would be to create circumstances in which financial organizations, their owners, suppliers and clients, faced the consequences of their decisions. In other words banking and financial services more generally would ideally be treated like any other industry and be subject to a system of regulation that encouraged competition – including provision for the regular entry and exit of firms.

As Wood and Kabiri (2010) note, the financial sector is exceptional in that regulators are focused mainly on the question of firm stability. In other sectors of the economy the encouragement of competition is the relevant focus, and the question of the strength of individual firms is of much less relevance. The reasons for this difference in treatment are of course precisely those discussed in the introduction to this chapter – the danger of a collapse in confidence across the sector and the disruptive consequences of a firm's failure on huge numbers of uncompleted transactions. Making financial services more like other industries therefore requires a method of ensuring that firms are never 'too big to fail' and that procedures are available at all times and well short of a crisis to enable the orderly departure of a firm from the market.

Reforms of this nature have already been introduced in the UK. Under the Banking Act (2009) the insolvency regime for banks has been modified and it is possible for regulators to take control of a bank from its shareholders before it is technically declared bankrupt. The aim is to achieve an orderly wind-down of a bank that fails to meet minimum financial requirements through sales to other banks or new investors. In a further development of the same idea it has been suggested (for example in the Turner Review undertaken by the Financial Services Authority (2009) in the UK) that 'systemically important banks' should draw up 'living wills' or 'recovery and resolution plans'. The analogy is with people who specify in a document what procedures should be followed with respect to the disposition and use of their assets in the event of their becoming incapacitated. A bank that fails to achieve certain minimum standards would find the provisions of its 'living will' invoked, control would be taken from its managers and shareholders, and new owners sought while operations continued. Again the aim of the procedure would be to threaten owners and managers with severe adverse consequences in the event of failure without jeopardizing the stability of the financial system as a whole.

CONCLUDING COMMENTS

At the heart of modern institutional economics is the distinction between 'made' or 'planned' order and 'spontaneous' or 'evolved' order.[5] When crises happen and order is threatened, an inevitable tension arises. Was the crisis induced by a failure of planning or regulation? Or was the crisis a result of spontaneous forces generating, not 'order', but dislocation and breakdown? The policy response to the crisis is heavily conditioned by how these questions are answered. In particular those who take the latter view will tend to favour the introduction of more determined efforts to regulate and plan the financial system. Those who trace the problem to regulatory failure will want to find ways of making the competitive system work more effectively.

This chapter has argued that the wrong lesson is likely to be learned from the global financial crisis. The important objective should be to enable rather than to inhibit the usual processes of competitive adaptation in the financial sector. In practice the imposition of greater regulatory intervention and further attempts at oversight are likely to be the main response. The crisis represented a failure of institutions in the broadest sense. Governance arrangements were insufficient to cope with transactional hazards in the financial sector. More regulatory intervention and centralized policing of financial markets can thus be anticipated. This trend can be seen in proposals to introduce more direct controls on the structure of banks, on the scope of their activities, on reserve requirements and on staff contracts. The information requirements of centralized systems are usually considerable, however, and these systems do not necessarily exhibit greater long-run stability than decentralized ones.

Competitive processes, on the other hand, will not generally result in the debasement of standards providing poor quality provision is eventually revealed and punished with sufficient severity. From this point of view, a system that permits the orderly winding up or disposal of financial institutions before they reach the point of technical insolvency has a great deal to commend it. It means that owners and managers would face somewhat different rules in the financial sector compared with other sectors. But this difference would simply reflect the problems of greater systemic risk to which firms in the financial sector give rise. The possibility of more rather than fewer 'failures', defined as institutions taken into administration according to the terms of pre-existing 'living wills', could potentially greatly add to the pressure on shareholders and others to ensure effective control and governance.

NOTES

1. For an extended discussion of the forces determining enterprise governance and ownership see Hansmann (1996).
2. See Morduch (1999) for a general review of the theoretical and practical issues associated with the microfinance sector in various countries up to the end of the twentieth century.
3. A basic statement of the theory of agency contracts reviewed here can be found in Ricketts (1986).
4. A well-known example is that of Nick Leeson, whose trading activities in Singapore in 1995 caused the liquidation of Barings, one of the oldest UK investment banks.
5. See the discussion, for example, in Kasper and Streit (1998: 142–55).

REFERENCES

Coase, R.H. (1937), 'The nature of the firm', *Economica*, **4**(16), New Series, November, 386–405.

Financial Services Authority (2009), 'A regulatory response to the global banking crisis', Discussion Paper DP09/4, Annex 1.

Hansmann, H. (1996), *The Ownership of Enterprise*, Cambridge, MA: Harvard University Press.

Kasper, Wolfgang and Manfred Streit (1998), *Institutional Economics: Social*

Order and Public Policy, Cheltenham, UK and Northampton, MA, USA: Edward Elgar Publishing.
Menger, C. (1871), *Principles of Economics*, trans. and edited by Jones Dingwall and Bert F. Hozelitz (1950), Glencoe, IL: Free Press.
Morduch, Jonathan (1999), 'The microfinance promise', *Journal of Economic Literature*, **37**(4), (December), 1569–614.
Ricketts, M. (1986), 'The geometry of principal and agent: yet another use for the Edgeworth box', *Scottish Journal of Political Economy*, **33**(3), 228–48.
Wood, G. and Ali Kabiri (2010), 'Firm stability and system stability: the regulatory delusion', paper presented at a conference on Managing Systemic Risk, University of Warwick, 7–9 April 2010.

11. Economics in the mirror of the financial crisis*

Rodolfo Signorino

1 INTRODUCTION

Famously, for Hegel ([1820] 2001: 20) '[t]he owl of Minerva takes its flight only when the shades of night are gathering', that is, philosophical reflection on the world runs behind the unfolding of events and is possible only *post festum*. Now that the world economy seems to be on the road to recovery from the global crisis which started about three years ago, conditions are favourable to the emergence of a less involved reflection on its possible causes in order to draw some useful lessons for the future. Another interesting subject to investigate is the search for economists' responsibility in the current events. Why were economists unable to foresee the crisis? Did mainstream economics influence regulatory and control policies in financial markets so as to favour (or at least, not hinder) the onset of the crisis? Has the crisis shown that heterodox economics, particularly that of Keynesian inspiration, is endowed with a better explanatory power than orthodox economics? Thorough analysis of the causes of the crisis and well thought-out answers to the above questions are yet to emerge from the ongoing debate. The actual dimensions of the phenomenon under study, in fact, will probably induce many non-economists and economists alike to a second thought on what, till a little while ago, appeared as established notions. The former (non-economists) may well wish to change their mind about the widespread belief according to which accepted economic theory considers the removal of any obstacles to free markets as the *conditio sine qua non* for efficient resources allocation. The latter (economists) should, at least, reconsider their prescriptions on the subject of financial regulation, prescriptions that manifestly proved unable to prevent or mitigate the present financial turmoil:

> [T]he trust in the ability of self-regulation of the financial markets belongs to political ideology, not to economic doctrine. Economists have been studying for thirty years the failures of financial markets, speculative bubbles, the information asymmetries that distort the incentives of managers and financial

> institutions, and liquidity crises. The lessons to be drawn concern the correct formulation and the contents of financial regulation, not its necessity. Evidence of this is the fact that the crisis has overwhelmed above all the banks, the most controlled sector of all. (Tabellini, 2009, my translation)

The structure of the chapter is as follows. In section 2 I discuss some of the factors that may have played a role in causing the crisis and emphasize that supporters of different economic theories will assign different weights to each factor in their analyses. As a consequence, suggested economic policies are highly sensitive to the economic theory employed in evaluating the set of causes. In section 3 I seek to defend economists from the common charge that their inability to foresee the crisis is a clear sign of the lack of scientific status of their discipline. In my view, the main liability of mainstream economics lies elsewhere, in its excessive trust on the self-equilibrating mechanisms of free-market economies. Mainstream macroeconomists may have been too hasty in dismissing the financial instability hypothesis proposed by Keynes and developed by Minsky. Section 4 briefly outlines Keynes and Minsky's contribution on this subject, while section 5 concludes. It hardly needs to be stressed that what follows is but a very tentative analysis to be duly developed in future works.

2 PROXIMATE AND REMOTE CAUSES OF THE PRESENT DISTRESS

The collapse of the US sub-prime mortgage loan market, starting in spring 2007, is generally acknowledged as the immediate cause of the present financial and economic crash, by far the worst experienced by free-market economies since World War II:

> There is some consensus on the proximate causes of the crisis: (i) the US financial sector misallocated resources to real estate, financed through the issuance of exotic new financial instruments; (ii) a significant portion of these instruments found their way, directly or indirectly, into commercial and investment bank balance sheets; (iii) these investments were largely financed with short-term debt. (Diamond and Rajan 2009: 606)

While there is substantial agreement on the proximate causes, identification of the remote causes appears more complex. Without claiming to be exhaustive, a possible list of the latter should include:

1. the strong *laissez-faire* bias generated by the so-called Great Moderation;

2. growing interdependence of economies due to the liberalization in the international movements of financial capital;
3. the Fed easy-money policy in the early 2000s;
4. radical changes in the nature and *modus operandi* of the banking system caused by financial innovations;
5. the changes in the incentives structure of financial managers;
6. the dynamics of income distribution and household indebtedness in the US economy.

The Great Moderation

The period of steady growth (mild recessions and local financial crises aside) starting at the end of the turbulent 1970s is generally labelled as the Great Moderation. The drastic reduction in the macroeconomic instability recorded for almost three decades preceding this crisis is generally ascribed to a plurality of factors, including (i) the structural changes occurring in real economies that made them more resilient to shocks; (ii) a substantial improvement in the performance of monetary policy in many industrialized countries which succeeded in reducing the volatility of inflation and GDP; and (iii) good luck, in the sense that, in the period under consideration, shocks were less frequent and wide-ranging (Bernanke, 2004). The Great Moderation brought with it, as a kind of by-product, improved trust in the thaumaturgical virtues of free markets and, by the same token, increased distrust in regulation and control policies by public authorities.[1] Along the way, the complacency of economists has sharply increased. In particular, macroeconomists have felt (and have been perceived by the public) increasingly able to comprehend the intricate mechanisms of free-market economies and thus formulate the appropriate policy recommendations when needed.

Liberalization in the International Movements of Financial Capital

The progressive abolition of barriers to the international movement of financial capital has allowed an extension of the potential market for – mainly US-made – financial products, thus stimulating financial innovation. At the same time, the growing Asian countries and the oil-producing Arab countries, with their surplus of savings, were inclined to purchase new US financial products, perceived almost as risk-free as US Treasury Bonds but yielding a higher expected return. A period of low real interest rates (Bernanke, 2005) and a considerable increase in the degree of financial interdependence in the world economy has followed. This has both positive and negative consequences. On the one hand, the possibilities of diversification and hence of risk management have become wider; on the other, low real interest rates favour the rise of speculative bubbles, and financial interdependence causes the potential for a domino effect (*simul stabunt simul cadent*):

> Since the only way diversification of idiosyncratic risks can happen is by sharing these risks among many companies and individuals, better diversification also creates a multitude of counter-party relationships. Such interconnections make the economic system more robust against small shocks because new financial products successfully diversify a wide range of idiosyncratic risks and reduce business failures. *But they also make the economy more vulnerable to certain low-probability, tail events precisely because the interconnections that are an inevitable precipitate of the greater diversification create potential domino effects among financial institutions, companies and households.* In this light, perhaps we should not find it surprising that years of economic calm can be followed by tumultuous times and notable volatility. (Acemoglu, 2009: 1–2, emphasis added)

The actual bursting of the crisis has shown that the risk distribution curve was indeed much more fat-tailed than the majority of financial brokers were then inclined to think.

The Fed Easy-money Policy in the New Millennium

The first few years of the new millennium in the USA were characterized by low nominal interest rates, too low for some commentators:

> The classic explanation of financial crises is that they are caused by excesses – frequently monetary excesses – which lead to a boom and an inevitable bust. This crisis was no different: A housing boom followed by a bust led to defaults, the implosion of mortgages and mortgage-related securities at financial institutions, and resulting financial turmoil. Monetary excesses were the main cause of the boom. The Fed held its target interest rate, especially in 2003–2005, well below known monetary guidelines that say what good policy should be based on historical experience. Keeping interest rates on the track that worked well in the past two decades, rather than keeping rates so low, would have prevented the boom and the bust. (Taylor, 2009a)[2]

Moreover, low interest rates usually induce firms to raise their debt-to-equity ratio (so-called *financial leverage*). The goal to maximize the return on equity together with the availability of cheap money encourages banks and firms to take on increasing risks. Thus, short-term indebtedness rose in order to increase the acquisition of long-term assets, while, at the same time, new and effective (from the point of view of banks and firms) procedures for managing such risks were developed:

> With very low interest rates, the only way of making intermediation by the banks profitable was to get into more debt to buy financial assets, that is, to increase the financial leverage. But to do this, banks had to find a way to get rid of the risk involved in such assets, both because in some cases the regulators did not allow a certain financial leverage for the riskiest activities to be exceeded and because banks themselves did not want to hold too risky assets. (Perotti, 2009, my translation)

The Process of Financial Innovation

The way to dispose of such risky assets was provided by financial innovations, in particular by the process of securitization and the seemingly endless creation of financial derivatives. Such innovations involve a structural change in the nature and *modus operandi* of the credit system:

> Mortgage loans are no longer granted [by banks] so as to maintain a relationship with the client throughout the life of the loan and hence assume the risk directly (in the finance jargon: *originate to hold*, to originate for holding until loan expiration). Rather, the loan is granted to be transferred as soon as possible to the widest possible set of investors (*originate to distribute*). This drastic change in bank strategy has had potentially positive effects, but it has also produced serious distortions. In particular, a breakdown in the relationship between bankers' risk and responsibility has ensued. Therefore, the criteria for credit-granting and risk-evaluation, which are the fundamental elements of a banker's duty, have been loosened. What is important [from the bankers' point of view] is no longer to grant loans that may be refunded at their expiration, but to maximize the volume of loans to be granted and hence the fees to be earned. (Onado, 2009: 12, my translation)

In other words, the 'prestige game' carried out by the new finance consists in converting the mortgage loan, a typical illiquid asset springing from an idiosyncratic relationship between a borrower and a lender, into an easily negotiable and thus highly liquid asset. Until the borrowers' insolvencies were circumscribed, the prestige game worked well:

> Home mortgages, credit card debt, automobile loans, student loans and the like were all pooled, or grouped together, and assets were issued that were backed by the groups. These asset pools were structured in a way that both reduced the risk faced by the buyer of the 'asset-backed' securities, and allowed borrowers access to credit they otherwise would not have had. It sounds like everyone wins; a pure efficiency gain. This all looked great, until 2007 when it became apparent that the quality of some of the loans in the residential mortgage pools might not be what they should have been. (Cecchetti, 2008: 2)

Hence, banks and other actors in the credit system became guilty of what Keynes stigmatized as one of the most antisocial practices in the financial world, the relentless search for the liquidity of one's own investments (see *infra* section 4).

The transformation in the *modus operandi* of the credit system (from the 'originate-to-hold' to the 'originate-to-distribute' model) brought with it a change in the structure of individual incentives and the rise of a considerable problem of information asymmetry among the various actors involved in the financial transaction:

> The 'originate and distribute' model destroys information compared to the 'originate and hold' model. The information destruction occurs at the level of the originator of the assets that are to be securitized. Under the 'originate and hold' model the loan officer collecting the information on the creditworthiness of the would-be borrower is working for the Principal in the investing relationship (the originating bank or non-bank lending institution). Under the 'originate and distribute' model, the loan officer of the originating banks works for an institution (the originating bank) that is an Agent for the new Principal in the investing relationship (the SPV [Special Purpose Vehicle] that purchases the loans from the bank and issues securities against them). *With asymmetric information and costly monitoring, the agency relationship dilutes the incentive for information gathering at the origination stage. Reputation considerations will mitigate this problem, but will not eliminate it.* (Buiter, 2007: 2–3, emphasis added)

Changes in the Incentives Structure of Financial Managers

As Keynes once wrote, quoting the old English proverb, you can lead a horse to water, but you can't make him drink. The availability of drinkable water is just one of the circumstances required so that the horse may drink; the other – essential – circumstance is that the horse is thirsty. Paraphrasing Keynes's dictum, it may be maintained that the Fed easy-money policy and the new financial products have led the horse of the financial brokers to water; but the latter has (abundantly) drunk because it had strong incentives to do so. This point has been analysed in great detail by Rajan (2005: 315 ff.). In short, his thesis is the following. Until the 1980s in the United States the coexistence of technological and legal elements caused the predominance in the financial sector of traditional operators (banks) and a strongly risk-adverse credit policy. Bank managers earned a basically fixed remuneration with very few incentives to take risks. Conversely, the risk that a credit management perceived as imprudent by the public could shake the trust of depositors and provoke a bank-run was overrated. As almost always happens in all those sectors in which 'tranquility' is bought at the price of a drastic competition squeeze, choice alternatives were nearly non-existent while inefficiencies spread: '[B]ankers [were] extremely conservative. This served depositors well since their capital was safe, while shareholders, who enjoyed a steady rent because of the limited competition, were also happy. Of course, depositors and borrowers had little choice, so the whole system was very inefficient.' (Rajan, 2005: 315)

Such a 'petrified forest' situation waned when new information technologies drastically reduced the costs of acquisition and elaboration of financial data and legislative deregulation opened up new opportunities for competition in the financial sector. The salient characteristics of this new scenario are: (i) the appearance in the financial sector of new, non-banking, operators; (ii) the disintermediation of the more traditional and standardized financial products (in the financial jargon, *plain vanilla*); and (iii) progressive specialization of banks in producing and marketing the more sophisticated and innovative financial products. Consequently, also the incentives structure of bank managers underwent a drastic change since the remuneration of the latter has always been more sensitive to the short-run performance of their portfolio choices. In particular, Rajan points out that the overall remuneration of a given financial manager increasingly depends on the differential between the rate of return of his/her portfolio and that of competitors' portfolios. This means that competition in the financial sector pushes financial managers (i) to take increasing risks, particularly those that may be more easily hidden or underscored in the periodic reports they are subject to (such as the tail risks quoted by Acemoglu, 2009); and (ii) to conform to the investment policy chosen by the majority of their colleagues/competitors. Such a herd behaviour strategy shields financial managers from any sanction for underperformance whatever the actual pay-off achieved by the ruling investment policy.[3] Such behaviour is indeed rational from an individual point of view but produces, at the aggregate level, some systemic results which are not necessarily benign:

> Taken together, these trends suggest that even though there are far more participants today able to absorb risk, the financial risks that are being created by the system are indeed greater. And even though there should theoretically be a diversity of opinion and actions by participants, and a greater capacity to absorb the risk, *competition and compensation may induce more correlation in behavior than desirable*. While it is hard to be categorical about anything as complex as the modern financial system, it is possible these developments may create more financial-sector-induced procyclicality than the past. *They also may create a greater (albeit still small) probability of a catastrophic meltdown.* (Rajan, 2005: 318, emphasis added)

Unfortunately, recent experience shows that it is precisely the worst scenario foreseen by Rajan that has actually come true.

Dynamics of Income Distribution

Finally, according to some 'heterodox' commentators, a basic role in the present crisis has been played by the dynamics of income distribution in the United States (Barba and Pivetti, 2009).[4] To put it in a nutshell, the gist of this line of reasoning is the following. Assume that, in a given economy, wealthy people have a decidedly smaller (marginal and average) propensity to consume than the poor. Therefore, in such an economy, an increase in the inequality of income distribution goes hand in hand with an increase in aggregate saving, that is, a reduction in aggregate consumption expenditure. The Keynesian evil of low aggregate demand, unable to foster full employment, comes true, unless the other components of aggregate demand (firms' investment expenditure, government expenditure and a surplus in the balance of international trade) act as a substitute for languishing household expenditure. The US economy in recent decades has witnessed an apparent paradox: the coexistence of stagnant labour income and rising consumption expenditure (together with rising inequality in income distribution). Such a paradox was made possible, according to the heterodox point of view, by a deliberate policy of easy credit by banks and other financial institutions that allowed increasing household indebtedness, and by the Fed low interest rate policy that provided the necessary fuel for various speculative bubbles in the real estate and financial markets. Rising market prices of property and financial assets have boosted household financial wealth. Households have generally replaced wage income with debt as the main source for financing consumption expenditure and have used financial capital gains as collateral to back a growing indebtedness. In short, many US households have got used to considering their (mortgaged) houses as an automatic cash dispenser. Also the Nobel laureate Joseph Stiglitz acknowledges that a heavy recourse to debt can only delay, but not resolve, the inherent contradiction between increasing relative impoverishment of working classes and increasing consumption expenditure:

> Growing inequality too has contributed to the lack of aggregate demand. We have redistributed income from those who would spend it to those that don't. For a while, we thought we could circumvent the problem by allowing Americans at the bottom and middle to continue spending anyway, by borrowing. But that was not sustainable. (Stiglitz, 2009: 285)

To conclude this section, it may be claimed that a host of US domestic factors and international factors have played a role in the present global financial turmoil. Careful evaluation of the right weight to assign to each of these factors will help devise future intervention policies. Of course, the results of this evaluation will heavily depend on the kind of economic theory employed.[5] Mainstream macroeconomists will likely side with Taylor (2009a and 2009b) and, accordingly, demand a tighter monetary policy to prevent future bubbles. New microeconomists will be likely to focus on the asymmetric information and moral hazard problems in financial markets highlighted by Buiter (2007) and Rajan (2005) and, accordingly, demand a drastic change in the incentives structure of financial managers. Finally, heterodox economists will probably argue that governments' most urgent task is the introduction of a set of fiscal and social security measures to achieve considerable income redistribution to the benefit of middle/low classes, while a restrictive monetary policy and/or new and more severe regulations of the financial markets may prove to be ill-advised decisions since such measures would depress the consumption capacity of poor families, typically those more credit-constrained.[6]

From the economists' perspective the basic question to be answered is: has the current crisis shown the urgency of a thorough review of the main pillars of accepted economic theory or, on the contrary, only an upgrade of its analysis of financial markets? What is thus at stake is the explanatory power of mainstream economics and its trust in the welfare-maximizing virtues of free-market economies as opposed to the much less confident outlook endorsed by heterodox economics (Laidler, 2010).

3 ECONOMISTS UNDER TRIAL: WHY DID THEY FAIL TO FORESEE THE CRISIS?

The main charge levelled against economists as a profession during the innumerable 'trials of economists' celebrated in the last two years is basically the following: *economists failed to predict the crisis*. Many critics have also maintained that economics is a pseudo-science, more akin to astrology than to astronomy, that economists' meetings are more like reunions of wizards than scientific assemblies, and that it would be best for economists to maintain silence, at least for a few years. (See the speech by the Italian Minister for Finance, Giulio Tremonti, at the People's Friendship Meeting, 2009.)

A possible line of defence against such a charge could consist in singling out some 'prophetic' contributions, that is, papers written by economists warning about the possible outbreak of the crisis before spring 2007. In this regard, the names heard most frequently are those of Rajan (2005) and Shiller (2000 and 2003). This line of defence is taken, for example, by Spaventa (2009) who nonetheless acknowledges that such 'prophets of doom' were few and far between in the economics profession: 'In general, dissenters were often treated as those boring old aunts always having something to grumble about at family parties' (pp. 2–3). Likewise, Perotti (2009) claims that 'the vast majority of economists neither foresaw nor understood the financial crisis because they were totally unaware of some fundamental developments in the credit market' (my translation). An unpublished paper by Imperia and Maffeo (2009) shows that it is very hard to find prophetic contributions published by the economic journals with the highest impact factor and thus representative of mainstream economics, while the situation is totally different as regards non-mainstream journals. From this evidence, the two authors draw the conclusion that heterodox economics, particularly that of Keynesian inspiration, is better equipped than orthodoxy to understand the causes of the crisis and to point out possible remedies.

In my view, the above remarks show that economists need a more robust line of defence than the search for single prophetic contributions. It should be pointed out to critics that the (incontrovertible) fact that the majority of economists were unable to foresee the US sub-prime collapse means neither that economics is a pseudo-science nor that economists should be sentenced to silence. In this regard, the philosophy of science may come to the aid of economists. The problem boils down to the following question: *Is it legitimate to adopt the capacity to foresee accurately as the dividing line between science and pseudo-science and to infer from only one, albeit macroscopic, case of failure the non-scientific nature of a discipline?* A thorough answer to such a question would require a whole volume on the logic and history of science. That said, any answer (whether positive or negative) would be highly controversial since, as epistemologists know, all scientific research programmes (to use Lakatos' terminology) grow 'in a sea of anomalies, and counter-examples are merrily ignored' (see the seminal work by Lakatos and Musgrave, 1970). Unfortunately, binding widely-shared criteria have not yet been devised to ascertain whether a given scientific research programme has entered into a (theoretically or empirically) regressive phase and therefore has to be abandoned. From this point of view, the allocation of public and private resources for financing one scientific research programme rather than another is partly a matter of chance (albeit not entirely random). In any case, the relationship between theory and facts is much more complex than recent critics of economics seem to hold.

Yet the critics' position (a discipline unable to predict accurately should not, *ipso facto*, be considered scientific) deserves further investigation. In my view, this claim is a naive version of the so-called *Symmetry Thesis*. According to the latter, a perfect logical symmetry exists between the operation called explanation and that called prediction within all truly scientific theories: 'explanation is simply prediction written backwards' (Blaug, 1992: 5). Therefore, taking the symmetry thesis to its logical conclusion, it may be maintained that the inability of a given discipline to foresee accurately implies its inability to explain adequately, hence its lack of truly scientific content.[7] The symmetry thesis takes its clue from the hypothetico-deductive model of scientific explanation, codified by Hempel and Oppenheim (1948). The latter claim that all truly scientific explanations involve an *explanans* constituted by two sets of elements:

a. a list of initial conditions; and
b. (at least) one universal law.

The explanation of the phenomenon *explanandum* comes from a correct application of the standard rules of deductive logic to (a) and (b): 'The event under discussion is explained by subsuming it under general laws, i.e. by showing that it occurred in accordance with those laws by virtue of the realization of certain specified antecedent conditions' (Hempel and Oppenheim, 1948: 136).

Within the hypothetico-deductive model a given wrong forecast could derive from the fact that the *explanans* of the theory under examination contains stochastic (that is, non-deterministic) universal laws and/or that initial conditions have not been duly specified. Therefore, within the model a given wrong forecast by no means implies that the theory under scrutiny is irreparably flawed. Such a conclusion holds, *a fortiori*, for a social science such as economics whose universal laws are stochastic in nature and an exhaustive list of initial conditions is nearly impossible. To put it in a nutshell, economics is a discipline, not a science: economic theories, being always subject to a *ceteris paribus* clause, can offer at best 'weak explanations' (Hicks, 1983: 371). Therefore, economists, when they participate in public debates, should make it clear that they do not possess any knowledge of Truth (with capital T). As is taught in any first-year course of statistics, stating that 'given a significance level of $\alpha\%$, available evidence does not allow the hypothesis H_0 to be rejected' in no way means that the hypothesis H_0 is true in the ordinary sense of the word.[8]

Intellectual modesty is a great virtue in economics also for the following reason. As recently emphasized by Gilles Saint-Paul (2009):

> [in the economic world] beliefs about the future and about how the economy works affect the trajectory [of the object under study]. [. . .] The actual behavior of markets, unlike an immutable deterministic law of nature, depends on the beliefs of the markets, including their understanding of economic phenomena and their consequences for asset prices.

Thus, when economists propose to the general public their models on how the economy works, their solutions to the economic problems of the day inevitably influence people's beliefs and expectations and thus heavily contribute to forging the very object of their study.[9] Here, in my view, is the main reason why economists are to blame for the present turmoil. Drastically simplifying the issue, it may be claimed that, in the pre-crisis years, the economic theory spread by the media and taught in first-year macroeconomics courses at the top universities was highly confident in the ability of free-market economies to determine an efficient allocation of economic resources, albeit in the long run. The macroeconomic consensus at the time is thus summarized by Taylor (2000: 90):

> First, the long-run real GDP trend, or potential GDP, can be understood using the growth model that was first developed by Robert Solow and that has now been extended to make 'technology' explicitly endogenous. Second, there is no long-run trade-off between inflation and unemployment, so that monetary policy affects inflation but is otherwise neutral with respect to real variables in the long run. Third, there is a short-run trade-off between inflation and unemployment with significant implications for economic fluctuations around the trend of potential GDP; the trade-off is due largely to temporarily sticky prices and wages.

Hence, cyclical fluctuations are traced back either to exogenous (mainly supply-side) shocks or to plain policy errors. From this theoretical perspective, active fiscal and monetary policies are considered more as part of the problem than as part of the solution:

> Fifty-some years ago, when I began to study economics, students were taught that the private sector had no tendency to gravitate to full employment, that it was prone to undesirable fluctuations amplified by multiplier and accelerator effects, and that it was riddled with market failures of various sorts. But it was also believed that a benevolent, competent, democratic government could stabilise the macroeconomy and reduce the welfare consequence of most market failures to relative insignificance. Fifty years later, in the beginning years of this century, students were taught that representative governments produce pointless fluctuations in prices and output but, if they can be constrained from doing so – by an independent central bank, for example – free markets are sure to produce full employment and, of course, many other blessings besides. (Leijonhufvud, 2009: 1)

Once it is granted that free-market economies provide an efficient resources allocation, a likely next step is to hold the belief that free markets are able to create *by themselves* the right 'rules of the game' and the right sanctions for misbehaviour. Supporters of this view usually claim that the necessity to keep and possibly increase one's own reputational capital is a sufficient deterrent against individual opportunistic behaviour. Accordingly, public authorities should only adopt a soft-touch regulation of markets.[10] Thus, a first lesson that the crisis may teach mainstream economists is that markets (particularly, financial markets) may not be able to solve by themselves the distortions caused by individual opportunistic behaviour. This means that both academic economists and those working for public authorities should reconsider the issue of regulation and control of the financial markets:

> Forgetting the institutional foundations of markets, we mistakenly equated free markets with unregulated markets. Although we understand that even unfettered competitive markets are based on a set of laws and institutions that secure property rights, ensure enforcement of contracts, and regulate firm behaviour and product and service quality, we increasingly abstracted from the role of institutions and regulations supporting market transactions in our conceptualisation of markets. [. . .] We must now start building a theory of market transactions that is more in tune with their institutional and regulatory foundations. We must also turn to the theory of regulation – of both firms and financial institutions – with renewed vigour and hopefully additional insights gained from current experience. (Acemoglu, 2009: 2)

A second lesson is that the results achieved by modern microeconomic theory in terms of sub-optimality of equilibria when markets are plagued with information asymmetries involve macroeconomic consequences that cannot be further neglected. As argued by Spaventa (2009: 3), contemporary macroeconomic models arising from the debate between the New Classical and New Keynesian economists are rigorously micro-founded. Yet their micro-foundations are hardly compatible with the rise and the bursting of financial crises. In particular, such models assume that (i) asset prices reflect the set of available information, thus ruling out the phenomenon of asymmetric information; and (ii) agents are always on their intertemporal budget constraint, thus ruling out the phenomenon of bankruptcy.[11]

4 A DIFFERENT VIEW ON FREE-MARKET ECONOMIES: THE FINANCIAL INSTABILITY HYPOTHESIS

The dissatisfaction with contemporary macro-models may provide a stimulus to elaborate a macroeconomic theory that (a) does not depict crises as exceptional or negligible events; (b) shows that crises may arise from purely financial motives; and (c) explains the mechanisms of the contagion from the financial markets to the commodity and labour markets:

> The macroeconomic models currently used fail to explain causes and consequences of the accumulation of financial imbalances and ample variations in asset prices. It is only recently that models describing the transmission channels of monetary policy have started to highlight the complexity of the intermediation process, interactions among intermediaries, the causes and effects of large-scale portfolio reallocations, the possibility of speculative bubbles, and the feedback relationships between the financial sector and the real sector of the economy. Assessment of the systemic risk that derives from the increasing interdependence among economies, sectors, economic agents, brought about by market liberalization and financial innovation, is the field in which it is urgent to invest. It is the challenge for the new generation of economists. (Draghi, 2009: 6, my translation)

To be equal to the task pointed out by the Governor of the Bank of Italy, Mario Draghi, inspiration may be drawn from a research tradition that, up to the bursting of the crisis, appeared definitively buried in the cemetery of the history of economic thought, in the section devoted to fallacious theories: Keynesian economics. In Chapter 12 of his *The General Theory of Employment, Interest and Money* (1936, now reproduced in vol. VII of *The Collected Writings of John Maynard Keynes*, (Johnson and Moggridge, 1971–89)) bearing the title 'The state of long-term expectation', Keynes emphasizes that financial markets, allowing the trading of securities representative of real capital goods, have made liquid for the individual investor what it is illiquid for society: investment. On the one hand, this favours the very same investment process: few entrepreneurs would bet their own money on long-term and uncertain investment projects if they did not have, at any moment, the opportunity to sell their own investment in the financial markets, that is, to turn it into liquid money. (As noted by Keynes, few men would get married in the absence of the institution of divorce!). On the other hand, such an opportunity provided by financial markets to any individual investor constitutes a strong element of instability for the investment process at the economy level (and, through the *multiplier* mechanism, for aggregate demand and aggregate income and employment) since it opens the way to short-term speculation. Keynes's thought in this regard is worth a full quotation:

> It might have been supposed that competition between expert professionals, possessing judgment and knowledge beyond that of the average private investor, would correct the vagaries of the ignorant individual left to himself. It happens, however, that the energies and skill of the professional investor and speculator are mainly occupied otherwise. For most of these persons are, in fact, largely concerned, not with making superior long-term forecasts of the probable yield of an investment over its whole life, but with foreseeing changes in the conventional basis of valuation a short time ahead of the general public. They are concerned, not with what an investment is really worth to a man who

> buys it 'for keeps', but with what the market will value it at, under the influence of mass psychology, three months or a year hence. [. . .] *Of the maxims of orthodox finance none, surely, is more anti-social than the fetish of liquidity, the doctrine that it is a positive virtue on the part of investment institutions to concentrate their resources upon the holding of 'liquid' securities. It forgets that there is no such thing as liquidity of investment for the community as a whole.* The social object of skilled investment should be to defeat the dark forces of time and ignorance which envelop our future. The actual, private object of the most skilled investment to-day is 'to beat the gun', as the Americans so well express it, to outwit the crowd, and to pass the bad, or depreciating, half-crown to the other fellow. (emphasis added)

In so far as speculative traders do not internalize all economic consequences arising from their trading activity, short-term speculative trading in financial markets involves a strong negative externality. Consistent with this formulation, Keynes proposes the introduction of a tax on Stock Exchange negotiations in order to close the gap between the private marginal cost and the social marginal cost of short-term speculation:[12]

> It is usually agreed that casinos should, in the public interest, be inaccessible and expensive. And perhaps the same is true of Stock Exchanges. That the sins of the London Stock Exchange are less than those of Wall Street may be due, not so much to differences in national character, as to the fact that to the average Englishman Throgmorton Street is, compared with Wall Street to the average American, inaccessible and very expensive. [. . .] The introduction of a substantial Government transfer tax on all transactions might prove the most serviceable reform available, with a view to mitigating the predominance of speculation over enterprise in the United States.

Keynes's lesson on the relationship between financial markets and the investment process in free-market economies was subsequently developed by Hyman P. Minsky, a long-forgotten economist today (re)discovered by many commentators (see Whalen, 2008 and Yellen 2009. For a thorough assessment of Minsky's heritage see Bellofiore and Ferri, 2001).

Perhaps the most surprising conclusion stemming from Minsky's contribution is that *economic stability is destabilizing* since a prolonged period of stable growth without inflation induces the actors in the financial markets to believe that future gross incomes will continue to rise and therefore an increasing debt-to-equity ratio will be sustainable: 'Stable growth is inconsistent with the manner in which investment is determined in an economy in which debt-financed ownership of capital-assets exists and in which the extent to which such debt-financing can be carried is determined by the market' (Minsky, 1977).

This is what Minsky calls the *Financial Instability Hypothesis*, that is a 'theory of how a capitalist economy endogenously generates a financial structure which is susceptible to financial crises and how the normal functioning of financial markets in the resulting boom economy will trigger a financial crisis' (ibid.). Minsky's analysis starts from the observation that accumulation of capital goods in modern capitalist economies is largely carried out through debt financing. Debt financing involves the exchange of present money (which is certain) for future money (which is, obviously, uncertain). Thus, behind the world of real commodities (consumption and capital goods), there is a 'paper world' made of liabilities to pay money at dates specified or as conditions arise, irrespective of whether or not the future profits expected by the borrowers are realized:

> The viability of this paper world rests upon the cash flows (or gross profits after out-of-pocket costs and taxes) that business organizations, households, and governmental bodies, such as states and municipalities, receive as a result of the income-generating process. [. . .] The validation of business debt requires that prices and outputs be such that almost all firms earn large enough surpluses over labor and material costs either to fulfill the gross payments required by debt or to induce refinancing. Refinancing takes place only if gross profits are expected to be large enough either to validate the new debt or to induce further refinancing (ibid.)

In this regard Minsky distinguishes between (a) hedge finance; (b) speculative finance; and (c) ultra-speculative or Ponzi finance. In the first case, in any given period, capital gross income exceeds the flows of debt payments by a safe margin. In the second case, in the initial periods the flows of debt payments exceed capital gross income, while in the following periods the opposite holds. However, the present value of expected cash receipts is greater than the present value of payment commitments (unless interest rates increase sharply and unexpectedly). Finally, in the third case, during the whole life of the debt, the flows of interest payments exceed capital gross income. Hence, units engaged in a Ponzi finance scheme are forced to make new debts just to be able to pay the interests on previous debt. As remarked by Minsky (1980), since such refinancing is available only if the total cash inflows expected by a Ponzi unit exceed its total cash outflows, the survival of a Ponzi unit often depends on the expectation that, at a given future time, certain assets may be sold at a sufficiently high price. The US sub-prime market bubble is thus a typical instance of a Ponzi finance. Banker α is willing to grant to the part-time worker β a mortgage loan even if the expected net income of β is uncertain or unable to match the interest payments (at least in some of the periods of the debt lifetime) since α expects a steady increase in the market value of the house purchased by β. Thus, α believes that, in the event of β's insolvency, he/she could get enough from the sale of β's house to recover the residual instalments of the loan unpaid by β:

> Understanding the subprime crisis requires understanding the role played by the GSEs (Fannie Mae and Freddie Mac). They increased the demand for the housing stock through subsidies that raised the homeownership rate to an unsustainable level, and, as a consequence of a relatively inelastic supply of housing due to land and local zoning constraints, contributed to a sustained rise in house prices. *That rise in housing prices made the issuance of subprime and Alt-A loans appear relatively risk free.* (Hetzel, 2009: 217, emphasis added)

> Part of the decline [in underwriting standards in the prime and subprime mortgage] may have stemmed from the rapid price escalation in the value of the underlying collateral – the land and structures that secured the mortgage. This led many strapped borrowers and their lenders/investors to believe that the borrowers could refinance their way out of any payment problems. Lenders and investors also came to believe that ever-escalating home prices would eliminate any loss in the event that a risky borrower defaulted and the loan was foreclosed. (Utt, 2008)

Obviously, as long as the house market price keeps rising, α's expectations are *ex post* confirmed. Increasing numbers of people are induced to invest their (own or borrowed) money in the real estate market so that the property demand curve becomes positively sloped (higher prices lead to higher demand) and a speculative bubble starts.[13]

As recalled above, for Minsky a typical feature of free-market economies experiencing a period of prolonged prosperity is the spread of expectations of further rises of Stock Exchange and further increases in corporate profits and dividends. Accordingly, people and firms are increasingly prepared to pass from hedge to speculative financing and from speculative to Ponzi financing. As a consequence, the economy's overall degree of financial fragility increases: 'Over a period of good years the weight of units with speculative and Ponzi positions increases, and the economy becomes more fragile: a minor shock may initiate a major debt deflation which, if not opposed by active economic policy, may lead to a deep and long depression' (Bellofiore and Ferri, 2001: 15).

Thus, from Minsky's perspective, it comes as no surprise that a minor shock such as the collapse of the US sub-prime mortgage loan market led the world economy into a long deep depression.

What, for Minsky, makes a substantial difference between the highly unstable pre-1929 economies and modern less-unstable economies are: (i) the dimension of government deficits; and (ii) the rapidity and extent of Central Bank interventions in the financial markets (see in particular Minsky, 1980). As regards point (i) modern large public deficits sustain aggregate demand (Keynes) and corporate aggregate profits (Kalecki) when private (consumption and investment) expenditure declines. As regards point (ii), mindful of the 1929 bank run and the consequent credit squeeze, debt-deflation spiral and mass unemployment, central banks take seriously their role as lenders-of-last-resort. Yet Minsky is aware that there are two sides to the coin: while modern fiscal and monetary interventionist policies make post-1929 free-market economies less prone to violent financial cycles, they bring about inflationary bias and a reduction in the economy's potential growth rate.

5 FINAL REMARKS

In this chapter I discussed some of the factors that may have played a role in causing the present financial turmoil. In particular, I focused on three different theoretical explanations: (i) errors in monetary policy management; (ii) asymmetric information and distortion of incentive structures in financial markets; and (iii) growing inequality in income distribution coupled with increasing working class indebtedness. Obviously, the explanation eventually gaining most consensus will set the policy agenda for the years to come. I also sought to defend economics from the recurrent charge of not being a truly scientific discipline since, according to critics, its practitioners were unable to foresee the crisis. I argued that economists' responsibility for the present financial dislocation lies elsewhere, in their over-optimistic attitude towards the way free-market economies actually work. Finally, as an alternative to mainstream economics I briefly sketched Keynes's and Minsky's contributions on the relationship between investment and finance. In particular, the latter depicts capitalism as a fragile system, prone to continuous wide-ranging booms and recessions, unless carefully regulated by public authorities and other economic institutions. Therefore, from a Keynesian perspective the crisis should remind economists that one of their most demanding tasks is to design the appropriate set of policies and institutions required to promote public prosperity and happiness in the ever-evolving environment generated by free-market economies.

NOTES

* An extended version of this chapter in Italian was presented to a Ph.D. seminar, 'Gli economisti allo specchio della crisi', organized by the Dottorato in Diritto Comunitario e Diritto Interno [PhD programme in European Community Law and Italian National Law], Law Faculty, University of Palermo, 11 February 2010. I wish to thank Laura Lorello for her kind invitation to the seminar, and Michele Battisti, Carlo Panico and Andrea Salanti for their comments on a previous version of this chapter. Usual caveats apply.

1. The global movement towards a softer regulation of financial markets also comes from the competition among countries in the attempt to attract the international flows of financial capital: 'While regulation is national, finance is global. The location of financial enterprises and markets is endogenous; many are very footloose. A thriving financial sector creates jobs and wealth, and is generally environmentally friendly. So regulators try to retain and attract financial businesses to their jurisdictions in part by offering more liberal, less onerous regulations. This competition through regulatory standards has led to less stringent regulation almost everywhere.' (Buiter, 2007: 6). Moreover, a role not yet sufficiently analysed in the implementation of 'easy-going' financial legislation has been played by the lobbying performed by private financial institutions (Igan et al., 2010).
2. Taylor has recently written a book (Taylor, 2009b) reproaching the Fed for deviating from the so-called Taylor rule in the years before the crisis. The Taylor rule (Taylor, 1993) prescribes how a Central Bank should adjust its interest rate instrument according to the differential between actual and planned inflation and between actual and potential output. For a critical assessment of the interpretations of the crisis based on the Taylor rule see Brancaccio and Fontana (2009).
3. The idea that brokers tend to mimic the behaviour of their colleagues/competitors is not new. In his 1937 essay 'The general theory of employment' (*Quarterly Journal of Economics*), in which he summarized the main tenets of his new revolutionary economic theory, Keynes wrote: 'Knowing that our individual judgment is worthless, we endeavour to fall back on the judgment of the rest of the world which is perhaps better informed. That is, we endeavour to conform with the behaviour of the majority or the average. The psychology of a society of individuals each of whom is endeavouring to copy the others lead to what we may strictly term a *conventional* judgment.' (Keynes's emphasis. This essay is now reproduced in *The Collected Writings of John Maynard Keynes*, vol. XIV, pp. 109–23). Recently, herd behaviour was analysed by Banerjee (1992).
4. In the past two decades, a rising debt-to-income ratio and the consequent rise in households' financial fragility has become a common feature of many industrialized countries besides the USA: see Rinaldi and Sanchis-Arellano (2006).
5. Sir John Hicks once claimed that economic theories are 'rays of light, which illuminate a part of the target, leaving the rest in the dark. As we use them, we avert our eyes from things that may be relevant, in order that we should see more clearly what we do see. It is entirely proper that we should do this, since otherwise we should see very little. But it is obvious that a theory which is to perform this function satisfactorily must be well chosen; otherwise it will illumine the wrong things' (Hicks, 1976: 208).
6. Though not declared heterodox economists, Fitoussi and Stiglitz (2009: 5) put at the top of their list of recommendations a series of fiscal and social security measures to reverse the present trend of income distribution in order to stimulate aggregate demand in the medium to long run.
7. The symmetry thesis has been submitted to harsh criticisms. In fact, *contra* it is possible to mention two of the best-known scientific theories, that is, Newton's theory of universal gravitation (a theory that predicts but does not explain) and Darwin's theory of the evolution of living species (a theory that explains but does not predict): see Blaug (1992: 5 ff).
8. In the statistics jargon $\alpha\%$ is the probability of committing a Type I error, that is, the rejection of an H_0 hypothesis which is actually true; while $\beta\%$ is the probability of committing a Type II error, that is, the failure to reject an H_0 hypothesis which is actually false. Making an analogy with the logic of criminal trial, it may be said that a Type I error is the conviction of an innocent, while a Type II error is the acquittal of a culprit. Given the amount of available evidence both in statistics and criminal law, an inevitable trade-off exists between these two kinds of errors.
9. This is particularly evident within the rational expectations approach in economics: 'expectations since they are informed predictions of future events are essentially the same as the predictions of the relevant economic theory' (Muth, 1961: 316).

10. For example White (2009: 39) explicitly supports the superiority of market discipline thesis over public supervision in the banking system.
11. Goodfriend (2002) provides an easily-accessible introduction to contemporary macro-models.
12. The proposed tax on financial transactions to mitigate short-term speculative fluctuations today takes the well-known name of the Tobin tax, from the US Nobel laureate, James Tobin, who proposed it in the early 1970s.
13. To have a complete description of what has happened in the last few years it is necessary to add to Minsky's analysis an element that, in his time, was still in its embryonic state: the securitization process, that is, the possibility of converting the idiosyncratic loan relationship between α and β into a negotiable instrument traded within an ample set of financial operators. Thanks to these operations of derived finance, lender α frees him/herself from the insolvency risk of borrower β and gets fresh liquidity to use in new financial operations.

REFERENCES

Acemoglu, D. (2009), 'The crisis of 2008: structural lessons for and from economics', *CEPR Policy Insight*, no. 28.

Banerjee, A.V. (1992), 'A simple model of herd behavior', *The Quarterly Journal of Economics*, **107**, 797–817.

Barba, A. and Massimo Pivetti (2009), 'Rising household debt: its causes and macroeconomic implications – a long-period analysis', *Cambridge Journal of Economics*, **33**, 113–37.

Bellofiore, R. and P. Ferri (eds) (2001), *The Economic Legacy of Hyman Minsky*, 2 vols, Cheltenham, UK and Northampton, MA, USA: Edward Elgar Publishing.

Bernanke, B.S. (2004), 'The great moderation', remarks by Governor Ben S. Bernanke at the meetings of the Eastern Economic Association, Washington, DC, available at http://www.federalreserve.gov/BOARDDOCS/SPEECHES/2004/20040220/default.htm.

Bernanke, B.S. (2005), 'The global saving glut and the US current account deficit', remarks by Governor Ben S. Bernanke at the Sandridge Lecture, Virginia Association of Economics, available at http://www.federalreserve.gov/boarddocs/speeches/2005/200503102/default.htm.

Blaug, M. (1992), *The Methodology of Economics. Or How Economists Explain*, 2nd edn, Cambridge: Cambridge University Press.

Brancaccio, E. and G. Fontana (2009), 'A critique of interpretations of the crisis based on the "Taylor Rule"', available at http://www.theglobalcrisis.info/docs/relazioni/BrancaccioeFontana.pdf.

Buiter, W. (2007), 'Lessons from the 2007 financial crisis', *CEPR Policy Insight*, no. 18.

Cecchetti, S.G. (2008), 'Monetary policy and the financial crisis of 2007–2008', *CEPR Policy Insight*, no. 21.

Diamond, D.W. and R.G. Rajan (2009), 'The credit crisis: conjectures about causes and remedies', *The American Economic Review*, **99**, 606–10.

Draghi, M. (2009), 'Gli economisti e la crisi', presentation at the Società Italiana degli Economisti, 50th Riunione Scientifica Annuale, Rome, available at http://www.adapt.it/acm-on-line/Home/documento3518.html.

Fitoussi, J.P. and J.E. Stiglitz (2009), 'The Shadow Gn*: The ways out of the crisis and the building of a more cohesive world', available at http://www.ofce.sciences-po.fr/pdf/dtravail/WP2009-17.pdf.

Goodfriend, M. (2002), 'Monetary policy in the new neoclassical synthesis: a primer', *International Finance*, **5**, 165–91.

Hegel, G.W.F. ([1820] 2001), *Philosophy of Right*, Kitchener, ON: Batoche Books, available at http://www.efm.bris.ac.uk/het/hegel/right.pdf.

Hempel, C.G. and P. Oppenheim (1948), 'Studies in the logic of explanation', *Philosophy of Science*, **15**, 135–75.

Hetzel, R.L. (2009), 'Government intervention in financial markets: stabilizing or destabilizing?', in Alfredo Gigliobianco and Gianni Toniolo (eds), *Financial Market Regulation in the Wake of Financial Crises: The Historical Experience*, Banca d'Italia, *Seminari e Convegni*, no. 1, pp. 207–21.

Hicks, J.R. (1976), '"Revolutions" in economics', in Spiro J. Latsis (ed.), *Method and Appraisal in Economics*, Cambridge: Cambridge University Press.

Hicks, J.R. (1983), 'A discipline, not a science', in *Collected Essays on Economic Theory*, vol. III, *Classics and Moderns*, Oxford: Basil Blackwell.

Igan, D., P. Mishra and T. Tressel (2010), 'Lobbying and the financial crisis', available at http://www.voxeu.org/index.php?q=node/4530.

Imperia, A. and V. Maffeo (2009), 'As if nothing were going to happen: a search in vain for warnings about the current crisis in economic journals with the highest impact factors', available at http://www.boeckler.de/pdf/v_2009_10_30_imperia_maffeo.pdf.

Johnson, E. and D.E. Moggridge (eds) (1971–1989), *The Collected Writings of John Maynard Keynes* (30 volumes), London and New York: Macmillan and Cambridge University Press. *The General Theory of Employment, Interest and Money* (1936) is available at: http://www.marxists.org/reference/subject/economics/keynes/general-theory/.

Keynes, J.M. (1937), 'The general theory of employment', *Quarterly Journal of Economics*, reproduced in *The Collected Writings of John Maynard Keynes*, vol. XIV, New York: Macmillan, St Martin's Press, pp. 109–23.

Laidler, D. (2010), 'Lucas, Keynes and the crisis', *Journal of the History of Economic Thought*, **32**, pp. 39–62.

Lakatos, I. and A. Musgrave (eds) (1970), *Criticism and the Growth of Knowledge*, Cambridge: Cambridge University Press.

Leijonhufvud, A. (2009), 'Macroeconomics and the crisis: a personal appraisal', *CEPR Policy Insight*, no. 41.

Minsky, H.P. (1977), 'The financial instability hypothesis: an interpretation of Keynes and an alternative to "standard" theory', reprinted as Chapter III of H.P. Minsky (1982), *Can 'It' Happen Again? Essays on Instability and Finance*, New York: M.E. Sharpe.

Minsky, H.P. (1980), 'Finance and profits: the changing nature of American business cycles', reprinted as Chapter II of H.P. Minsky (1982), *Can 'It' Happen Again? Essays on Instability and Finance*, New York: M.E. Sharpe.

Muth, J.F. (1961), 'Rational expectations and the theory of price movements', *Econometrica*, **29**, 315–35.

Onado, M. (2009), *I Nodi al Pettine. La Crisi Finanziaria e le Regole non Scritte*, Roma-Bari: Laterza.

Perotti, R. (2009), 'Economisti alla sbarra, ecco l'atto di accusa', *Il Sole 24 Ore*, 27 May, available at http://www.ilsole24ore.com/art/SoleOnLine4/dossier/

Economia%20e%20Lavoro/2009/lezioni-per-il-futuro/27-maggio/economisti-sbarra-atto-accusa.shtml.

Rajan, R. (2005), 'Has financial development made the world riskier?', *Proceedings, Federal Reserve Bank of Kansas City*, August, pp. 313–69.

Rinaldi, L. and A. Sanchis-Arellano (2006), 'Household debt sustainability. What explains household non-performing loans? An empirical analysis', *European Central Bank Working Paper Series*, no. 570.

Saint-Paul, G. (2009), 'A "modest" intellectual discipline: in defence of contemporary economics', available at http://www.voxeu.com/index.php?q=node/3996.

Shiller, R.J. (2000), *Irrational Exuberance*, Princeton, NJ: Princeton University Press.

Shiller, R.J. (2003), *The New Financial Order: Risk in the 21st Century*, Princeton, NJ: Princeton University Press.

Spaventa, L. (2009), 'Economists and economics: what does the crisis tell us?', *CEPR Policy Insight*, no. 38.

Stiglitz, J.E. (2009), 'The current economic crisis and lessons for economic theory', *Eastern Economic Journal*, **35**, pp. 281–96.

Tabellini, G. (2009), 'Il mondo ritorna a correre, l'Italia non si fermi', *Il Sole 24 Ore*, 24 June, available at http://www.ilsole24ore.com/art/SoleOnLine4/dossier/Economia%20e%20Lavoro/2009/lezioni-per-il-futuro/24-giugno/tabellini.shtml.

Taylor, J.B. (1993), 'Discretion versus policy rules in practice', *Carnegie-Rochester Conference Series on Public Policy*, **39**, pp. 195–214.

Taylor, J.B. (2000), 'Teaching modern macroeconomics at the principles level', *The American Economic Review, Papers and Proceedings*, **90**, pp. 90−94.

Taylor, J.B. (2009a), 'How government created the financial crisis', *The Wall Street Journal*, 9 February, available at http://www.stanford.edu/~johntayl/How_Government_Created_the_Financial_Crisis-WSJ-2-9-09.pdf.

Taylor, J.B. (2009b), *Getting Off Track: How Government Actions and Interventions Caused, Prolonged, and Worsened the Financial Crisis*, Stanford, CA: Hoover Press.

Tremonti, Giulio (2009), Speech at the People's Friendship Meeting, 28 August, available at http://it.wikipedia.org/wiki/Giulio_Tremonti.

Utt, R. (2008), 'The subprime mortgage market collapse. A primer on the causes and possible solutions', available at http://www.heritage.org/Research/Reports/2008/04/The-Subprime-Mortgage-Market-Collapse-A-Primer-on-the-Causes-and-Possible-Solutions.

Whalen, C.J. (2008), 'The credit crunch: a Minsky moment', *Studi e Note di Economia*, no. 1, pp. 3–21.

White, E.N. (2009), 'Lessons from the history of bank examination and supervision in the United States, 1863–2008', in Alfredo Gigliobianco and Gianni Toniolo (eds), *Financial Market Regulation in the Wake of Financial Crises: The Historical Experience*, Banca d'Italia, *Seminari e Convegni*, no. 1, pp. 15–44.

Yellen, J.L. (2009), 'A Minsky meltdown: lessons for central bankers', presentation to the 18th Annual Hyman P. Minsky Conference on the state of the US and world economies, 'Meeting the challenges of the financial crisis'; available at http://www.frbsf.org/news/speeches/2009/0416.html.

12. Human resources: the key to institutional economics after the Great Recession

Charles J. Whalen

INTRODUCTION

In the wake of the recent global financial crisis, many economists have asked what went wrong, how can economists do a better job of anticipating or preventing financial trouble in the future, and how can economic theory better incorporate financial institutions into macroeconomics? Addressing those questions is appropriate, and this author has even led one inquiry of that sort (Whalen, 2011).

But learning from the global financial crisis and what has become widely known in the USA as the Great Recession must involve more than recognizing what can go wrong. It must also involve learning as the crisis winds down and as the economy moves into the recovery phase and then into the next expansion. If, as is almost certain, the jobs that will be required in that expansion will be different and often even in different places from where they were before, then unless we take these issues into account we will not have properly or fully addressed the recession problem. This chapter leaves a retrospective analysis of the downturn to others and instead takes an institutional economist's perspective on what we can learn from how the crisis was brought to a close.

From an institutionalist perspective, resolving the Great Recession required a two-pronged strategy: recovery and reform. The recovery agenda included monetary stimulus and expansionary fiscal policy to stabilize aggregate demand, Federal Reserve (Fed) 'lender-of-last-resort' action to stabilize financial markets, and temporary financial market policies to address dimensions of the Great Recession that required more extensive intervention. The reform agenda included financial regulatory reform, a national commitment to the challenges facing USA's working families, and US participation in efforts that promote international economic stability and job creation (Whalen, 2010a). Most of this was addressed by US policy-makers in response to the recent crisis, but a key part was given short shrift in both the recovery and reform agendas: the part focusing on working families.

Writing in *Macroeconomic Theory and its Failings* (*MTIF*), the precursor to the current volume, this author stressed that 'the overarching policy objective should be greater macroeconomic stability and *broadly shared prosperity* in the USA and abroad' (Whalen, 2010a: 250, emphasis added). This is consistent with the view he expressed in an essay co-written in the mid-1990s with the late Hyman Minsky. They wrote:

> In the current era, economic success requires more than economic growth, low unemployment and minimal inflation. It requires that every citizen has the opportunity to develop and utilize his or her talents and capacities, and it requires an economy that rewards workers with rising standards of living and the prospect of an even better life for their children. (Minsky and Whalen, 1996: 161)

In the institutionalist reform agenda presented in *MTIF*, attention to issues affecting American workers and their families was impossible to miss, but the recovery agenda was also supposed to help millions of American families by reducing unemployment and resolving the mortgage crisis.

As the Great Recession wound down in late 2009, however, unemployment rose to 10 per cent (nearly hitting its post-war peak) and stayed above 9 per cent into mid-2010 as this chapter was written. Meanwhile, the federal effort to address the mortgage problem remained inadequate – indeed, an independent bank analyst called it a 'dud' (Puzzanghera, 2010). Thus, what resolution of the global financial crisis and Great Recession reveals is that the recovery and expansion ahead are shaping up to look like the previous expansion, which left most middle-class and working families behind (Weller, 2006).

How should institutionalism respond? In the wake of the Great Recession, among the most promising ways forward for institutional economists involves focusing on what American institutionalist Vernon M. Briggs calls *human resource economics* (HRE). HRE is a policy-oriented field that views human resources as the key to economic progress and personal development and is one that is frequently ignored and neglected. It also puts the attention of economics squarely on workers, their capacities and contributions, and their well-being.

This chapter explores the emergence, evolution and contemporary relevance of HRE. Following the lead of Briggs, a pioneer in HRE, the discussion of contemporary relevance has five dimensions: labor supply and demand, workforce quality, employment opportunities, personal development, and international well-being. HRE offers insights for dealing with future downturns, but is also relevant to preparing adequately for future expansions.[1]

A DISTINCT FIELD

Economists and politicians have long pointed to human resources as the source of national strength and prosperity. Adam Smith ([1776] 1935: 734) put worker 'skill, dexterity and judgment' at the heart of his explanation for the wealth of nations, and other economists followed his lead. As a result, the labor theory of value was a cornerstone of classical economics.

Despite that long history, HRE emerged as a distinct field within economics only in the wake of World War II. The breakthrough came when post-war economists conducted research to explain economic progress in industrialized nations. Their research demonstrated that the human resources side of the resource base has 'enormous implications for national and international well-being' (Briggs, 1987).

Yet the story of HRE does not begin entirely after World War II. That is because institutional economist John R. Commons (1862–1945) provides HRE with vital intellectual grounding. Commons responded to the economic booms and depressions of the early twentieth century by forging a 'third way' between laissez-faire and a planned economy (Whalen, 2008a: 45). HRE takes that path as its starting point.

The centerpiece of this 'third way' is pragmatic reform. Commons believed that economic and human adjustment problems are an inevitable part of the advance of industrialization. Thus, he concluded that social institutions and public policy have to evolve to deal with the changing circumstances. There is no utopia beyond a dynamic, 'reasonable' and harmonious society. In short, Commons put the aim of practical problem-solving at the heart of institutional economics, and this is where HRE gets its reformist bent.

GROWTH AND STABILIZATION

HRE emerged from the post-war work of labor economists influenced by institutional economics. It originated with research on the relationship between human resources and economic growth. But these labor economists soon realized that human resource development could also play a constructive role in addressing other difficult economic issues, including stabilization of employment, output and prices.[2]

A starting point for HRE is *Education, Manpower, and Economic Growth*, by Frederick H. Harbison and Charles A. Myers (1964).[3] It examined 75 countries on the basis of a composite human-resource development index and compared those findings with national indicators of economic development and growth. Its main conclusion was that nations could make the greatest strides in growth and development by crafting and implementing a coherent strategy for human resource development. According to Harbison and Myers, that strategy would set clear priorities for an economic agenda that recognizes and reflects broad social goals, not merely narrow economic objectives.

The link between human resources and aggregate economic growth has remained a focal point for HRE. For example, Briggs demonstrated in 1987 that although much post-war economic research assumed physical capital was the main source of productivity increases and long-term growth, human resource development was actually the major contributor. 'It is a fact of economic life that deserves prominence in policy formulation', concluded Briggs (1987: 1213–14). This emphasis continues to influence the work of US human resource economists such as Robert Glover and Christopher King (2010), and on a global scale it drives the human development research agenda of the United Nations, which has kept attention on the matter for over two decades in its reports on human development (United Nations Development Program, 2010).

HRE also emerged as economists began to grapple with structural unemployment in the 1960s. Careful observers of the early post-World War II economy noted that the average US unemployment rate was rising with each successive period of cyclical prosperity. This 'creeping prosperity unemployment' triggered a debate among economists over whether structural economic change posed a growing problem (Marshall and Briggs, 1989: 590).

The two economists at the center of this debate were Walter Heller, President John Kennedy's chief economic adviser, and Charles Killingsworth, a professor at Michigan State University. Heller argued that expansionary fiscal policy, in the form of a tax cut proposed by Kennedy, would be sufficient to reduce unemployment. Killingsworth countered that an increasing proportion of unemployment was structural and would not respond to tax cuts. He argued that automation, the emergence of computers, and other technological changes were affecting more and more workplaces, reducing demand for unskilled workers and increasing demand for engineers, programmers, repairmen and other skilled workers.[4]

In the wake of Kennedy's assassination, policy-makers passed both the tax cut supported by Heller and experimental programs consistent with Killingsworth's position. The latter included worker-training and labor-market assistance for the jobless, initiatives initially called 'manpower' policies and later renamed employment and training policies. Other programs with structural components would follow, especially under the Comprehensive Employment and Training Act of 1973 (CETA), but also the Job Training Partnership Act of 1982 and the Workforce Investment Act of 1998.

Another aspect of HRE emerged in the 1970s: use of employment and training policies to counteract recession. In the 1960s, US policies aimed at the labor market were applied 'without any countercyclical intent' (Levitan et al., 1972: 359). But that changed with the Emergency Employment Act of 1971 and then CETA, which sought to address business-cycle fluctuations by offering workers temporary positions in periods of high unemployment. Such work is often called public-service employment, and the same strategy was part of the American Recovery and Reinvestment Act of 2009 (ARRA). In February 2010, the US Congressional Budget Office estimated that ARRA boosted real US gross domestic product by as much as 2 per cent in 2009 and 4 per cent in 2010 and that it lowered the unemployment rate by as much as 0.5 percentage points in 2009 and 1.8 percentage points in 2010 (US Congressional Budget Office, 2010: 9).

Under CETA, local governments (and later also non-profits) hired the unemployed to serve in any of a range of positions, including teacher's assistant, home-health aide, and police dispatcher. Program participants also worked on community conservation and weatherization projects. ARRA was designed to provide similar employment. Assessments of CETA found that it boosted aggregate spending and employment more quickly than tax cuts. The assessments also found little evidence that federal spending merely substituted for local spending (Marshall and Briggs, 1989, 598–601).

In the late 1970s, employment and training policies were also implemented to help stabilize prices in the face of stagflation. Since economists and policy-makers feared that merely stimulating aggregate demand further would worsen inflation, Ray Marshall, President Jimmy Carter's Labor Secretary, and other human resource economists proposed attacking joblessness through targeted employment and training programs. The aim was to eliminate labor bottlenecks in the economy, and thus ease inflation pressures, while simultaneously reducing unemployment. The same goal was, and remains, a key driver of active labor market policies in Western Europe.

CIVIL RIGHTS AND EQUITY

The civil rights movement was another major development that contributed to emergence of HRE and national human-resource policy in the United States. Human resource economists such as Marshall and Briggs viewed civil rights as a matter of human rights and social equity, but also as a matter of enhancing economic efficiency. For these economists, ensuring equal opportunity meant tackling not only overt discrimination but also institutional forms of discrimination, which range from procedural matters that affect hiring decisions to 'the preparation of people for jobs' (Marshall and Briggs, 1989: 593). Moreover, this group of economists was not interested in equity and opportunity for racial and ethnic minorities alone; they also supported equal opportunity for women – indeed, equal opportunity for all.[5]

In the 1970s, new structuralist research demonstrated that minorities, women, and youth were entering the labor force in larger numbers and often faced employment challenges. Marshall and Briggs (1989: 592) responded by emphasizing that this structuralist research dovetailed with Killingsworth's earlier findings. They argued that both research streams point to 'the necessity of human-resource policies as the most equitable and efficient way to reduce aggregate unemployment rates'.

CONTEMPORARY RELEVANCE

Drawing on a 1987 essay by Briggs titled 'Human resource development and the formulation of national economic policy', one can identify five policy dimensions of HRE. They are: labor supply and demand, workforce quality, labor-market opportunities, personal development, and international well-being. An examination of these dimensions reveals the contemporary relevance of HRE.

Labor Supply and Demand

One way to look at the labor supply or quantitative dimension of human resources is to begin with the number of employed people in the United States. In August 2010, the official number was just under 139.3 million. Following the international standard set by the template produced by the ILO, to be counted among the employed by the US Bureau of Labor Statistics (BLS), as in all other economies following the ILO standard, a person must first be viewed as part of the civilian labor force. To be included in the labor force, one must be sixteen or older, reside in one of the fifty states or the District of Columbia, and not be confined to an institution (home for the aged, prison, or mental-health facility). In August 2010, the US labor force totaled 154.1 million (US BLS, 2010).

Of course, not everyone in the labor force is counted as employed, a category that requires paid employment within a certain BLS reference period, which again follows the ILO standard. A member of the labor force can also be 'unemployed', which requires one to be available and either searching for work or waiting to be recalled by an employer. As of August 2010, the unemployed comprised 14.9 million, 9.6 per cent of the US labor force (US BLS, 2010).

The 9.6 per cent unemployment rate in August 2010 is one measure of unutilized labor, but there are also potential workers who are part of the US population and not currently part of the labor force. Many of those potential workers fall within a BLS category of people considered 'marginally attached' to the labor force. They are

> persons not in the labor force who want and are available for work, and who have looked for a job sometime in the prior twelve months (or since the end of their last job if they held one within the past twelve months), but were not counted as unemployed because they had not searched for work in the four weeks preceding the [most recent BLS employment] survey. (US BLS, 2008)

Marginally attached workers in August 2010 numbered 2.4 million, including 1.1 million 'discouraged workers', who were no longer looking because they believed no jobs were available to them (US BLS, 2010).[6]

There is also underutilized labor. For example, in August 2010 the BLS identified 8.9 million of the employed labor force as involuntary part-time workers. These people would like to work full-time, but had their hours cut back or were unable to find full-time jobs (US BLS, 2010). Another category of underutilized labor is underemployment, which involves people in positions that require less skill and education than they possess.

Surveying this terrain, human resource economists such as Briggs and Marshall have often called for a comprehensive, national human resource strategy that would include a commitment to full employment. They envision a strategy that would address not just the unemployment rate, but also the challenges surrounding marginal attachment and underutilization. That strategy would have a macroeconomic component, involving fiscal and monetary policies, but also a battery of labor-market and education policies that recognize the need for remedies tailored to fit different circumstances.[7]

Workforce Quality

In addition to a quantitative dimension, HRE has a qualitative dimension. A nation interested in the qualitative dimension of human resources would address the needs of its most economically disadvantaged residents, but would also engage in preventive maintenance and embrace the notion of long-run educational development.

For those who cannot find employment on a regular and self-supporting basis, or who must rely on the underground economy, Briggs (1987: 1225) envisions a *lifeline of opportunity*. This would include job training and other employment preparation, which he sees as both just and economically pragmatic. Writing in the late 1980s, he described the case for an opportunity lifeline by focusing on three US economic problems: the declining labor-force participation of black males, the poverty challenge facing female-headed households, and increasing adult illiteracy. These problems still exist.

In fact, the problems remain serious and economic conditions since the global financial crisis have only made them worse. A 2006 volume edited by Ronald B. Mincy (2006) found that the labor force participation rate of black men continued to decline even during the economic boom of the 1990s. A 2004 report by Andrew Sum and his colleagues at Northeastern University found an ongoing decline in the employment-to-population ratio of black men that began in the mid-1950s. It also found a high and rising rate of year-round joblessness among black men (one out of every four were idle all year in 2002) (Sum et al., 2004). Both studies conclude by recommending the sort of targeted education and workforce-development strategies that Briggs has been promoting for decades.

Poverty among female-headed households and the illiteracy problem are also worrisome. In 1985, one out of every three families headed by a woman was living in poverty (Briggs, 1987: 1225–6). In 2005, the poverty rate for such families was 29 per cent, ten times the rate found in two-parent families (Gosling, 2008: 175–6). A 2002 report on an adult literacy survey, sponsored by the US Department of Education, concluded that about 44 million of the 191 million adults in the United States – nearly one out of four (23 per cent) – have skills that place them in the lowest of five possible proficiency levels for reading, comprehension of documents, and quantitative reasoning. The skills of many respondents were so limited that 'they were unable to respond to much of the survey' (Kirsch et al., 2002: 18). The following year, another literacy study estimated that 50 million Americans cannot read or comprehend above the eighth-grade level and that nearly 75 per cent of the unemployed were illiterate (Morry, 2003). (Note that the study was conducted prior to the Great Recession.) Viewing the labor force in this light puts a wholly different dimension on our labor force problems.

Along with a lifeline for the unemployed and working poor, Briggs envisions a *preventive maintenance* component that offers assistance to anyone who becomes vulnerable to unemployment, regardless of salary history. This is warranted, he argues, by the increasingly dynamic nature of the workplace and the economy's increasing skill and educational requirements. Believing it is impractical to expect the entire workforce to adjust to these changing employment patterns on its own, Briggs suggests a network of initiatives to assist individuals with the labor-market adjustment process. They would include providing reliable information on labor-market trends and job requirements, and offering workers opportunities for educational upgrading, job retraining, employment counseling, and even relocation when appropriate (Briggs, 1987: 1227–30).

Since education is at the heart of Briggs's understanding of what is needed to achieve national success in a dynamic, global economy, he also envisioned *long-run educational development* as contributing to the qualitative dimension of human resources. He offered five educational objectives: preventing students from dropping out of school; boosting the average literacy and educational proficiency level across American society; ensuring that education is contingent on ability to learn, not ability to pay; making educational opportunities accessible to adults throughout their working lives; and linking education reform to a national industrial policy.[8] Briggs recognized this would require extensive changes within US educational institutions (affecting administrative practices, teacher certification and compensation, school decision-making, student assessment methods, and more), but he insisted such changes would enable education to 'contribute to the answer and not worsen the problem' of contemporary labor-force adjustment (Briggs, 1987: 1230–31).

Equal Employment Opportunity

A workforce-opportunity dimension to human resources exists alongside the quantitative and qualitative dimensions. Conventional economics argues that discrimination is irrational and thus should not persist. On the basis of extensive research, Briggs responded that experience 'has demonstrated that it cannot be realistically assumed that labor markets function solely on the basis of merit and productivity'. He added: 'The roots of discrimination run deep into the institutional practices that prepare workers to compete in the labor market' (Briggs, 1987: 1231).

In Briggs's view, equal employment opportunity should be supported by anti-discrimination mechanisms that monitor hiring patterns and offer redress in the event of discriminatory actions. In some cases it is enough to insist that hiring requirements are job-related and that employment practices are fair. Other times, however, biases and discrimination go much deeper, and help explain why certain groups within the labor force might not appear in the applicant pool of a fair-minded employer.[9] Thus, Briggs stresses that active outreach, training, apprenticeship, and placement programs contribute to pursuit of equal employment opportunity (Briggs, 1987: 1231–4; Curington, 2007).

Personal Development and International Well-being

The two remaining dimensions of human resources look beyond the national economy and focus on personal development and international well-being. Some individual benefits of human resource development come from being adequately prepared for employment. Indeed, this is where HRE touches on worker incomes, retirement security, and quality of working life, all of which deserve attention from human resource economists.[10] However, there are also other benefits associated with education and the development of individual talents and abilities, some accruing to the individual and some to society.

Economists have long recognized there are social as well as individual benefits of an investment in human resources. In fact, education offers the classic case of a good that generates a positive externality. Yet Briggs (1987: 1235) suggests that the need for an educated citizenry has become increasingly great, owing to the awesome ability of science and technology to create, destroy and 'reshape the relationship of human beings to their natural environment'. He writes that 'it is imperative that the uses of these forces be the result of the decisions made by an informed citizenry and not by an opinionated or indifferent society'.

That last point connects the personal to the political, but it also connects the individual to the rest of global humanity. Most HRE has focused on well-being at the national level, suggesting that a prosperous and humane US economy, for example, provides Americans with the best position from which to address problems on an international scale. Over the years, however, these institutionalists have given increasing attention to international issues, especially international coordination, global standards and worldwide codes of conduct. Not surprisingly, their message centers on leveling the global economic playing field to bring up those at the bottom and prevent a global race *to* the bottom.

THE WEALTH OF NATIONS

In response to the Great Recession, economists and policy-makers devoted much attention to shoring up the financial sector of the economy and introducing reforms that might help anticipate or even prevent future financial crises. That was appropriate.[11]

After the Great Recession, however, it seems useful for economists to turn their attention to human resources, the ultimate source of the wealth of nations. HRE, rooted in institutional economics, offers one way forward. It is pragmatic, aimed at practical problems, and attuned to the multiple dimensions of human resources. There are certainly plenty of human resource issues to explore, and devoting attention to them now will pay off at all stages of the business cycle.[12]

NOTES

1. For an excellent discussion of HRE, see Briggs (1987). For more on HRE, see Whalen (2010b). Some other economists in the HRE tradition include Eileen Appelbaum, Barry Bluestone, Christopher King, Robert Glover, Garth Mangum, Ray Marshall, Paul Osterman, Michael Piore, Richard Santos and Andrew Sum, though these individuals often disagree on policy specifics. The late Eli Ginzberg and Sar Levitan can also be considered part of this tradition.
2. HRE was not the economics profession's only post-World War II tradition to focus on the importance of human skills and knowledge. The other tradition, called human-capital theory, emerged from neo-classical economics and is associated with the work of Theodore Schultz and Gary Becker. For critical assessments of human-capital theory from the perspective of HRE, see Briggs (1987) and Piore (1974).
3. See also Ginzberg (1958) and Harbison (1973).
4. On structural unemployment, see Killingsworth (1965a; 1965b; 1979). On the Heller–Killingsworth debate and its continuing relevance, see Bluestone (1996).
5. HRE is concerned not merely with the *level* of employment, but also with the *composition* of employment (Marshall and Briggs, 1989: 594). Reflecting on the civil rights era from the vantage point of the mid-1980s, Briggs wrote: 'There had to be changes in the racial and gender composition of employment patterns, as opposed to an exclusive policy focus merely on the level of employment. As a black leader once expressed it, "After all, we had full employment back on the plantations"'. At the same time, Briggs recognized that any successful equal-employment opportunity strategy would need to be accompanied by a full-employment strategy, or the former would only heighten job-security concerns among groups that previously benefited from exclusionary employment practices (Briggs, 1987: 1233–4).
6. Other marginally attached workers indicate they have not recently looked for work due to reasons such as family responsibilities and school attendance (US BLS, 2010).
7. Immigration is also an important part of the quantitative dimension of human resources. For more on this, see Whalen (2010b).
8. On linking education and training with industrial policy, Briggs writes: 'There can be little purposeful long-term educational preparation of the labor force for employment if there is little direction provided as to where the economy is thought to be going' (Briggs, 1987: 1231).
9. For example, recruitment and job-posting practices can be structured (even inadvertently) in a way that favors some groups over others. In addition, inequality and discrimination can shape the institutions that educate, train and prepare people for employment. Past patterns of discrimination can cause even those with educational or training opportunities to temper their occupational aspirations and forgo some opportunities out of discouragement.
10. For a related discussion of income and retirement insecurity in recent decades, see Whalen (2008b).

11. But, as suggested earlier in this chapter (and in Whalen, 2010a), the mortgage crisis deserved greater attention than it received, as did unemployment.
12. This chapter was prepared in the spring of 2010 (and updated in the summer), when there was widespread agreement among economists that the US economy was in a recovery, although the unemployment rate, at over 9 per cent, remained close to its post-World War II peak.

REFERENCES

Bluestone, Barry (1996), 'Economic inequality and the macrostructuralist debate', in Charles J. Whalen (ed.), *Political Economy for the Twenty-First Century: Contemporary Views on the Trend of Economics*, Armonk, NY: M.E. Sharpe, pp. 171–94.

Briggs, Vernon M. (1987), 'Human resource development and the formulation of national economic policy', *Journal of Economic Issues*, **21**(3), 1207–40.

Curington, William P. (2007), Interview with Vernon M. Briggs Jr, conducted via telephone, May, deposited in the Martin P. Catherwood Library, Cornell University, Kheel Center for Labor Management Documentation and Archives.

Ginzberg, Eli (1958), *Human Resources: The Wealth of a Nation*, New York: Simon & Schuster.

Glover, Robert W. and Christopher T. King (2010), 'Sectoral approaches to workforce development: toward an effective US labor-market policy', in Charles J. Whalen (ed.), *Human Resource Economics and Public Policy: Essays in Honor of Vernon M. Briggs Jr*, Kalamazoo, MI: W.E. Upjohn Institute for Employment Research.

Gosling, James J. (2008), *Economics, Politics, and American Public Policy*, Armonk, NY: M.E. Sharpe.

Harbison, Frederick H. (1973), *Human Resources as the Wealth of Nations*, New York: Oxford University Press.

Harbison, Frederick H. and Charles A. Myers (1964), *Education, Manpower, and Economic Growth: Strategies of Human Resource Development*, New York: McGraw-Hill.

Killingsworth, Charles. C. (1965a), 'Automation, jobs, and manpower: the case for structural unemployment', in Garth L. Mangum (ed.), *The Manpower Revolution: Its Policy Consequences*, Garden City, NY: Anchor Books, pp. 97–117.

Killingsworth, Charles C. (1965b), 'Unemployment after the tax cut', in William G. Bowen and Frederick H. Harbison (ed.), *Unemployment in a Prosperous Economy*, Princeton, NJ: Industrial Relations Section, Princeton University, pp. 82–97.

Killingsworth, Charles C. (1979), 'The fall and rise of structural unemployment', in Barbara D. Dennis (ed.), *Proceedings of the Thirty-First Annual Meeting*, Madison, WI: Industrial Relations Research Association, pp. 1–13.

Kirsch, Irwin S., Ann Jungeblut, Lynn Jenkins and Andrew Kolstad (2002), *Adult Literacy in America: A First Look at the Findings of the National Adult Literacy Survey*, 3rd edn NCES 1993–275, Washington, DC: National Center for Education Statistics, Office of Educational Research and Improvement, US Department of Education.

Levitan, Sar A., Garth L. Mangum and Ray Marshall (1972), *Human Resources and Labor Markets: Labor and Manpower in the American Economy*, New York: Harper and Row.

Marshall, Ray and Vernon M. Briggs (1989), *Labor Economics: Theory, Institutions, and Public Policy*, 6th edn, Homewood, IL: Irwin.

Mincy, Ronald B. (ed.) (2006), *Black Males Left Behind*, Washington, DC: Urban Institute Press.

Minsky, Hyman P. and Charles J. Whalen (1996), 'Economic insecurity and the institutional prerequisites of successful capitalism', *Journal of Post Keynesian Economics*, **19**(2), 155–70.

Morry, Chris (2003), 'Illiteracy in the United States', Communication Initiative Network (Summary of Findings of the Words are Your Wheels Literacy Program), available at http://www.comminit.com/en/node/17040, accessed 13 February 2009.

Piore, Michael J. (1974), 'The importance of human capital theory to labor economics: a dissenting view', in Barbara D. Dennis (ed.), *Proceedings of the Twenty-Sixth Annual Winter Meeting*, Madison, WI: Industrial Relations Research Association, pp. 251–8.

Puzzanghera, Jim (2010), 'Foreclosure prevention program is struggling', *Los Angeles Times*, 21 August, available at http://articles.latimes.com/2010/aug/21/business/la-fi-obama-foreclosures-20100821, accessed 24 August 2010.

Smith, Adam ([1776] 1935), *An Inquiry into the Nature and Causes of the Wealth of Nations*, New York: Modern Library.

Sum, Andrew, Iswar Khatiwada, Frimpomaa Ampaw, Paulo Tobar and Sheila Palma (2004), *Trends in Black Male Joblessness and Year-Round Idleness: An Employment Crisis Ignored*, Chicago, IL: Alternative Schools Network, available at http://www.nlc.org, accessed 13 February 2009.

United Nations Development Program (2010), 'Summary – the real wealth of Nations: pathways to human development', available at http://hdr.undp.org/en/reports/global/hdr2010/summary/, accessed 31 May 2010.

US Bureau of Labor Statistics (BLS) (2008), 'Marginally attached workers (Current Population Survey)', in 'BLS Information Glossary', available at http://www.bls.gov/bls/glossary.htm, accessed 13 February 2009.

US Bureau of Labor Statistics (2010), 'The employment situation: August 2010', Washington, DC: US Department of Labor, available at http://www.bls.gov/news.release/empsit.nr0.htm, accessed 4 September 2010.

US Congressional Budget Office (2010), *Estimated Impact of the American Recovery and Reinvestment Act on Employment and Economic Output From October 2009 Through December 2009*, February, Washington, DC: Congressional Budget Office.

Weller, Christian E. (2006), 'America needs a more balanced economy', *Perspectives on Work*, **10**(1), 14–16.

Whalen, Charles J. (2008a), 'Post-Keynesian institutionalism and the creative state', *Forum for Social Economics*, **37**(1), 43–60.

Whalen, Charles J. (2008b), 'Post-Keynesian institutionalism and the anxious society', in Sandra S. Batie and Nicholas Mercuro (eds), *Alternative Institutional Structures: Evolution and Impact*, New York: Routledge, pp. 273–99.

Whalen, Charles J. (2010a), 'An institutionalist perspective on the global financial crisis', in Steven Kates (ed.), *Macroeconomic Theory and its Failings: Alternative*

Perspectives on the Global Financial Crisis, Cheltenham, UK and Northampton, MA, USA: Edward Elgar Publishing, pp. 235–59.

Whalen, Charles J. (ed.) (2010b), *Human Resource Economics and Public Policy: Essays in Honor of Vernon M. Briggs Jr*, Kalamazoo, MI: W.E. Upjohn Institute for Employment Research.

Whalen, Charles J. (ed.) (2011), *Financial Instability and Economic Security after the Great Recession*, Cheltenham, UK and Northampton, MA, USA: Edward Elgar Publishing.

13. What should a financial system do? Minskian lessons from the global financial crisis

L. Randall Wray

Before we can reform the financial system, we need to understand what it *should* do. The global financial collapse makes it clear that the system has gone seriously astray. This chapter will examine the approach taken by Hyman Minsky, who was arguably the most prescient observer of the evolution of the financial system in the post-war world. Indeed, the global financial crisis has frequently been called a 'Minsky crisis' (Cassidy, 2008; Kregel, 2008; Whalen, 2007). More specifically, Minsky argued that a new form of capitalism had emerged in the last quarter of the twentieth century – money manager capitalism (Minsky, 1992a; 1992b; 1992c; 1992d; Minsky and Whalen, 1996; Wray, 2009). This evolution was promoted by policy changes, what might be called a move toward self-regulation that replaced New Deal regulation and supervision. This was accompanied by an increasing financial dominance over the economy – what some call 'financialization'. We could point to a transition away from traditional 'banking' and toward 'market-based' provision of finance. That, in turn, was encouraged by the development of new economic theories about the operation of the financial system. The most important of these was the 'efficient markets hypothesis'.

In this chapter I will not present and critique the orthodox approach – interested readers are directed to an excellent overview by John Cassidy (2010). Instead I will first look at what the financial system has been doing, and then will look at what it ought to be doing. That will lead to general policy recommendations for reform. To put it as simply as possible, Minsky always insisted that the proper role of the financial system is to promote the 'capital development' of the economy. By this he did not simply mean that banks should finance investment in physical capital. Rather, he was concerned with creating a financial structure that would be conducive to economic development to improve living standards, broadly defined. The position taken in this chapter is that as currently constituted, the financial system is poorly structured to serve that purpose. Substantial reform is required.

WHAT DO BANKS DO? THE BASICS

According to Minsky, 'A capitalist economy can be described by a set of interrelated balance sheets and income statements' (Minsky, 1992a: 12). The assets on a balance sheet are either financial or real, held to yield income or to be sold or pledged. The liabilities represent a prior commitment to make payments in the future. Assets and liabilities are denominated in the money of account, and the excess of the value of assets over the value of liabilities is nominal net worth. All economic units – households, firms, financial institutions, governments – take positions in assets by issuing liabilities, with margins of safety maintained for protection.

Financial institutions are 'special' in that they operate with very high leverage ratios: for every dollar of assets they might issue 95 cents of liabilities; their positions in assets really are highly 'financed' positions. Further, some kinds of financial institutions specialize in taking positions in longer-term financial assets while issuing short-term liabilities, that is, they intentionally put themselves in the position of requiring refinancing because of a maturity mismatch. An extreme example would be an early 1980s-era US thrift institution that held 30-year fixed rate mortgages while issuing demand deposits (convertible 'on demand' to cash). Such an institution requires continuing access to refinancing on favorable terms because the interest rate it earns is fixed and because it cannot easily sell assets. This can be described as an illiquid position which requires access to a source of liquidity – Federal Home Loan Banks or the Fed in the case of the US. Normally it would refinance using some combination of insured deposits and uninsured short-term liabilities; with deposit insurance a modern bank run takes the form of a run on the uninsured liabilities (such as commercial paper) and is stopped by borrowing from the central bank that acts as 'lender-of-last-resort'.

Other kinds of financial institutions specialize in arranging finance by placing equities or debt into portfolios using markets. They typically rely on fee income rather than interest. In normal circumstances they would not hold these assets directly, but if markets become disorderly they can get stuck with assets they cannot sell (at prices they have promised) and thus will need access to financing of their inventories of stocks and bonds. Some might hold and trade assets for their own account, earning income and capital gains, or might do so for clients. Still others provide insurance and retirement savings accounts.

Thus there are many kinds of financial institutions. Minsky distinguished among traditional commercial banking, investment banking, universal banking and public holding company models. A traditional commercial bank makes only short-term loans that are collateralized by goods in production and distribution. The loans are made good as soon as the goods are sold; this is the model the Real Bills doctrine had in mind (1992c). The bank's position is financed through the issue of short-term liabilities such as demand and savings deposits (or, in the nineteenth century, bank notes). The connections among the bank, the 'money supply', and real production are close, the sort of relation the quantity theory of money supposed. Essentially, the firm borrows to pay wages and raw materials, with the bank advancing demand deposits received by workers and suppliers. When the finished goods are sold, firms are able to repay loans. Banks charge higher interest on loans than they pay on deposits, with the net interest margin supplying bank profits.

If the bank is to remain solvent, losses on assets must be very small because the commercial bank's equity must absorb all asset value reductions. It is the duty of the commercial banker to be skeptical; as Minsky loved to say, a banker's cliché is 'I've never seen a pro forma I didn't like' – borrowers always present a favorable view of their prospects. This is why careful underwriting (credit assessment) is essential. While it is true that loans can be made against collateral (for example, the goods in the process of production and distribution), a successful bank would almost never be forced to take the collateral. A bank should not operate like a pawn shop. As Martin Mayer (2010) says, banking has always been a business where profits come over time as borrowers pay principal and interest. He alludes to the morality of a loan officer, whose success depends on the success of the borrower. It goes without saying that betting on the failure of one's borrower is inimical to the duties of a commercial bank.

In the pre-1870 period that Minsky called the commercial capitalism stage, productive capital was owned directly by individual entrepreneurs and purchased out of accumulated savings (from profits). Banking was limited to commercial banking plus offering savings accounts. In the next stage, finance capitalism, capital goods had become too expensive for individual ownership so that the corporate form emerged. External finance in the form of shares and bonds financed the ownership of capital assets. This leads to the second type of bank, the investment bank. The function of an investment bank is to provide the external finance needed to put the produced capital goods into the hands of the entrepreneur.

We can distinguish between two investment banking models. In the first, the investment bank holds the equities and bonds issued by the corporation that requires financing of its capital stock. The investment bank in turn finances its position by issuing debt held by households. If the investment bank's debt is shorter term than the assets it holds, it must be able to refinance its position as discussed above. Mayer's aphorism still applies: the investment bank will be successful only to the extent that its corporate borrowers are successful. Alternatively the investment bank simply places debt and equities of corporations into the portfolios of households. This model of investment banking does not require borrower success; rather than asking whether the borrower will repay the loan, this investment banker only worries whether he or she can sell the stocks and bonds. Underwriting is no longer an essential activity; indeed, careful underwriting can be ensured only if the households that purchase the debt and equity marketed by the investment bank have recourse.

Of course, investment banks can combine both models: owning the equities and bonds that households do not wish to hold. Today in the US households mostly hold the bonds and equities of firms only indirectly, through professionally managed funds (Minsky, 1992c: 37-8). We will return to this below when we examine Minsky's final stage of capitalism, the money manager phase.

This second investment bank model is often referred to as a 'markets' model as opposed to a 'banks' model because it largely relies on investment banks selling debt to households and fund managers. The development of the asset-backed securities markets is the best example, in which originating banks (of a wide variety) package loans (again, of a wide variety) to serve as the collateral behind marketed securities. Originally the idea was that originating banks would shift the risks off their balance sheets, but they ended up retaining interests in a lot of the securities, a point we will return to. Essentially, the development of securitization of all kinds of loans (including mortgage loans, student loans, auto loans and even credit card debt) turned commercial banks into investment banks of the second type; rather than holding the loans on their balance sheets, they marketed them.

Minsky analyzed two alternative arrangements to the commercial bank plus investment bank model (Minsky, 1992c). The first is the universal bank that was adopted in Germany and Japan; the second is the public holding company (PHC). A universal bank model combines commercial banking and investment banking functions in a bank that provides both short-term lending and long-term funding of the operations of firms. It issues liabilities, including demand deposits, to households and buys the stocks and bonds of firms. A universal bank might also provide a variety of other financial services, including mortgage lending, retail brokering and insurance. The final alternative is the PHC model in which the holding company owns various types of financial firms with some degree of separation provided by firewalls. The PHC holds stocks and bonds of firms and finances positions by borrowing from banks, the market and households.

Minsky argued that the development of money manager capitalism has led to a convergence of these three models. This prescient recognition in 1992 helps to explain the current crisis, in which problems with mortgages first brought down investment banks and then the short-term lending market (such as commercial paper) that bank holding companies had relied upon for financing their positions in assets – including collateralized debt obligations held by 'special purpose vehicle' subsidiaries – and then spread on to the commercial banks and 'shadow' banks that invested in the securitized loans.

BANKING IN THE MONEY MANAGER PHASE OF CAPITALISM: THE RETURN OF FINANCE CAPITALISM

In an important sense, money manager capitalism represents a return to the pre-war finance capitalism stage. So let us first briefly look at the condition of the financial system in 1929, on the precipice of the Great Crash. Then we will look at transformation of the financial system toward money manager capitalism. In the next section we examine in more detail the condition of the financial system that collapsed in 2007.

We have already examined the rise of external finance of a firm's capital assets after 1870. As J.M. Keynes famously described in his *General Theory*, separation of nominal ownership (holders of shares) from management of enterprise meant that prices of equities would be influenced by 'whirlwinds of optimism and pessimism'. Worse, as John Kenneth Galbraith (2009) makes clear, stocks could be manipulated by insiders – Wall Street's financial institutions – through a variety of 'pump and dump' schemes. Indeed, the 1929 crash resulted from excesses promoted by trust subsidiaries of Wall Street's investment banks. Since the famous firms like Goldman Sachs were partnerships, they did not issue stock; instead they put together investment trusts that would purport to hold valuable equities in other firms (often in other affiliates, which sometimes held no stocks other than those in Wall Street trusts) and then sell shares in these trusts to a gullible public.

Effectively, trusts were an early form of mutual fund, with the 'mother' investment house investing a small amount of capital in their offspring, highly leveraged using other people's money. Goldman and others would then whip up a speculative fever in shares, reaping capital gains (Galbraith,

2009). However, trust investments amounted to little more than pyramid schemes (the worst kind of what Minsky called Ponzi finance); there was very little in the way of real production or income associated with all this trading in paper. Indeed, as Galbraith showed, the 'real' economy was long past its peak; there were no 'fundamentals' to drive the Wall Street boom. Inevitably, it collapsed and a 'debt deflation' began as everyone tried to sell their stocks, causing prices to collapse. Spending on the 'real economy' suffered and we were off to the Great Depression.

The New Deal's reaction to the Great Crash was to prohibit commercial banks from handling equities – a response to the excesses of the 1929 boom. The banking crisis had been made very much worse because banks were caught holding stocks with little or no value, many of them issued by these investment trusts. Ironically, even the investment banks that had created the trusts got burned because they also held the worthless stocks. In some cases, this was because they got caught holding stocks they were trying to sell when the market crashed. However, many had invested in the pyramid schemes they created, following the greater fool theory that they would recognize the peak and sell out before the crash. That will sound familiar to anyone who has studied the dot.com boom of the late 1990s, or the 2007 crisis – the banks that originated the toxic waste in the mid-2000s for sale to customers got caught holding it for precisely the same reasons.

In other words, the problem and solution are not really related to functional separation but rather to erosion of underwriting standards that is inevitable in a speculative boom, and especially when a trader mentality triumphs. If a bank believes it can offload questionable assets before values are doubted, its incentive to do proper underwriting is reduced. And if asset prices are generally rising on trend, the bank will try to share in the gains by taking positions in the assets.

Minsky argued that the convergence of the various types of banks within the umbrella bank holding company and within shadow banks was fueled by growth of money manager capitalism. It was also encouraged by the expansion of the government safety net; indeed, it is impossible to tell the story of the current crisis without reference to the implicit guarantee given by the US Treasury to the mortgage market through its GSEs (Fannie and Freddie), through the student loan market (Sallie), and even through the 'Greenspan Put' and the Bernanke 'Great Moderation', which gave the impression to markets that the government would never let markets fail. Gradually, the Glass–Steagall separation was circumvented and then gutted, and investment banking, commercial banking, and all manner of financial services were consolidated in a single financial 'big box' superstore with explicit government guarantees over a portion of the liabilities. Financial institution indebtedness grew to some 120 per cent of GDP, with complex and unknowable linkages among chartered banks and mostly unregulated financial institutions. It was always clear that if problems developed somewhere in a highly integrated system, the Treasury and Fed would be on the hook to rescue the shadow banks, too.

As late as the 1990s the big investment banks were still partnerships so they found it impossible to benefit directly from the run-up of the stock market, similar to the situation in 1929. An investment bank could earn fees by arranging initial public offerings for start-ups, and it could trade stocks for others or for its own account. But in the euphoric irrational exuberance of the late 1990s, that looked like small change. How could an investment bank get a bigger share of the stock market action? In 1999 the largest partnerships went public to enjoy the advantages of stock issue in a boom. Top management was rewarded with stocks, leading to the same pump-and-dump incentives that drove the 1929 boom.

Traders like Robert Rubin (who would become US Treasury Secretary) had already come to dominate firms like Goldman. Traders necessarily take a short view: you are only as good as your last trade. More importantly, traders take a zero-sum view of deals: there will be a winner and a loser, with the investment bank pocketing fees for bringing the two sides together. Better yet, the investment bank would take one of the two sides, preferably the winning side, and pocket the fees and collect the winnings. Before this transformation, trading profits were a small part of investment bank revenues; for example, before it went public, only 28 per cent of Goldman's revenues came from trading and investing activities. That grew to about 80 per cent of revenue after it went public (see Wray, 2009).

In some ways, things were even worse than they had been in 1929 because the investment banks had gone public, issuing equities directly into the portfolios of households and indirectly to households through the portfolios of managed money. It was thus not a simple matter of having Goldman or Merrill Lynch jettison one of its unwanted offspring (special-purpose vehicles that got stuck with mortgage backed securities and collateralized debt obligations); problems with the stock or other liabilities of the behemoth financial institutions would rattle Wall Street and threaten the solvency of pension funds and other invested funds. This finally became clear to the authorities after the problems with Bear Stearns and Lehman Brothers. The layering and linkages among firms – made opaque by over-the-counter derivatives such as credit default swaps – made it impossible to let them fail one-by-one, as failure of one would bring down the whole house of cards.

The problem was that total financial liabilities in the US rose to about five times GDP (versus 300 per cent in 1929), so that every dollar of income must service five dollars of debt. That is one (scary) way to measure leverage. Another measure, of course, is the ratio of debt to assets. This became increasingly important during the real estate boom, when mortgage brokers would find finance for 100 per cent or more of the value of a mortgage, on the expectation that real estate prices would rise. That is a trader's, not a banker's perspective because it relies on either sale of the house or refinancing.

A traditional banker might feel safe with a capital leverage ratio of 12 – with careful underwriting to ensure that the borrower would be able to make payments. With equity at risk, underwriting is essential. However, for a mortgage originator or securitizer who has no plans to hold the mortgage, what matters is the ability to place the security (this is the 'originate to distribute' model in which mortgages are pooled and held in trusts as collateral against securities). Many considerations then come into play, including prospective asset price appreciation, credit ratings, monoline and credit default swap 'insurance', and 'overcollateralization' (markets for the lower tranches of securities). We need not go deeply into the details of these complex instruments. What is important is that income flows take a back seat in such arrangements, and acceptable capital leverage ratios are much higher. For money managers, capital leverage ratios are 30, and reach up to several hundred.

Total risk exposures can be very much higher than this because many commitments are not reported on balance sheets. There are unknown and essentially unquantifiable risks entailed in counter-parties – for example in supposedly hedged credit default swaps in which one sells 'insurance' on suspected toxic waste and then offsets risks by buying 'insurance' that is only as good as the counter-party. Because balance sheets are linked in highly complex and uncertain ways, failure of one counter-party can spread failures throughout the system.

BANKING ON THE PRECIPICE: THE FINANCIAL SYSTEM THAT COLLAPSED IN 2007

On the eve of the 2007 crash, we no longer had any sharp distinction between investment banking and commercial banking in the US. Bank holding companies could engage across the spectrum of financial activities. Some activities were farmed out to independent or quasi-independent specialists (independent mortgage brokers, special-purpose vehicles). Many financial services were supposedly taken out of financial institutions to be performed by 'markets'. However, this was more apparent than real because the dominant financial institutions controlled those markets and set prices of financial assets (often using complex and proprietary models). For our purposes, there was a handful of behemoth financial institutions that provided the four main financial services: commercial banking (short-term finance for business and government), payments services (for households, firms and government), investment banking (long-term finance for firms and government), and mortgages (residential and commercial real estate). A lot of the debts were securitized and ultimately held in pension funds, university endowments, mutual and money market funds, and sovereign wealth funds – the main money managing institutions.

The originate to distribute model virtually eliminated underwriting, to be replaced by a combination of property valuation by assessors who were paid to overvalue real estate, by credit ratings agencies who were paid to overrate securities, by accountants who were paid to ignore problems, and by monoline insurers whose promises were not backed by sufficient loss reserves. As Jan Kregel (2008) has argued, the mortgages were Ponzi from the very beginning – they required rising real estate prices as well as continual access to refinance because borrowers did not have the capacity to service the loans. Much of the activity was actually off the balance sheets of banks and thrifts, with mortgage brokers arranging for finance, with investment banks packaging the securities, and with the 'shadow banks' or 'managed money' holding the securities.

When delinquencies and defaults on mortgages rose, problems immediately came back to the banks through several avenues: they were stuck with securities they were trying to sell, they had sold credit default swap 'insurance' or had provided 'buy-back' guarantees on securities they had sold, they had special-purpose vehicles with loads of bad assets, and they could not refinance positions in assets because the market for short-term debt had practically disappeared. But that was only the beginning of problems for the financial sector. Shenanigans similar to those that had occurred in 1929 took place over the decade of the 2000s as traders adopted the 'greater fool' theory: they were sure the whole thing would inevitably collapse, but each trader thought he could sell out position at the peak, shunting toxic assets off to the greater fools. Just as in 1929, traders found that selling into a collapsing market meant losses, and falling asset prices meant collateral calls with no access to finance.

As of the end of 2010, no fundamental reform of the financial sector had occurred; if anything the biggest banks were even bigger, and were still holding most of the toxic waste assets. They were still searching for greater fools to buy the junk, and still focused on earning fees and trading profits for asset turnover. Meanwhile, virtually no loans for productive activities were being made. We were very far, indeed, from Martin Mayer's vision of banking, or Hyman Minsky's banks that finance the capital development of the economy. In the following section we return to Minsky's insights on banking, trying to identify what banks should be doing in our new millennium. The previous discussion should make it pretty clear that banking as practised in the first decade of the new millennium had gone seriously astray.

WHAT *SHOULD* BANKS DO?

Let us first enumerate the essential functions to be provided by the financial system.

1. a safe and sound payments system;
2. short-term loans to households and firms, and, possibly, to state and local governments;
3. a safe and sound housing finance system;
4. a range of financial services including insurance, brokerage, and retirement savings services; and
5. long-term funding of positions in expensive capital assets.

There is no reason why any single institution should provide all of these services, although the long-run trend has been to consolidate a wide range of services within the affiliates of a bank holding company. The New Deal reforms had separated institutions by function (and state laws against branching provided geographic constraints). Natural evolution plus deregulation allowed growth of a handful of dominant behemoths that play a key role in provision of all of these services. However, economies of scale in banking are exhausted at a relatively small size. And large 'too big to fail' banks are systemically dangerous, too large and complex to regulate, supervise or manage. Hence, reforms ought to aim for downsizing. This does not necessarily mean a return to Glass–Steagall separation by function, but it does mean that policy should favor small institutions over large ones.

In the remainder of this section I will briefly comment on each of the five functions identified as essential by Minsky. In each case, the current arrangements fall short of what is needed.

The Payments System

Clearing checks at par requires access to the central bank; only it can guarantee that bank liabilities used in payment always maintain parity against cash. And if we are to use bank deposits as the basis of payments, we must have deposit insurance to prevent bank runs at the first hint of crisis. Nothing less than 100 per cent coverage will do – as the UK found out when the crisis hit because its insurance covered only 90 per cent of a depositor's funds (it was forced to increase coverage to 100 per cent to stop bank runs). If we use 'private' banks to run our payments system, we must 'backstop' them with government guarantees. Effectively, then, they are playing with 'house money'; issuing claims on government to make loans and to purchase risky assets. They cannot really be private, rather they are public–private partnerships. If they lose their gambles, government pays (bank owners absorb 5 to 8 per cent of the losses; deposit insurance covers the rest). So the other side of the coin must be close regulation and supervision of the kinds of assets they are permitted to buy.

The alternative is a public payments system, based on the old 'postal savings bank' model. This is a cost-efficient and safe way of providing payments services (still used in many countries, including Japan and Italy): wages are deposited directly in the post office, utilities bills are deducted from accounts, and checks can be written for other payments. The postal savings bank would hold only the safest assets – similar to the Milton Friedman–Irving Fisher '100% reserves' model – such as cash and federal government debt (see Phillips, 1995). Direct access to the central bank ensures par clearing. Government policy would determine the interest rate paid on safe and secure savings.

Short-term Lending

Turning to short-term lending, when banks are back-stopped by government, market incentives are weak because holders of insured deposits do not care if the banks take risky bets. And owners are putting up only 5–10 cents on every dollar bet – with government taking the rest of the risk. Since most of the liabilities issued to make loans or buy risky assets are guaranteed by government, the only justification for using the banks as intermediaries is if they do proper underwriting, and can do a better job than the government can. In the case of commercial loans, that is highly probable but only if the banks hold the loans to maturity and develop relations with their customers. In other words, originate-to-securitize is inimical to proper underwriting. Relationship banking provides the proper incentives, with banks holding the loans and thus making profits only if borrowers succeed.

This reverses the trends of the past three decades, during which financial institutions have done everything they could do to shift risks. As we now know, all these efforts failed – for a variety of reasons – as all the risks came right back to the banks. Further, the belief that someone else would bear the risks changed bank behavior in a way that greatly increased systemic risks. For these reasons, chartered banks should be forced to bear the risks they create. There is still room for institutions and practices outside the realm of chartered banks, but these would not have access to deposit insurance or to par clearing at the Fed. The problem has been that unchartered 'shadow banks' had lower costs, which gave them a competitive advantage over regulated banks that were subject to more constraints and that had to operate a costly payments system. This can be rectified in two ways: compensating chartered banks for operating the payments system and charging shadow banks for access to it. Alternatively, as discussed above, the payments system could be taken away from banks and operated directly by government savings banks. In that case, commercial banks would finance positions in assets by issuing non-deposit liabilities and perhaps by borrowing directly from the central bank.

Housing Finance

The third function is housing finance, particularly important in a nation in which a large majority of households are homeowners. US experience is that simplest is best: the 30-year fixed rate mortgages originated and held by thrifts (savings and loans institutions) operating as mutuals worked exceedingly well – homeowners almost never defaulted and mutuals almost never failed. Incentives of shareholders (technically, the liabilities were not deposits) and borrowing homeowners were well aligned. The thrifts were killed by a combination of change of ownership (gradually rules were relaxed until an individual could own a thrift, opening the floodgates of control fraud as real estate developers bought thrifts to finance fraudulent schemes) and Chairman Volcker's experiment in monetarism (raising short-term rates above 20 per cent, resulting in insolvency of most thrifts with long-term low interest rate mortgage assets). It may not be possible to bring back the mutuals, but it is relatively easy to promote safe practices. Government insurance of mortgages should be restricted to those originated and held by financial institutions that conform to approved practices. Only fixed rate mortgages subject to proper underwriting would be included, and only mortgages held by the originator would retain government insurance. Eliminating mortgage brokers, credit raters, securitizers and various other links in the home finance food chain would increase efficiency and safety.

Note, however, that where government takes most of the risk for lending that is seen to be in the public interest (mortgage loans, student loans), the social value of underwriting might be low. Default rates of 5 or

10 per cent on such loans might be seen to be acceptable so long as there are strong public benefits of financing an activity like home ownership or college education. In that case, it may not be desirable to use financial intermediaries; it might make more sense for the government to cut out the middleman and to make the loans directly. The higher default rates that might result from lower quality underwriting done by government could be more than offset by the reduced costs of intermediation. This seems to be the case for student loans in the US, where policy is moving away from reliance on intermediaries and back to direct lending by government.

The other thing to note is that if we are to promote long-term fixed rate mortgages by banks there must be a promise that the central bank will not embark on any Volcker-esque experiments that drive short-term borrowing rates to 20 per cent. Since mortgage lenders will be stuck with long-term fixed rate assets, there must be a social compact to keep the central bank's overnight rate target within reasonable bounds.

Financial Services: Insurance, Brokerage and Retirement Savings

The financial system also provides a range of financial services, including brokerage, retirement and insurance. The argument to consolidate these in 'big box' financial superstores was always based on supposed 'synergies'. In reality, as Minsky and many others have argued, economies of scale in banking are reached at a very small size. Supposed economies of scope have proven to be mostly the ability to dupe customers with 'bait and switch' schemes. Charles Keating's Lincoln Savings used its FDIC seal of approval to sell risky and ultimately worthless assets to its elderly widows who thought they were buying insured certificates of deposit (CDs). More recently, Goldman Sachs allowed hedge fund manager Paulson to design sure-to-fail synthetic collateralized debt obligations (CDOs) that Goldman sold to its own customers, allowing both Goldman and Paulson to use credit default swaps (CDSs) to bet on failure (Eisinger and Bernstein, 2010). In other words, the 'synergy' allows the institution to bet against its customers.

Worse, large institutions invariably become too complex to manage, regulate or supervise. This allows top management to run the institution as a control fraud, duping owners of equity while top management is enriched. And, finally, since the institution is thought to be 'too big to fail', government will also get swindled when it is called in for the inevitable bailout.

Hence, following Minsky, all large chartered banks should be prohibited from diversifying across the range of financial services. Instead, they should be narrowly focused in their activities, forced to spin off any business not closely related to making short-term commercial loans and commercial and residential real estate mortgages.

On the other hand, Minsky proposed creation of a network of local community development banks (CDBs) that would be permitted to engage in a wide range of services, targeted to their communities (Minsky et al., 1993). He wanted to include payments services, small business and consumer loans, mortgages, retirement savings, and financial advice within each CDB. The CDBs would be public–private partnerships, with the federal government providing some of the capital base. They would be run by a community board of directors, with representatives of government sitting on the boards. Banking would be 'intensified': rather than the megabank holding company with affiliates and branching, each CDB would be local but loosely linked to the network through its relation to a government-owned Federal Bank for Community Development Banks that would regulate and supervise its members.

Investment Banking

Finally, the financial system needs to help fund long-term positions in complex and expensive capital assets. As discussed above, historically there are three main approaches to investment banking. Minsky (1992a; 1992b; 1993b) argued that the move to money manager capitalism essentially merged these forms. The crisis revealed two related problems. First, underwriting standards deteriorated when investment banks were transformed from partnerships to publicly held firms. The investment banks got caught up in the same 'maximization of shareholder value' delusion that gripped all publicly traded firms in the stock market euphoria. Since top management was rewarded with stocks and options, 'pump and dump' schemes dominated strategy as short-term trading profits triumphed over longer-run returns. A 'trader mentality' was promoted, and traders like Bob Rubin actually rose to the top ranks of many of the investment banks.

Second, complex – and opaque – linkages among firms were created because of financial dependency (for example, positions in securities were financed in the commercial paper market) and counter-party risks (for example, risks were supposedly hedged through use of CDSs). When problems arose in mortgages, the securities were downgraded, affiliates such as special-purpose vehicles were denied access to the commercial paper market, and CDS 'insurance' became worthless when counter-parties could not pay. The entire financial system froze because the linkages were broken.

It will be very difficult to reorient investment banking toward a long-term horizon with proper underwriting when debt is securitized and subject to lax oversight, and when the average stock is held less than a year (and the stock market taken as a whole is a negative source of funding of capital assets, because firms are caught up in the casino, purchasing their own equity to share in the gains of a speculative bubble). Still, it is necessary to do so.

Minsky emphasized that the capital development of the economy can be ill-done in two ways: the Smithian way and the Keynesian way. It can be misallocated – Smithian way – for example, by too much residential real estate investment. And the aggregate level of investment can be too low – Keynesian insufficient investment. Keynes called for socialization of investment – with government determining the aggregate scale. John Kenneth Galbraith also endorsed socialization of investment to resolve the Smithian problem, with much more investment flowing into public infrastructure. We might pose a new 'TINA' to Margaret Thatcher's TINA (there is no alternative to free markets): there is no alternative to socialization of investment, to resolve the Smithian and Keynesian problems.

In any event, what is needed is to change the incentive structure at investment banks so that good underwriting is rewarded. Compensation of top management and traders must be linked to longer-term results. Neither higher capital ratios (as mandated in Basel III), nor requirements that banks put some 'skin in the game' will help. When investment banks originate to distribute, capital ratios are irrelevant (they do not hold the assets on their books). And in a speculative boom, investment bankers are happy to take positions in the dodgy assets that are booming – on the expectation they can offload them at the peak. Hence, compensation must be tied to longer-term returns; say, five-year income flows, with 'claw-backs' for losses. Underwriting is encouraged when banks hold assets on their books, hence policy should also favor that practice over the 'originate to distribute' model. This means that investment banks would play more of an intermediary role, holding long-term debt and issuing their own debt to savers.

CONCLUSION

Over past decades the belief that 'markets work to promote the public interest' gained in popularity. Minsky questioned: but what if they don't? Then a system of constraints and interventions can work better. He also believed that we need to make 'industry' dominate over 'speculation' (recalling Keynes's famous dichotomy), and not vice versa, or the capital development of the economy will be ill-done in two ways: the Smithian/Neo-classical way or the Keynes/Aggregate demand way. If investment is misdirected, we not only waste resources but we get boom and bust. If investment is too low, we not only suffer from unemployment but also profits are too low to support commitments – leading to default. Further, when profits are low in 'industry' then problems arise in the financial sector because commitments cannot be met. In that case, individual profit-seeking behavior leads to incoherent results as financial markets, labor markets and goods markets all react in a manner that causes wages and prices to fall, generating a debt deflation.

Unfortunately, things are not better when investment is too high: it generates high profits that reward innovation, generating greater risk-taking and eventually producing a financial structure that is too fragile. As Minsky always argued, the really dangerous instability in the capitalist economy is in the upward direction, toward a euphoric boom. That is what makes the debt deflation possible, because asset prices become overvalued and too much unserviceable debt is issued.

Perhaps the biggest flaw in the orthodox approach is the treatment of 'finance' as if it were a scarce resource that is to be allocated through a price system. But finance is not scarce at all – it is simply a matter of accepting a liability and financing a position in that asset by issuing another liability. In the modern era, this all takes place electronically, essentially keystrokes on a computer, something we can never run out of. What *are* scarce are creditworthy borrowers. The key role that banks can serve is to assess creditworthiness, and the best way to do that is to develop relations with customers. This is fundamentally a non-market activity. Markets failed spectacularly at their attempt to eliminate the relations by substituting credit raters and the originate-to-distribute model, with various risk hedging strategies that actually morphed into bets that customers would fail, then rigging loan terms to ensure they would. And fail they did!

The 'free market' ideal is that debt deflations are not endogenous; rather they must result from exogenous factors, including too much government regulation and intervention. So the solution is deregulation, downsizing government, tax cuts and making markets more flexible. The Minsky–Keynesian view is that the financial structure is transformed over a run of good times from a robust to a fragile state as a result of the natural reaction of agents to the successful operation of the economy. If policy-makers understood this, they could formulate policy to attenuate the transformation – and then deal with a crisis when it occurs.

REFERENCES

Cassidy, John (2008), 'The Minsky moment', *The New Yorker*, 4 February, available at http://www.newyorker.com, accessed 29 January 2008.

Cassidy, John (2010), *How Markets Fail: the Logic of Economic Calamities*, New York: Picador: Farrar, Straus and Giroux.

Eisinger, Jesse and Jake Bernstein (2010), 'The Magnetar trade: how one hedge fund helped keep the bubble going', ProPublica, 13 April, available at http://www.propublica.org/feature/the-magnetar-trade-how-one-hedge-fund-helped-keep-the-housing-bubble-going.

Galbraith, John Kenneth (2009 [1954]), *The Great Crash 1929*, New York: Houghton Mifflin Harcourt.

Kregel, Jan (2008), 'Minsky's cushions of safety: systemic risk and the crisis in the US subprime mortgage market', Levy Public Policy Brief no. 93, January.

Mayer, Martin (2010), 'The spectre of banking', *One-Pager* No. 3, 20 May, Levy Economics Institute.

Minsky, Hyman P.

A) Levy Working Papers:

(1992a), 'Reconstituting the United States' financial structure: some fundamental issues', Working Paper no. 69, January.

(1992b), 'The capital development of the economiy and the structure of financial institutions', Working Paper no. 72, January.

(1996), 'Uncertainty and the institutional structure of capitalist economies', Working Paper no. 155, April.

B) Manuscripts in Minsky archives at Levy Institute:

(1993a), 'The essential characteristics of post-Keynesian economics', 13 April.

(1993b), 'Financial structure and the financing of the capital development of the economy', The Jerome Levy Institute Presents Proposals for Reform of the Financial System, Corpus Christie, TX, 23 April.

(1992c), 'The economic problem at the end of the second millennium: creating capitalism, reforming capitalism and making capitalism work' (prospective chapter), 13 May.

(1992d), 'Reconstituting the financial structure: the United States', (prospective chapter, four parts), 13 May.

Minsky, Hyman (1986), *Stabilizing an Unstable Economy*, Yale University Press.

Minsky, Hyman (1996), 'Uncertainty and the institutionalist structure of capitalist economies: remarks upon receiving the Veblen–Commons Award', *Journal of Economic Issues*, June, pp. 357–68.

Minsky, Hyman P. and Charles J. Whalen (1996), 'Economic insecurity and the institutional prerequisites for successful capitalism', Levy Working Paper no. 165, May.

Minsky, Hyman P., Dimitri B. Papdimitriou, Ronnie J. Phillips and L. Randall Wray (1993), 'Community development banking: a proposal to establish a nationwide system of community development banks', Public Policy Brief no. 3, Jerome Levy Economics Institute.

Phillips, R.J. (1995), *The Chicago Plan and New Deal Banking Reform*, Foreword by H.P. Minsky, Armonk, NY: M.E. Sharpe.

Whalen, Charles (2007), 'The US credit crunch of 2007: a Minsky moment', Levy Public Policy Brief, no. 92, available at http://www.levy.org.

Wray, L. Randall (2008a), 'Financial markets meltdown: what can we learn from Minsky?', Levy Public Policy Brief no. 94, April.

Wray, L. Randall (2008b), 'The commodities market bubble: money manager capitalism and the financialization of commodities', Levy Public Policy Brief no. 96, October.

Wray, L. Randall (2009), 'The rise and fall of money manager capitalism: a Minskian approach', *Cambridge Journal of Economics*, **33**(4), July, pp. 807–28.

Index